The Thar Articles

The Thar Articles

B. B. Dandekar

A Sequel to “Rampaging Lovers”

This is the way it could have been……
This is the way it might have been……

GYAN

ISBN : 978-81-212-1341-7

Price : ₹ 980

First Published, 2016

Published by

Gyan Publishing House
5, Ansari Road
Daryaganj, New Delhi-110002
Phone: 9811692060
E-mail: books@gyanbooks.com

Printed at: G. Print Process, Delhi.

Cataloging in Publication Data—DK
Courtesy: D.K. Agencies (P) Ltd. <docinfo@dkagencies.com>

Dandekar, B. B., 1938- **author.**
The Thar articles / B.B. Dandekar.
pages cm
Novel.
"A sequel to "Rampaging lovers."
ISBN 9788121213417

1. American fiction. I. Title.

PS3604.A53T43 2016 DDC 813.6 23

Prologue

The two men met in an abandoned, disused Fort just inside the border on the Indian side, in the Thar Desert. The Fort had changed hands several times in its history, eventually ending up, for now, under Indian control, the battered red-sandstone walls and gun emplacements showing the damage over the years that neither side had attempted to repair or conceal. It had become a point of honour. Whoever held the Fort held the Thar. Each side had fought fiercely to retain it, and the shattered, pock-marked walls and the steps leading into it still carried the stains of victory and defeat. Of the same colour. Slashes of death and valour, triumph and dishonour, all painted on the dull red background with the careless brush of artillery shells. No pattern or conformity. No chance to redo or repaint. All strokes final.

Not that there had been much to fight over in that desolate, barren piece of God-forsaken territory. Sand and scrub stretching for miles in every direction, the scrub precariously eking out its existence by tenaciously clinging to the sand—not unlike the people in the area. A wistful longing to stay alive, as a pleading, sometimes defiant, act of survival.

But all that had been a long time ago. Almost thirty years ago. Long forgotten by both sides, like the Fort itself. Most of those who had survived had since died, taking their honour and their valour with them. Their hatreds too. A chapter long since closed—and better kept that way.

Otherwise it would not have been possible for the two men to have met at all.

They seemed so different from each other. The Pakistani General with the soldier's bearing, the slightly receding hairline adding to the commanding figure, the military moustache curling away at the tips. The khaki uniform with the brown belt across the chest, shiny with well-polished buttons, spoke of his pride in it.

The Indian Prime Minister was quite the opposite. A short, slightly dumpy, pudgy figure with a rich, full head of hair that sat comfortably under the white cloth cap. The Nehru-style jacket and the churidar trousers didn't add much to his stature or commanding presence. He didn't look like the leader of 700 million people; more like a grocer's assistant or, if one was prepared to be charitable, maybe a stockbroker.

Then the similarities began. In the eyes. Cold, hard, shrewd, given to flashes of impatience and irritation, capable of smiling when the need arose, probing each the other behind the façade and devising strategy as they did, uncertain of the limits to which the other might be comfortably pushed without outright rejection. Each came as the representative of his government. For a meeting that had been called by both sides with an urgency that had bypassed the usual coyness of wrangling over meeting times and meeting places and the shape of the negotiating table. Both sides had dispensed with usual protocol arrangements so that the two men could meet swiftly without the hassles of intermediaries. Not that security had been compromised in any way, by either side. Intelligence agents from both sides had inspected the Fort, checking the red-sandstone walls and the wood roof for bugs. Each side assured the other it was not they who were suspect; precautions had to be taken against third parties. The Americans and the Russians too had an interest in these discussions.

The room in the Fort had been hastily furnished. A woven wool carpet was spread out from one side to the other, adding a touch of warmth to the bare, harsh walls. It had been provided by the Pakistanis. In the centre of the room, on the carpet, was a couch, with rounded cushions, that could be leaned against, even with the feet drawn up. It had been provided by the Indians. A low table was set in the front of the couch. On it, at one end, was an unopened bottle of scotch, an unopened bottle of club soda, and a tall glass. It had been provided by the Indians. At the other end was an unopened bottle of lemonade and a tall glass. It had been provided by the Pakistanis. In between were two canisters of ice cubes, with tongs; neither side knew who was supposed to provide the ice cubes, so each side had brought its own.

Outside the Fort, in the broiling sun, sheltering for shade against the heavily-armed military vehicles from both sides, were the retinues that had brought both men from opposite directions to the Fort.

But inside the Fort there were only the two of them.

The military man added a cube of ice to his lemonade; the minister took his scotch neat on two cubes of ice; the club soda bottle remained unopened. They turned towards each other, raising their glasses in welcoming gesture; settled back comfortably into the couch, and appeared to relax.

The General spoke first. He appeared to be in no hurry to make his case, taking a long drink from his tall glass, wiping the drops of moisture from his forehead with a white handkerchief from the upper pocket of his uniform.

"I'm so glad you could come, Prime Minister," he said, in tones of genuine appreciation that were not lost on his adversary at the other end of the couch.

"It concerns us as much as it concerns you, General. If you had not asked for this meeting, I most certainly would have! I apologise for this rather makeshift arrangement," the Prime Minister said, waving his hand around the bare walls, "but it had all to be done so quickly, we did not have the time for much beautification."

They refilled their glasses. The General had another long drink, then placed his glass with an air of finality back on the table.

"I have a problem. I want you to help me solve it. It cannot be solved by anyone else but you. It is as simple as that."

"I will, if I can. I know what your problem is. My aides have already briefed me on it. But you must know that the position of my government is very delicate in the matter. The Soviets are our friends; our allies. We receive a lot of arms shipments from them. Aid too. Helps to keep us neutral in the matter. We cannot overtly work against them. I'm sure you understand. We have already indicated to them, privately and publicly, that they ought to get out of this region—and stay out of it!"

"Doesn't seem to have done much good—if you will forgive me saying so."

"I forgive you. Because you are quite right. And that is, precisely, the reason I am here. If they will not listen to reason, then we have to resort to other means—but I cannot be involved, you understand?"

"I understand, I understand," the General said, patiently, causing the Prime Minister to smile softly.

"India cannot be involved in all this. Leave it to the bloody Pakistanis to help their Muslim brothers in Afghanistan! But I'm not asking for an official involvement by the Indian government in the matter. That would even be counterproductive by defeating the purpose I had in mind. But a little help? On the side? Given by private individuals? Without the knowledge and approval of the Indian government?"

The Prime Minister rose from the couch and walked to the vertical slits in the walls that had been the artillery gun emplacements thirty years ago. Looking out on the desert sands and the sparse scrub as far as the eye could see. He then walked up and down the room oblivious to the General still seated on the couch, who was following him, his head turning slowly, as the movement of a gun-sight tracking a moving enemy.

He had been told about this behaviour of the Prime Minister. When he thinks, he will walk, his aides had said. The more intense the thought, the slower the pace, until he has thought it through, when he will come to an almost stop. But not quite, because he is still thinking about it all the time, even when he faces you.

As now. Could one be really neutral in all this? Did not neutrality itself imply acquiescence? The doubts, like the drops on his forehead, peered out again and the General wiped them away.

"You are quite right, General," the Prime Minister said softly. "It does concern us. Very much so! I would like to help—and I will. Quite unofficially of course. Goes without saying. This is the way I think we could do it. That is if you agree."

He came to the couch and sat on it, kicking off his sandals and pulling his feet up so that he could face the General.

"You will name one man; I will name the other. Men you and I can both trust. Implicitly! With our lives, let alone our reputations. Because that is precisely what we will be doing. They will have my full confidence—and yours. A carte blanche! They will meet with each other to determine the way we can best meet this 'Bear' threat on our northern borders. They will draw up articles of agreement, setting out in detail the means to accomplish their objectives and the resources they will need. Two copies only. Just two! One with my man; one with yours. Not with us. We will be briefed by our two men on its contents, of course, but we will be unaware of the existence of such a document—and if it ever comes to light, why, we will both strenuously deny any knowledge of it! Is that agreed?"

The General permitted himself to smile for the first time that afternoon. The sun slanting its rays in through the slits had started to make that room in the Fort uncomfortably warm. Soon it would be hot in there. Just as well to have a quick resolution to their problem. The General would have been able to withstand it, but the Prime Minister would most certainly have not. And meeting again under such secrecy was out of the question—at least until the success or failure of their mission was more obvious to the both of them. 'Oh!' thought the General, 'that all negotiators met under such trying conditions!' No, that was not the real reason why resolution had been quick. It was because both men had wanted it to be so. No arguments, no fuss, no silly squabbling about the shapes of tables or the preconditions to the conditions. When both sides desperately wanted it, all that remained to be ironed out was the method of operation. And for that two other trusted men, fully aware of the urgency, and far more competent than the two in the room, would meet under vastly different conditions and sort out the details. These would be set down in a document. Only two copies; one for each side, held by these two men, as private individuals and not as official representatives of their respective governments.

It seemed so simple. That is where its merit lay, for the two men in the room. Making the resolution too complex only invited trouble, mired in details that threatened to doom the mission to failure. Far better to let two others, far more knowledgeable about the realities in the field to work out the details, knowing full well that resolution had already occurred at the highest levels.

Except for one detail. And the General thought of it first.

"What shall we call this agreement? Of which we know nothing. Of which we do not, quite rightly, wish to know anything. A name? So that we may refer to it if ever the need arises."

The Prime Minister broke into a broad smile, showing the whitest of teeth in the strong mouth. The plumpish cheeks made him seem almost boyish.

"What would you suggest General? Yes, we ought to give it a name. This document—of which we know nothing. Except we have sanctioned it, and with that sanction, who knows, we may be putting into motion a new era, heralding a new age of friendship between our two peoples?"

"I can see why you win elections, Prime Minister," the General said dourly. But a smile peeped out through his bushy eyebrows.

"And I can see why you never hold any," the Prime Minister said with equal composure. "But seriously, and I am serious, perhaps the success of this joint, illicit, venture is all we may need for better feelings on both sides? Yes?"

"I hope so. And if it fails? Will Indo-Pak affairs go the same way?"

"I hope not. Did you have a man in mind for this?"

"Yes."

"You wouldn't care to tell me who?"

"No."

"I thought not," the Prime Minister said with mock dejection. "I have a person in mind too. One of the very best! Shall we arrange for them to meet somewhere?"

"Why not here? This is safe enough. And close enough. And equally distant for the both of them. This Fort. This very room! Yes?"

The Prime Minister nodded. "But the name?"

This time it was the General who waved his hand carelessly about the room. But it was not about the room that he waved it at, but the sands around them.

"Here we are," he said, "in the middle of the Thar Desert. A most forbidding piece of land, inhospitable, particularly to foreigners who would attempt to violate it. Shall we call this document—of which there will be only two handwritten copies, and of which we know nothing—THE THAR ARTICLES? And why, after the operation is well under way, my dear Prime Minister, I would like to meet with you here again, say a year from now, and have a drink with you, while we review and retain, or set fire, to those two copies in this room?"

"THE THAR ARTICLES," the Prime Minister said, raising his glass to the General.

CHAPTER 1

The couple sauntering down the main street in Georgetown didn't attract much attention. Except, perhaps, some envy in the young men who passed them. Seeing the tall, elegant, stunningly beautiful English girl, with brown hair and brown eyes, holding tight the arm of the not too tall, not too handsome, not too well built, East Indian gentleman with the unruly mop of black hair and the mild, tired-looking black eyes that peered out from behind the large spectacles. Julia had no time for them. She was used to young men cast appreciative glances at the richness of her. At one time, when she was much younger than twenty-eight, the same glances had bothered her—almost as if she felt ashamed of herself for being so beautiful. But as she grew older, a serenity came that made allowances for the weaknesses in men and, while she never encouraged it by being suggestive in any way, she had learned to pass them by with a mature look of indifference.

That is until she fell in love with Joshua Samuelson, an East Indian doctor in Hampstead, and married him. Then she found yet another change in her attitude to the glances she seemed to so wantonly attract. She found herself holding Joshua's arm even tighter, pulling him into her so that she could feel it pressed into the softness of her breast, sending into her a warm and enduring glow. Into him too, as he responded by patting her arm to reassure her that he understood. It was not of her doing—the stares she attracted. A stunning woman had an obligation to share that beauty with strangers in the street—in the most harmless sort of way. Unless she came from some exotic society in which women, beautiful or not, were hidden behind the burkha.

"I rather fancy seeing you in one, Julia," Joshua said, laughing gently. "Keep all that fine figure and lovely face, those liquid eyes and long eyelashes, those sensuous lips, only for my private viewing!"

"I almost believe you would," she replied. "But do they have air-conditioned ones? It must get rather hot in there, darling."

It was as if her pressing into Joshua, at such times, was almost an act of contrition. Gratitude too for his understanding. His reward? He was not slow to respond at this expression of her desire, stopping abruptly sometimes, so that she bumped into him in the most pleasurable sort of way, bringing her at times onto him and into his side, right there in the middle of the sidewalk.

It was a slow sauntering walk. They peered into shop windows that sold antiques, bakeries that wafted the smell of freshly baked bread into the street, a bookstore, where Julia begged to be allowed to enter, pouting when Joshua firmly steered her past it, past a hairdresser and a jewellers, until he brought her up sharply at the angled window of a female clothing store with dressed mannequins; mirrors at the back showing the dresses from behind. He stopped to linger, looking long and hard into the bay window, shifting his position slightly to get a better view of a rather low-necked evening gown.

"I didn't know you had a thing going for female mannequins, darling," Julia said lightly, turning her nose up at the offending woman who had attracted his attention.

"I have now," he said, holding her by the arm, pressing her up against him, reaching as if in endearment, to kiss her cheek past the curl of brown hair, close to her ear.

"Don't turn around," he whispered. "Look in the angled mirrors and tell me what you see. Quick!"

She did not argue, stop to consider, or remonstrate. The years of training she'd had with MI-6 told her instinctively when the seconds counted. As now.

"There's a man. Stopped. As we are. Looking into the bookstore twenty yards back."

"Look across the street."

She moved her position slightly. Ignored the mannequin with the low-necked evening gown to look into the straight mirror at the back.

“There’s a lady. An Indian woman, wearing a sari. Stopped. Looking into the store across the street. Can’t quite see what store it is.”

“That’s not important. A shoe store, actually. We’re being followed, Julia. I sort of got that feeling the minute we stepped out of the hotel, but I wasn’t sure until the bookstore—and I didn’t want to go in there until I was sure. With so many people browsing—or pretending to browse—we become easy targets. Sorry about that, darling. Forgive me?”

Julia looked into the mirror again. The man had not moved; neither had the woman. They appeared to be looking just as intently into their shop windows. The woman across the street moved one store up toward them. Stopped again.

Julia held him by the arm, drawing him up close.

“The next shop up here is another bakery. Where they appear to be serving tea as well. Isn’t it almost four? Time for tea, darling, wouldn’t you say?”

Joshua looked ostentatiously at his watch, holding it at a firm distance from his eye.

“Why, so it is! What a splendid idea, Julia. Tea it is and right here too. Take the table by the window as you enter. It seems to be available.”

Joshua parted the curtains at the window just a crack. The man was not visible from where they were sitting, but the woman across the street was. Not too tall, blue sari with a gold edge and border, draped around her showing the bare back of the short blouse closing in front tight underneath her breasts. They could not see the face; her back was turned toward them. The traffic sometimes obscured her from their view, until a baker’s truck pulled up against the curb, opposite their window, and blotted her out.

“Well, now what?” Julia said. “We can’t sit here all evening. On second thoughts, darling, why not? Just let’s sit here until they grow tired of it. The waiting game! Yes?”

Joshua shook his head.

"It isn't as simple as that," he said. "Why are there two of them? Is she tailing him? Or is he tailing her? Or are they both tailing us? Why separately? And then again it seems all wrong. Not like a normal tail. Because we could hop into a taxi and lose them both quite easily. It's as if they know we're having a nice leisurely afternoon stroll, and won't stray far from the hotel."

Joshua placed the order—two cups of hot tea and a plate of Danish pastry. As the blonde waitress reached forward to straighten the cutlery, he touched her on the hand. She looked down at him inquiringly.

He drew out a five-dollar bill.

"My wife and I would like you to help us out. See your truck parked on this side of the street?"

The girl nodded.

"It blocks our view of the other sidewalk. There is an East Indian lady standing there, looking into one of the shop windows on the other side. A shoe store. If you'll just nip outside and confirm it, why, the fiver's yours."

The young girl nodded once more, straightened the blond hair underneath the white cap, tightened the belt around her waist one notch, and stepped out the door. They saw her disappear round the side of the truck. Moments passed, turning into minutes. They had almost risen to their feet, when they saw her reappear on their side of the truck and come toward the door.

"She's there alright, Sir," the girl said, reaching for the fiver. "I went right up to her to make sure I had the right one. Only one there with a sari, looking into the window. Blue sari with gold all over it. That's the one, right?"

Joshua nodded.

"She's not looking for shoes in there, if you ask me, Sir. Turned around three times, even in the short minute or so I was there, to look this way."

"What does she look like?" Joshua said.

"Smashing! Really beautiful, if you ask me. But then, maybe, all those sari-clad women look smashing to me. Young. About my age. Twenty? Twenty-five? Oval face. Doe-like large eyes. Has a small, red, round dot on her forehead, between the eyes. Right there!"

The girl touched her index finger to her forehead at the level of the eyebrows and between the eyes.

"Anything else you noticed?" Julia said. "Is she waiting for someone?"

"Couldn't say, Miss. But I thought she looked once or twice at the man across, on our side of the street, further up at the bookstore. Will that be all, Sir?"

"Yes, thank you. May we sit here, my wife and I, for a while longer than is absolutely necessary, after our tea is done?"

The waitress waved her hand as if hurt at the question even being asked.

"Hey! Sit as long as you want. It's my father's bakery; I run this side of it for him. When you're through with these cups of tea, I'll bring you two new tea bags and another pot of hot water—on me."

She winked at Julia, and disappeared.

"I wonder what that was for?" Julia said, almost absent-mindedly. "I wonder what she thinks of it all."

"All what?"

"A beautiful, sari-clad woman who is tailing her errant husband, who is, no doubt, having an illicit love affair with a rather simple-minded English girl; the husband and his mistress caught, red-handed, in hiding, in her bakery café."

Joshua burst out laughing loudly. An elderly East Indian gentleman, who had followed them in, gave him a benign smile. Foreigners were permitted that sort of behaviour in the capital city. The presence of so many embassies almost assured the streets of aberrations in behaviour. And Americans, thank God, were getting almost as bad as foreigners these days.

"You've got an overactive imagination, darling. Now I always knew that—with you being a writer and a good one too—but, darling, don't you think this version of her thinking is a little far-fetched?"

"Oh! I don't know. Shall I go and ask her?"

"I believe you! I believe you!" Joshua said hastily, as Julia prepared to leave her seat. "Please, will you concentrate on the matter in hand? We are being tailed; we know that now. By a man and a woman who know each other and are working together. Question? Who are they tailing?"

"Us."

"Maybe, and then maybe not."

Julia threw up her hands in dismay—which gesture was not lost on the young girl at the counter making out the checks for the customers in the café.

"Are all Indians so enigmatic?" she asked. "Heaven help me! What have I married into? Am I condemned to spending the rest of my life working out the puzzles in your speech?"

"Sorry, darling."

He was about to plunge into a long and protracted apology for his thoughtlessness, when he noticed the wicked smile lurking in her eyes, and so he slapped her hand lightly in chastisement instead.

"They need not be following the both of us," Joshua said. "Maybe only the one? You or me? But they are working together—that's for sure."

"Why don't we find out, who?"

"Oh! And how do we do that, Holmes?"

"Very simple, Watson. One of us leaves this little place; the other stays. And let us agree to meet back in our hotel room in, say, twenty minutes?"

"Julia, my darling, what would I do without you? But of course! Why don't I think of such things?"

Julia blushed. High praise had always made her feel a little uncomfortable; indifference devastated her—and in between was the fine line that gave her a warm glow. He had not yet found that line. Give him some time. After all they had been married only two weeks. There lay, hopefully, a lifetime ahead for the nuances in marriage.

"Who shall it be?" Julia asked.

"Me! Quite definitely just me. No arguments about that, my love. Please?"

"And why you?"

"Because I'm an Indian man, and a male chauvinist, and your husband, and I love you, and you're not going out there into that street without us knowing who they are, and I forbid it! Please?"

Julia would have argued the point, but she relented. Besides she might learn just as much from behind the curtain watching him walk out into the street. So she nodded assent.

It didn't turn out quite that way, and a few minutes later she bitterly regretted having come up with the idea in the first place. At least they had been together in the café, affording each other protection by being together. And it was she who had suggested they break up! What if they were after him?

She saw Joshua step out of the cafe, the bell above the door tinkling as it closed behind him. He stepped onto the sidewalk, then walked casually past the bakery window where their eyes met for one brief moment of understanding. As she expected he did not walk past the window, choosing that exact spot to cross the street, constantly keeping himself in line with the bakery window, and always in her sight—as any newly married husband might?

The baker's truck had moved along. She could see clear across the street to the sidewalk on the other side. The Indian lady with the blue and gold sari turned around swiftly showing herself for the first time to both Joshua and Julia. Joshua stopped in the middle of the street as he saw her; then broke into a fast run across it. From the corner of her eye she saw the man, who had been loitering outside the bookstore, come within range, as he raced across the street too, catching up with both Joshua and the lady at the curb, on the far side of the street.

She told herself—bitterly blamed herself—several times that evening that she could still have made it across the street in the few seconds that ticked by, while she sat, idly, by the window with the drawn curtain, watching the three of them talk. She saw Joshua gesticulate wildly, as if remonstrating, his hands pointing towards the bakery and the window on the other side of the street. Towards her.

And still she sat there, not fully comprehending, until a car pulled up and, with what appeared to be no resistance at all, Joshua entered it with the other two—all three in the rear seat, the woman in between. Perhaps he had a gun in his ribs? That is when she slid out of the bench seat; had barely reached the door and opened it when the black Ford flashed past toward the intersection. The light turned green, the Ford turned the corner and was lost from view. She went back to the bakery café, to the table beside the window, to think things out. They had agreed to meet back in their room at the hotel in twenty minutes. The Inn was just round the corner, barely three minutes away. She had a few minutes to spare. She could think more clearly here than in a closed hotel room listening anxiously for the sound of his key in the lock—and not hearing it.

The blonde waitress, who had served them, seeing her dash out the door and then come back to her seat dejectedly, came up to clear away the tea things, lingering awhile as if in sympathy. Despite the worry that creased her forehead, the mournful look on the young face brought Julia a faint smile of amusement. There was not much she could do for the next ten minutes.

"May I talk about it?" Julia said, looking up at her.

The girl slid into the seat opposite her, where Joshua had been sitting a few minutes before.

"Why not? It always helps."

"It isn't as it seems," Julia said. "What you're thinking, I mean."

"Oh! And what am I thinking?"

"That she's his wife and I'm his—shall we say girl friend? But it isn't like that at all. I'm his wife. We've been married twice in the last two weeks."

"Twice?"

"Yes, twice. Once in a lavish affair in a synagogue in Bombay—Indians never do things by half!—and then once again in a private ceremony in a little chapel on the family estate in Bromfield, England, with a few close friends in the front row, and all of our devoted servants at the back."

"And she?"

"I don't know who she is! I've never seen……"

Julia stopped in mid-sentence. Strange how fickle memory could be. It always failed you when you needed it. Names, dates, places, people. They all seemed to sink into its bottomless store that no amount of frantic dredging could bring to the surface—when you needed it most. And then, when you were about to deny it, knowing a person or at least having seen her before, memory mocked you by flashing, even dancing, the unwelcome scene before you—as if it had never been lost.

Of course, Julia knew who she was. At the very least, Julia had seen her before. Once. It had been at the time Julia had gone to Bombay more than a year ago. They had formally announced their engagement in the social columns of the London Times. Julia Rayburn-Spencer, granddaughter of the eleventh Earl of Bromfield to Col. (Dr) Joshua Samuelson of Bombay, India, and now a London GP. The announcement had created quite a stir—and not all of it unwelcome. Her Majesty, the Queen, had called her grandfather to convey her warm wishes to the happy couple, with an invitation to tea at the Palace. Julia, who had been to tea several times with the Queen, took it in her stride, but Joshua turned belligerent and would have, not-so-graciously, turned down the invitation, had Julia not threatened him with similar dire consequences in Bombay. That brought him to his senses. As it turned out the Queen and Joshua found, to mutual surprise, that they had a common interest in "the realm of Jane Austen" as she put it. They found, further, that each had an in-depth knowledge of her characters, and ended up with a detailed dissection of Darcy and Elizabeth—the Queen pointedly drawing a parallel between Joshua—his pride as a commoner—and Darcy, while Joshua suggested, to the Queen's delight, that Her

Majesty was like her namesake—in all that made her so endearing an heroine! The Duke and the eleventh Earl had been discussing cricket scores and the chances of England in the upcoming Test Series with India, while Julia smiled, as a Queen might, at the four of them, stifling a yawn or two at the same time. Tea being long over, the Queen leaned over to Julia and begged her to come again soon; she had a priceless collection of Jane Austen first editions that she would love to show to Joshua. Could they, please, come back again, soon? Before Julia could reply, Joshua accepted promptly, and Julia curtsying to the royal monarch smiled acquiescence.

They had then gone to India to meet with his family. His mother had enfolded Julia in her arms as if she was an eleven-year-old, without as much as a 'by-your-leave'. Joshua's sister, Susan, whispered shyly: "How ever did you manage it?" There was one other member of the family—a brother in England, Joe—and Julia had met him already, knew him quite well, and was fond of him.

There had to be a reception. The old Mother insisted on it. What better way for all of Joshua's relatives and friends—close and distant—in India to meet with the lovely English girl he was planning to marry? Not just from Bombay. They would come from wherever they were—some as far away as New Delhi, where Joshua had worked before he'd emigrated to London. Not a quiet affair—Oh no!—Susan confided to Julia: 'Indians didn't do things by half!' An occasion like this helped to bring everyone together and was not to be missed. It helped to bury past hurts between relatives and friends, hurts that were begging to be buried, just awaiting a gathering like this one.

It was held in the assembly hall of the local school, which hall had been rented for the occasion and festooned with coloured ribbons and helium balloons, more appropriate to a child's birthday party than for a reception for grown-ups. Of course children were invited, and ran around unconcernedly dropping crumbs of cake-icing and dripping mango ice-cream all over their newly-bought party clothes.

Joshua and Julia stood at one end of the hall to welcome the guests, who lined up to shower their blessings (if older relatives) or their good wishes (if same-generation friends), or if very young, to shyly put forth their hand to the beautiful English Lady—not quite knowing what it was for nor what it was all about. Garlands rained down her neck in profusion. Woven with roses and marigolds and local sweet smelling flowers with exotic names like mogra and juie. She was glad she had worn a long, formal dress with the boat collar turned up to her neck, or she would have been collecting petals in her cleavage. She had declined the sari that Susan was persuading her to wear for the occasion.

"Mother taught me how to wear one, Susan, and I will, with pride, but not for the very first time in public, on a formal occasion such as this! I might trip over it and fall, and if it comes apart on me, whatever will Joshua's friends think of me?"

Whoever heard of being weighted down with flowers? But after the first six garlands, she certainly felt that way. Joshua, seeing her plight, got rid of his garlands onto a chair alongside and advised her to do likewise.

She shot him a grateful glance, which he misread.

Was she tired? Of all the effusiveness, perhaps? Did it jar on her, the way all his relatives and friends were inspecting her as his choice of wife? He could soon put a stop to all that. By bringing the evening to a close. After all she had been on her feet for more than an hour! Mother would understand—and she was the only one that mattered.

Julia restrained him.

"Darling," she said, depositing yet another garland onto the chair beside her, "where and when will I ever observe, firsthand, another Indian reception of this sort?" The food, the exotic-sounding music, the laughter, the conversation, the looks—some warm and encouraging; others dubious, as if, sorrowfully, predicting a disastrous marriage. Wouldn't their own daughters have been a far more suitable match for the doctor?

The men wore suits, mostly. A few were dressed in the Indian Nehru-style jacket and tight trousers, with white caps made popular by the Congress Party. One older, Hindu gentleman wore the *dhoti*—

a white garment that straddled his legs and was tucked in at the waist—with a simple white cotton shirt above it.

The children wore spanking new clothes. Some of the older girls had on a short blouse with a long skirt separated by bare back and mid-riff.

Most of the women wore saris. There had been so many in saris, she would have been unable to distinguish between them. They all looked alike—and very beautiful. His first and second cousins, distant relatives, friends from his college and later years. All strangers to her. Very well known to Joshua, as they chatted and joked with him after giving her a friendly greeting. She couldn't blame them. What could they talk to her about? The weather? With him they shared memories filled with nostalgia of the years gone by. Little incidents that had caused them amusement, pleasure or joy, even tears. The tears were no longer painful; the memory sweet to relive with him up close.

There was not much he could do either, without hurting them by constantly steering the conversation away from them and toward her. Ignore them! He need not have worried. This was no different than cutting a red ribbon at a local bazaar. As the granddaughter of the eleventh Earl of Bromfield, she had been called upon to hostess many of the same types of receptions thrown by her grandfather for visiting dignitaries. Since her grandfather and a few close friends, like Cecily and her brother Viscount Edward Andrew, were all she had known, those receptions had been just as prone to loneliness.

The guests had started to leave. The band, hired by the family for the dancing, were packing up their instruments. The floor was littered with ribbon that had worked its way loose from the ceiling. Some of the balloons had lost their helium and floated to the ground.

Joshua had disappeared.

Perhaps he had gone to the restroom. She sat in the chair for a while and slipped her feet out of her shoes, stretching her toes with the painted toenails that Susan had insisted on painting as a service to her. After the music, the silence was so much of a relief. Joshua's mother had disappeared too; so had Susan. The last guests drifted out of the hall; she was now alone in it. The farewells between the old Mother and her last guests in the anteroom across the hall, drifted in faintly. The couple welcomed the guests as they came; farewells were for the Mother. That is when she heard Joshua's voice raised in anger. Just the once. Then it died away, as if it were aware of itself, and promptly hushed. It seemed to come from the room on the other side of the hall, leading into the corridor that opened into the classrooms.

Julia walked, leisurely, towards the door. Unprepared. Unconcerned too. She had never heard Joshua's voice raised in anger, ever, in the time she had known him. Either with her or with anyone else. How much did she know about him? His past life? His inner life—and the actors within? She stopped at the door, unsure of whether she ought to open it and walk in boldly, or turn around and walk away. She did neither. Instead she put her fingers to the door and pressed it open the merest crack. Enough for her to see them at the far end of the room; unseen to them because they were so far away from her. Like some peeping Tom she told herself miserably, when she thought of it later. Curiosity, and MI-6 training, didn't let her see it that way then.

It was a woman in a bright red sari, wearing a yellow halter blouse tied into a knot at the front, underneath her breasts. The sari had slipped off her shoulders in the altercation, and the tightness of the blouse emphasised the fullness of her breasts. The edge of the red sari that should have muted that fullness trailed the stone floor. The face was the most beautiful she had ever seen, the doe-like large eyes cringing in fear, the large lips open, as she stifled back a scream, showing perfect teeth. The high cheekbones and the sharp chin gave her the elegance of a model. Yet, somehow, there was no softness to her. Cold, hard and frightened was Julia's first impression of her, and Julia was rarely wrong in such matters. Joshua held her roughly by the arm and was pushing her toward the door on the far side and into the corridor.

She did not appear very willing to go.

"Not now!" she heard Joshua whisper fiercely. "I cannot consider it now! All that is over. Finished! I am engaged to be married. Now, will you go?"

"No," she hissed. "And let go of my arm before I scream the place down!"

She saw Joshua turn around and look anxiously at the door behind which she was standing, causing her to, instinctively, step back away from it.

"Alright, I'll meet you later. But not now! If you'll just go!"

The hand that Joshua had on her arm tightened. She closed her arm to her side, plunging his fingers into the side of her breast. She raised her other arm to strike him; he did not defend himself as she rained blows on him. Ineffective and weak. He pushed her roughly toward the door and out of it. She heard their footsteps die away.

Joshua came back two minutes later, his hair ruffled. But he appeared composed as if nothing unusual had occurred.

I am not the perfect fiancée, Julia thought, because such a one would have suffered in silence, until he chose to tell who she was and what that was all about. No one could disown the past. That she understood. There were incidents and people—men too—in her own life that could not be disowned. That was natural. Even mistakes could be forgiven. Silence was really the best course of action about events and people in their past—until they surfaced into the present. As one had now. And then honesty could at least still the doubts, if not ease the pain.

He took her home by taxi, stopping briefly on the way to dash into a pharmacy close to home, emerging with a brown paper package that appeared to hold a small bottle. He was a registered doctor—in both India and the United Kingdom—and obtaining full service at a pharmacy was one of the perks of his profession.

He held it up to her.

"You must be tired," he said. "This will help you to sleep better."

She had been given a whole room to herself for the time she was with the family. The old Mother had accomplished that by the simple expedient of throwing everyone else—including Joshua—out of it.

In a small apartment that meant cramped quarters for everyone else, but they were used to it and would survive. Julia was an honoured guest—and the granddaughter of an English Earl; nothing could be too good for her! The old Mother apologised for lack of proper accommodation and hoped she would be comfortable.

Julia had done all she could to allay their fears.

Joshua came to say goodnight, sitting on the edge of the bed as she lay across it. Julia sat up, went to the dressing table and, looking at him in the mirror, brushed her shoulder length brown hair, tying it into a becoming pony tail that bobbed behind her head.

"Darling," she said, "you have a fine family. And some nice friends. And I'm really sorry if I can't remember all of their names. You will forgive me, won't you?"

"Of course."

"Take all those beautiful women. In their gorgeous saris. I'd never seen so many beautiful women in one room. Ravishing! Some of them were."

"Really?"

"Now who was the one in the green sari and the matching green blouse? You know the one whose garland broke, sending those fragrant white flowers all over my feet?"

"That was Nirmala. One of Susan's college friends. They used to study trigonometry together. And since neither of them was very good at it, I ended up playing tutor to the both of them."

"Ah! And the beautiful woman in the pale yellow silk sari and the red blouse?"

"Darling, I had eyes only for you! Do you think I can remember what every woman wore? To identify her?"

"You know the one who stepped on my toes when she hugged me?"

"Ah! That was my cousin Miriam. She was married last year to a nice boy from Delhi. Her husband was there too, you remember? He was the one who insisted on kissing you on both cheeks."

"Oh, yes."

"Darling, let's not talk about them," Joshua pleaded. "Not tonight, darling. If I wanted to be melodramatic about it I would have said: 'Our betrothal night!'—but I won't. Though it is."

"One more? And then no more. Please!"

"Alright. Fire away."

"Who was the ravishingly beautiful woman in the bright red sari with the yellow halter-style blouse tied tight in front under her breasts? The one you were talking to in the room off the hall? I couldn't help overhearing a few words, Joshua. What did she want? Why did you want her to leave? Why did she strike you? Is there something I ought to know? Joshua, I'd like to start us off with a warm and trusting feeling, and while you have filled my heart with so much more than just warmth, fill it with trust as well. Please?"

He came round to her side, touching her gently on the shoulder, sliding his hand over her soft, brown hair and past her cheek to the back of her head. He turned her head up to him and kissed her, long and tenderly, on the lips.

"Julia, you were with MI-6. I was with Indian Military Intelligence. We agreed to give each other one full year to settle our obligations with those agencies—then throw it all up to get married and settle down. I would be a doctor; you would be my wife. We'd have children—the number as yet to be determined. But for sure we'd try for at least one son and one daughter. Our son would one day be the Earl of Bromfield! Remember, once, in Paris with Henri and Farnsworth, we promised each other that we would no longer work with the agencies? Well, I've kept my word. I've resigned from IMI. I no longer work for them. Did you resign from MI-6?"

"I did. Oh, I did! I want to trust people, Joshua; not be looking over my shoulder at every other human being with distrust. Least of all—you!"

"Her name is Devika Rani—Devika for short. Comes from a fine family of Rajput warriors. Her father is a General in the Indian Army. My commanding officer at one time, though I no longer work for him. When I moved over to IMI, we recruited her and trained her. She was attached to the Indian Embassy in D.C., where her father was the military attaché. Our contact with the CIA. So now you know who she is. She worked for me."

"I see. Is that all?"

"Yes. She asked me to meet her in the room beside the hall. Urgent, the message said. So I went. Out of sheer curiosity, I suppose. Maybe I shouldn't have, but I did. Forgive me."

"But you were with me the whole time! How could she have sent you an urgent message to meet her?"

"In the garland, darling. IMI code. In the type and the arrangement of the flowers. I'll explain it all to you, if you wish. Three red roses in the pendant at the base of the garland meant 'Urgent'. So I went. They want me to work for IMI again, and I rejected it. Outright. Angrily too! You heard me. She didn't take too kindly to that; threatened to make a scene. I didn't like that—only you, and Mother, can threaten me; no one else!—so I threw her out of there."

"And none too gently."

"She has always been the excitable type. Easily becomes hysterical. That's all there is to it, darling."

Julia hesitated before she asked the next question. He must have been expecting it because his reply was immediate.

"Are you in love with her?"

"No!"

"Is she in love with you?"

He spread out his hands in dismay.

"Darling, I can speak only for my own emotions, not for anyone else's—not even yours! Do you love me today? I think so. Will you love me tomorrow? Or a year from now? How can I know?"

"Did she love you once?"

"May be."

"Did you love her back then?"

"No! I was already in love with you. Oh, Julia! How can you doubt it?"

"I don't doubt it."

"You don't?"

"Of course not," Julia said, smiling deliciously. "But, as a woman, I reserve the right to grill you, and give you a rough time, and be bitchy about it too! Are you going to accept their demands and work for IMI?"

"Not a chance. I gave you my word on that one."

Julia lay back on the bed feeling herself relaxing, the tensions of the evening drifting away, still leaving behind a tired body. He sensed her trust in him, because he reached for the package he had bought at the pharmacy and untied the string.

"What's in the bottle, darling?" Julia asked. His back was turned toward her as he deposited the wrapping in the waste paper basket.

"Something that is guaranteed to make you sleep so very well tonight, my darling."

"I'm sure I'll be able to sleep without it."

"But with this, it is assured," he said, turning around to face her. In his hand was a bottle of perfumed oil. She did not understand until he said:

"Take off your clothes, my love, and let me anoint you with oil. It will ease your tiredness away—trust me. We are only engaged—not yet married—so keep your bra and panty on, if you wish. I'll understand. But this will work wonders for your tired back and thighs, and your white arms too."

"Will it work wonders for you too?" Julia asked, shyly, her eyes dancing with merriment as she slipped off her dress and slip, unhooking her bra and depositing it with her other clothing at the foot of the bed. She kept her lacy panty on.

"Unquestionably!"

She lay on the bed, bare above the waist, while he massaged her back, and her neck, and the backs of her thighs. He then turned her over and did the same to her front, starting with her hands and arms, and into her armpits, then moving abruptly to her toes and feet, before moving upwards in long strokes on the insides of her strong thighs. Her eyes were open. He was deliberating how far he should go, when with a swift movement, she slipped off the lacy panty and flung it across the room.

He squeezed a generous stream of oil onto her chest. Then, using both hands, he moved over all of her, from her neck and over the fullness of her generous breasts—over the pink areolas and firm nipples—past her navel, and into the richness of her dark-brown hair. The oil felt cool and soothing; the aroma of the mogra flower wafted upwards to her.

She closed her eyes.

The waitress seeing her with closed eyes, touched her again on the arm, in sympathy, and retreated behind the counter. The elderly East Indian gentleman was ready to pay his check.

Julia went back to the hotel. Twenty minutes she had said to Joshua. It was more than thirty. She entered the elevator; it was empty. As the door of the elevator closed, she opened her handbag and put her hand inside it, slipping the safety catch on the gun. It made her feel a lot safer.

Joshua had rented a suite of rooms on the top floor of the hotel. The suite had a lounge and a bedroom with an attached bathroom. Joshua had insisted on taking it, even though she knew he could ill-afford it. Nothing was too good for their honeymoon, and to hell with the cost! The money would come later; a honeymoon came only once—that is if you stayed in love. At the door, that first time, they had paused. Julia had saved him embarrassment by opening the door and quickly stepping over the threshold. He could not have carried her over it. He was five feet seven and weighed one hundred and twenty pounds; She was five feet eight inches and weighed somewhat more than that—nearer one hundred forty—the way he liked it and the way he wanted her to be! So he'd reassured her, when she'd contemplated going on a diet on that night he'd seen all of her for the first time, as he'd anointed her with perfumed oil—on the night of their engagement.

This time, she inserted her electronic key into the lock and with the other hand drew out the gun.

Joshua was sitting on the sofa, facing the door, with a scotch and soda in his hand.

"Come in, darling," he said, rising from the sofa. "We've been expecting you."

CHAPTER 2

Julia walked into the room without hesitation, the gun still in her hand. She knew there were other people in it, besides Joshua, behind the closed door of the bedroom. His eyes motioned to the bedroom and she nodded in understanding.

"You can come out now," Joshua called out. "I think Lady Julia will receive you without shooting you for having ruined her evening."

They came out sheepishly. It had been their idea not to face her at the door, and the gun in her hand made that decision a wise one. The man was about fifty, balding, clean shaven, short and with a stocky build, wearing a tailored, custom-fitted, expensive suit. He carried his felt hat in his hand, nervously shifting it from one hand to the other, feeling the brim with his fingers as he did. She put away the gun and held out her hand to him. He bowed low over it as he shook it. He seemed overawed in the presence of royalty.

She saw the woman for the first time, and marveled at the sight of her. She may have been, at one time, her rival, but even Julia could admire the beauty in her. Not just in the well-formed body or the exquisite mouth and eyes, but in the femininity of her. The daintiness; the walk and movements. Many men must have admired her and desired her. Joshua too?

He was unconcernedly sipping his scotch and soda, waving them all to the liquor on the table. Not much there; a rather cheap scotch that he fancied, a bottle of soda, and a rather expensive sherry—the one Julia liked. She helped herself to a glass of it, settled into the sofa beside him, slipping off her flat-heeled shoes, drawing up her feet onto the sofa, discreetly tucking them under her. It had every indication of being a long evening.

"Will someone tell me, please, what this is all about?" Julia asked. It was not a petulant, plaintive complaint; rather a friendly inquiry.

"This is Colonel Max Roberts, darling, a link between IMI and the CIA. An old friend of mine. You might as well know that because it is going to come out anyway!"

"Oh? And what else is going to come out?"

"And this," Joshua said, waving his hand toward the woman, "is Devika Rani."

"Yes, I know," Julia said, "Devika for short. What does it mean—the name, I mean?"

"Goddess," she replied in a soft voice. "And a Queen."

"How very appropriate," Julia said. Meant it too.

"I don't feel like either, Mrs Samuelson,"

"Please call me, Julia. My husband has told me a great deal about you and the time you worked with him—in India."

"Yes. With IMI. You can speak freely before Colonel Roberts here. Besides being our link with the CIA, he is also a personal friend of my father."

The Colonel glowed with pleasure.

"Well, well. So now we all know each other. As friends," Julia said. But she wasn't going to let them get away that easily. No scenes or raising of her voice or flashing of her eyes in anger, to make her point. Just a few questions, politely asked.

"Why were the two of you tailing us? Or may I not ask?"

The Colonel squirmed uncomfortably. Devika left all the answering to him, hiding herself behind a glass of sherry and an enigmatic smile.

"We wanted to talk to Colonel Samuelson—beg pardon, Dr Samuelson—alone. It seemed we would never succeed. We've been tailing you for three days now, and the two of you were inseparable. Stuck with glue to one another, you were! Even walked so close, it was impossible to, accidentally, bump into him and slip him a note. Until today that is when, like a miracle, he left the café and walked into the street."

"Oh! And why did you wish to see my husband alone?"

"Because you are not involved," Devika said.

"And he is? Is that it?"

"Yes. But he refused to hear us out except in your presence, which is why we have ended up here instead of in Langley, Virginia."

Julia slid her arm into Joshua's drawing him close, leaning her head on his shoulder. He was surprised but reciprocated immediately to this public show of affection by putting an arm around her and kissing her on the head. Devika Rani pretended not to see.

"Then you had better tell us, hadn't you?" Julia said. "I see no harm in us listening to what you have to say. If he is involved, it is better for the both of us to hear of it now."

Colonel Roberts cleared his throat, took another scotch, neat, mentally resolving to encourage Devika Rani to drink up too, before they left.

"The problem is the Soviet invasion of Afghanistan.'

'You know about all the horrors there; I won't convert this into a political diatribe by recounting them. No one who is even half-informed can sit back and be indifferent to it. Certainly not the President! Not when our Pakistani friends came to us for help for the mujahidin. They didn't mean money—though we sent them that too. They meant arms. Shoulder fired anti-tank grenades, surface-to-air missiles for bringing down Soviet helicopters—that sort of thing.'

'Easily boxed and crated and shipped innocuously by the Department of Defense to Pakistan."

Colonel Roberts looked into his glass; liked what he didn't see, and refilled it. Wiped his brow with a large handkerchief. "At first the problem was simple enough. DoD shipped the arms to Karachi. They were moved, without much fuss being made about bills of lading, and invoices and import documents, and what have you, to the railway goods terminal; then mainly at night, so as not to interfere with the normal running of Pakistani Railways, they were shipped to Peshawar—and on to the mujahidin, who played havoc with the Russians! It is one of the few times I have seen the President delighted with the news we gave him. And he promptly doubled the amounts DoD had budgeted for those arms. I can't tell you the exact amounts—national security and all that—but I can tell you that it runs into the hundreds of millions of dollars. There was an unofficial slogan we bandied around in the CIA: 'Afghanistan—their Vietnam!'"

He stopped. It was a personal involvement. The face had changed. Perhaps it was the whiskey, but the eyes now flashed with anger and hatred, the eyebrows, dark lines, in an otherwise bald head, acting like horizontal shades of awning over windows of fire, directing his gaze at them.

"Well, quite naturally as we would have expected, the KGB tumbled to it, and started a counter-offensive of their own. Very subtly done, I must say. Unobtrusively. Reports started to trickle in from our agent in Pakistan—I can't tell you his name—that the arms weren't reaching the mujahidin as they were supposed to. Okay in the quantity, but not in their usefulness! Guns would have firing pins missing; shoulder fired anti-helicopter surface-to-air missiles would backfire, sending the freedom fighter and his buddies around him sky high—that sort of thing. Some of the heavy equipment would arrive in a severely damaged condition—and unusable. That we couldn't understand until we found out that a crane operator—at night—dropped all the crates from a height of sixty feet! Carpenters then hastily patched the crates together, after which he loaded them— very gently—onto the railway wagons bound for Peshawar.'

'Sabotage! That is what the KGB were carrying out in Sind in Pakistan, using their Pakistani agents very effectively. There was little we could do about it, because it was out of our hands; the President—I can tell you—was mad as hell! He blamed us—the CIA—for the failure of intelligence, and threw the Director out of the discussions."

"Really?" Joshua said. "Then what happened? Or is that the state of affairs as of now? What do you want me to do about it anyway? Get your Pakistani contacts in the CIA to investigate matters at that end. You'd be better off doing that—than ruining our honeymoon!"

"Please hear me out. That is not the end of the story. All of this took place more than a year ago."

"Then even I don't know what transpired, because the CIA was out of the loop. Something at levels far higher than mine—possibly at Presidential level. But the matter suddenly seemed to right itself. Shipments were reaching the mujahidin—and in pristine condition too—and once more the mujahidin were giving the Soviets hell. Everything went smoothly for about nine months—until about two months ago."

"Oh, and what happened two months ago?"

"No shipments."

"What do you mean by no shipments? Did DoD stop the shipments?" Joshua asked.

"No! DoD was making the shipments as usual—about one a month; they just weren't reaching the mujahidin."

"What?"

"You heard me. The shipments used to leave Norfolk, on Pakistani vessels, and somewhere along the way, they were being hijacked."

"Hijacked?"

"You heard me? That's what we found out when we received this from our agent with the mujahidin in Peshawar."

He reached into an inner pocket for what appeared to be a cable in code. The code had been deleted and the cable unscrambled. The message was explicit.

Joshua reached forward for it, his eyes rapidly scanning the lines. Julia leaned over his shoulder, pressing herself into his arm. He moved the paper so she could read it as well.

NO SHIPMENTS LAST TWO MONTHS STOP NOT EVEN SMALLS STOP PLEASE EXPEDITE STOP URGENT NEED FOR FALL OFFENSIVE MESSAGE ENDS

The agent's code name had been deleted.

"Smalls?" Julia said.

"Our code for small arms—bullets, hand grenades, spares, that sort of thing," Devika Rani said.

"And how are you involved in all this?" Julia asked.

"Ah! I was wondering when you would come up with that question," Devika Rani said.

Am I that transparent, Julia thought, or does every woman read every other woman in such matters?

"We will be coming to my involvement in all this soon, Mrs Samuelson," Devika Rani said, with a laugh, "and why we need Colonel Samuelson's help in the matter. But Colonel Roberts has not finished yet."

"Yes. There is more. And now it gets real ugly too. We could hardly take this lying down. The President saw that and so he called in the CIA—remember he blamed us for the previous failure in intelligence and the White House had been working directly with the Secretary of Defense; we weren't in the loop. He suspected then there were moles in the CIA, and he was probably right, because he did solve the problem for about nine months. So what went wrong? Sabotaged arms were one thing; arms that vanished were quite another. So he brought us in again.'

'We did the usual. A bait and trial run. We prepared a special shipment of sorely needed material, with the usual DoD secrecy—no more than usual. The Pakistani freighter, THE EMPEROR, had pulled into Norfolk, ostensibly for agricultural machinery. We loaded the containers in precisely the same way as we'd loaded dozens of earlier freighters; even let it leave port in precisely the same way—an unheralded departure at three in the morning. With one difference. We had on board an agent. A Pakistani who had worked for us before and who knew how to operate a ship's radio, because that is precisely what he had been, before we recruited him in Pakistan—a ship's radio officer on a Pakistani freighter."

"Well?" Joshua and Julia posed the question simultaneously.

"Well, nothing happened for about three weeks. The ship made the usual calls at Gibraltar, then entered the Mediterranean. It was an innocuous-looking ship, one freighter of many on the high seas, Nothing that would make it suspicious at all."

"Except that it left Norfolk, Virginia," Julia said, "and if there are moles in the CIA, they'd know."

"Possibly. But still nothing happened. It flew the Pakistani flag with the crescent and the star. Safe passage through the Middle East. It reached Port Said and the Egyptians let it through the Suez Canal. Sometimes they demand inspection of the cargo, but they didn't—not for this one. After Suez, it had a straight run down the Red Sea to Aden. Everything seemed fine and clear."

Colonel Roberts paused to take a generous swallow of his scotch and soda; not because he'd finished.

"Where did it call? Aden? Or Djibouti?" Joshua asked looking into his empty glass, deliberating whether he should have another; deciding against it.

"Aden. It was after Aden that the first hint of anything unusual came. We got a cable from our man on the freighter. He'd been communicating with us at regular intervals with meaningless messages. Progress reports really. He'd made friends with the regular radio officer on board, who was delighted to have the company. I suppose it can get pretty boring on a slow freighter on the Indian Ocean. Our man offered to help out—which gave him some use of the radio equipment.'

'Then, in code, for the first time, we got an urgent message. It said quite simply: ARMS FOR DOP STOP MESSAGE ENDS."

"DOP? Is that D.O.P. or DOP?" Julia framed the question but Joshua asked it. It is strange, she thought. We've been married two weeks—with a little more than a year's engagement—and he is already reading my mind? Am I reading his too?

"We don't know. It came over the air as 'DOP', without the periods. Two days later we received half a message. I say 'half', because it got cut off in mid-sentence. Mid-word actually! All he sent was a brief '19N73E', and then the radio went dead. We haven't heard from him since—and if you want my opinion, we're not likely to."

This time Colonel Roberts stopped, because he had finished. Devika Rani reached for his glass, and her own, and refilled them. Is that what an Indian wife would do, Julia thought? Should I be refilling Joshua's glass? Or would I take it away from him if he's drinking too much?

Devika Rani motioned with her hand for Joshua's glass, but he turned her down. She looked to refill Julia's drink—out of courtesy—but Julia declined as well.

Joshua had two options. He could play dumb. Ask all the questions. Or he could give them some answers—at least the ones he knew, and which he knew Julia knew too. What will he do, Julia thought, knowing that I know what he knows about 19N73E? Will he deliberately lie, or play stupid, before his wife of two weeks? After several years of marriage a man could be forgiven for such behaviour—but after two weeks?

Unless his safety was threatened in some way. Or hers. Is that why he hesitated to come up with an answer?

"I can tell you what 19N73E means," Joshua said slowly. "And so can Julia. And you know it too. So you can quit playing games. Otherwise Devika Rani wouldn't be here anyway."

"You are very quick on the draw, Colonel Samuelson," Roberts said, "as we Texans might say. But I didn't expect you to know without, at the very least, a reference to a map."

"I travelled from Bombay to London a great many times, Max. In the early years by sea. The old P&O liners. The SS Strathnaver was one of them. After the first day of being out at sea, no one much cared for what the course was. Either one was so seasick, death seemed to be a welcome recourse, or one was having such a fine time with the food and the dancing, what difference did it make where the hell the ship was going! If, after the first day, neither of these disasters had occurred, the passengers always asked for the ship's speed and the coordinates of the end points, so the ship's position could be plotted on large maps in the ship's several lounges. It sticks. That sort of information. Coordinates of Aden 13N45E;

coordinates of Bombay 19N73E. Your ship was headed not for Karachi in Pakistan but for Bombay in India. If memory serves me right, leaving Aden, the ship travels along the coast of Yemen, keeping well outside the 12-mile limit; then just after passing the coast of Oman, the course is set for Bombay. The coordinates of Karachi are less to the East and more to the North, than for Bombay."

"25N67E actually," Colonel Roberts said. "You're quite right. We figured that out as quickly as you did—with a map of course. So now you see why Devika Rani is involved. Quite naturally we got in touch with her at IMI, to find out what's happening to our arms, because, quite simply, damn it Joshua, they're being hijacked on the High Seas!"

"And what did IMI find out, Devika?" Joshua asked.

"Nothing! Not a thing. A conspiracy of total silence. But that's only to be expected. The bloody IMI is all pro-Russian anyway. They aren't going to lift a finger to help us. They became that way after you resigned from it. IMI is going down the drain, Joshua. All of the agents who are pro-Western are being eased out; Major Patel has resigned. Some are even being murdered. Mansingh had an accidental death on the Bombay-Poona highway. His car was hit by a military truck and plunged two hundred feet into a ravine in the Western Ghats, before it caught fire. The body was burnt to a cinder. We couldn't even identify it properly—who, in India, goes to the dentist? They're starving—the dentists I mean—or emigrating to England. Abdul has disappeared. We don't even have a body to show for it! Now, will you come back?"

"No."

"Why not?"

"I promised my wife I would resign from IMI if she resigned from MI-6. I gave her my word."

"I'm sure Lady Julia will let you break it." Devika Rani did not attempt to hide the scorn in her voice.

Julia refused to be drawn into it. She untucked her feet from under her, and reaching for Joshua's glass she refilled their glasses at the table. She did not sit beside him, this time perching herself on the armrest of the sofa so that Joshua's head was only inches away from her breast.

"You should never have left us!" Devika Rani said bitterly, the effects of the sherry now beginning to tell. The face was flushed with emotion. She became hysterical easily—isn't that what Joshua had told her on the night of their engagement in India? Wasn't that the reason he had thrust her bodily out of the room? Or was it just an act by a very fine actress—or a well-trained agent? Trained by whom? It was Joshua who had recruited her for IMI.

"Let me then appeal to you, Lady Julia," Roberts said.

"Please call me Mrs. Samuelson, Colonel Roberts. I leave the title at the family estate in Bromfield. For people who have called me that way since early childhood. For others, I am Mrs. Samuelson."

"Your pardon, Mrs. Samuelson. May we have the loan of your husband? For a few weeks, perhaps? The arms are ending up in India, and they are not finding their way to the Afghan border—where they should rightfully be. In the hands of men who are willing to back their struggle with their lives. There is very little we can do in the Indian arena because we are persona non-grata. But Joshua? He worked for IMI. He knows all there is to know. He knows everyone there. Bombay is his home. His city! Go with him, if you wish. Complete your honeymoon there. But let him find out a few simple answers for us. Where are our arms? Not just this last shipment but two previous shipments too. Worth hundreds of millions of dollars. Please?"

It was an impassioned speech. An appeal that seemed to be well-directed. No one spoke for a while. When finally Joshua spoke it was far from being final. That, she knew, would be left to her.

"May we, my wife and I, sleep on it for a while? I wouldn't want her to rush into deciding anything, and then, who can say, she may have made up her mind already."

Julia passed her hand over his hair, sliding it down to his shoulder, pressing his head into her so that the top of it cuddled into her breast. He leaned into it with delight, not expecting such a public demonstration of affection.

She, absent-mindedly, plucked at a lone white hair, separating it from its black brethren before excising it swiftly and painlessly. Is that what marriage would mean to him? Bound by his promises. Unable to act with freedom in matters that were so dreadfully important. And if she held him to his word—because she was afraid for his life—would he, forever, see her as his jailor? A prison of some delight? And what if she gave him his full freedom? To act without hesitation as if she did not even exist? Would that be a marriage at all? Or just a live-in arrangement, each with separate lives that met in a bed? How did one keep one's identity as a person—and yet mesh so completely with another? Separate, but tied. Together, but apart when they pleased. Free—with conditions. Incompatible! The concept of marriage itself was incompatible. Two could never be one.

Unless they both just happened to be pulling the same way.

They showed their guests out. Colonel Roberts seemed pleased. The last silence had seemed encouraging. Devika Rani seemed happy too. Perhaps it was the sherry. It did not matter they'd had too much to drink; the Ford, with the chauffeur was downstairs—and the evening wasn't over yet, for either of them. Devika Rani folded her hands together, in front of her chest, to Joshua in the Indian 'namaste'; impulsively kissed Julia on the cheek, one hand sliding behind Julia's back.

Joshua ordered dinner to be sent up to the room. With a bottle of champagne. Julia asked, anxiously, if their budget could stand it.

"Let's live it up, darling," he said. "At this rate, I'll soon be up to my neck in debt; a little more can hardly hurt much more, can it?"

But she knew he was kidding. Because he had opened up his bank balances to her when they were married, and all of them had been quite healthy. Otherwise she would never have agreed to such an expensive honeymoon in Georgetown.

They talked desultorily for a while, sometimes nostalgically about the times they had spent together in the past year after their engagement in Bombay. She had flown back soon after that to be with her grandfather in Bromfield—and had resigned, as she had promised him, from MI-6. He too had kept his word and had resigned from IMI. But he could not leave them suddenly, on very short notice, because he was far higher up in IMI than she had been with MI-6. She understood. How had he broken his links with IMI? With people he'd known and worked for so long? Had it been painful? Even traumatic? He didn't seem to show any lasting effects, but was he good at concealing his emotions? After all he had been an agent before? But then, so had she.

After dinner they decided to stay in for the evening. The weather had turned nasty, and the first of large raindrops spattered against the windows. It made the hotel suite cozy.

Two weeks of marriage, she thought, and already the air is strained between us. Could they survive fifty years of this?

"Darling," she said at last, "I would like you to make up your own mind in this business. Act as if there were no promises involved. No marriage between us either."

"That's impossible," he said quickly. "I wouldn't want it that way. But thanks anyway."

"So what are you going to do about it, Joshua?"

Before he could reply, the phone rang. It was Colonel Roberts. He picked up the receiver. She could not hear what Colonel Roberts had to say—and he had quite a lot to say, because Joshua was silent and listening for a long time—but she heard Joshua's reply. Brief, and to the point.

"No, Max. The answer is 'no'!"

He replaced the receiver, watching her as he did, smiling as he came towards her—almost like a young adolescent boy asking for his reward.

She kissed him on the lips, holding him tight, with an arm around his waist as she moved him to the bedroom.

"Do you have any of that fragrant oil?" she asked shyly. "The one with which you anointed me in Bombay? The night we got engaged? Or have you forgotten already?"

"I won't ever forget it," he said. "As it happens, I have several bottles of it packed in one of my suitcases. Quite by accident, of course."

"Of course. Just in case I had trouble sleeping at night? How thoughtful of you, darling. You do think of everything. But I thought I might anoint you for a change. If it will work wonders for you, that is—as it did for me."

His face flushed with amusement—and anticipation of delight. He undressed completely. She thought he might leave his underwear on—almost to pay her back for her initial reticence that night—but he didn't hold grudges, he told her. Never against her; never where sex was concerned. She could do with him as she wished.

She arranged two pillows under his back so that he arched in a smooth curve over them, his arms stretched over his head. The wispy black hair in his armpits, and elsewhere, seemed all desperately in need of oil. All of his body cried out for the oil.

She undressed too. No point in getting oil stains over her clothes, she said, as she dropped the articles of clothing, one by one, in the steps she took towards him, heaping the slip and the lacy bra and lacy panty over his clothes at the foot of the bed.

He lay on the bed and watched her every move, marveling, as he had done these past two weeks, at the newness of her. She would always be that way to him. A delight! The brown hair everywhere, the curl of it sometimes falling over her forehead. She blew it away with a puff of her breath.

She sat on the bed beside him, her feet tucked underneath her thighs, and poured a generous pool of oil onto his belly. It was a pool she would dip into when her fingers had run dry. Using both hands in circular motion, she spread it all over him. She was not adept at it—not having done it before—but he guided her hands to where he felt it was most needed.

He was not as passive a subject as she had been. He would insist on dipping his fingers into that same pool of oil and anointing her at the same time. He had little control, because he could reach only selected areas of her, such as her breasts and thighs.

She let him, except when his hand interfered with her smooth oiling of his body, when she retaliated by gripping the offending hand in her armpit. She held it there for longer than necessary, and he let it be, feeling the passion surge within them both, until the sheer touch between them, became an unbearable "agony" to both of them, when he forced her back on to the bed and covered her body with his own.

He remembered in time, and stopped.

"I'm not protected," he said.

"Does it matter?"

"You might get pregnant?"

"Isn't that the general idea?"

She held his head away from her so she could kiss him on the lips. Passionate, demanding, hungry kisses that surprised, even her, in their intensity. She had not known such desire before.

"Are you quite sure? So soon after marriage."

"Darling, if I wasn't quite sure, I wouldn't have married you, would I? I'm twenty-eight years old; you're thirty-five. I want children, Joshua. Please!"

Without hesitation he pulled her up, slipping into her, then straightening her thighs under him, as the surges erupted within the both of them.

He lay for some time on her, his head lost among her brown hair, nuzzling the side of her neck, occasionally murmuring words of endearment in English, which she understood, and in some Indian language, which she did not—but which were just as sweet.

Dear God, she thought, how will I ever be able to repeat the joy of this—if I lose him? And the thought made her grip her arms round his neck and back and press him down to her.

Did he feel the same way too? This was not the time to ask, when he was almost asleep on top of her. It would have to be that way, she decided—his being on top—not because he couldn't have taken her weight on top of him, but because it was the way she liked it! He felt he might be making her uncomfortable, and so he would have rolled off her—that is if she would let him. So after a wrestling match—which he won; she weighed more than him but he was stronger than she was—he rolled triumphantly off her. They lay side by side, his hand across her breast, his thigh over hers, savoring the presence of a naked spouse beside, like dying ripples spreading a glow of consummated pleasure, unwilling to see the evening come finally to a close. He fondled her breasts, passing his hand over her nipples; she played with the hair on his chest.

"Darling," she said, "what did Colonel Roberts have to say?"

His voice, buried from somewhere below, in the region of her neck, sounded sleepily vague.

"Nothing much, my love. He wanted an answer and I told him 'no'."

"Yes, I heard that. But he seemed to go on for ever so long."

"You know what Max is like? Uses a paragraph where a sentence would do. Long-winded! That's Max for you. Went on and on about how important the matter was to Indo-Pak relations. These CIA types, that's all they think about—political fallout!"

Julia's hand froze on his chest.

"What did you say, Joshua?"

"Political fallout. Between India and Pakistan if Pakistani arms are being hijacked to India. He has a point though."

"No! No! I mean about Indo-Pak?"

"Indo-Pak relations. Why, does that interest you?"

"Say it again, darling. Just the first word."

He did not understand, but he would have denied her nothing—not now when it felt so good with her.

"Alright, here goes." He closed his eyes. "Indo-Pak, Indo-Pak, Indo-Pak, Indo-Pak. Shall I stop now? I'm beginning to sound like a parrot or a bloody Indian mynah."

She laughed, slapping him gently across the chest as loving chastisement. She turned towards him, raising herself so that she was able to look him in the face, a few inches away.

"I like to write, Joshua. You've always known that. Not very successfully—though the Editor of the London Times did tell Grandfather my work was good. When I write, I live with words. Play with them; dream with them. You could say I even have an 'affair' with them! You're not jealous, are you?"

He shook his head, waving his hand in generous approval. She had his full permission to sleep with them whenever she wished!

"They ring in my head sometimes. Phrases, sentences; sometimes even a single word—like Indo-Pak. Drop the first two and the last two alphabets—and you have DOP."

He sat up in bed, pushing her aside gently, swinging his legs to the floor, his back to her.

"You're right! Of course, you are. Oh, you're so clever, darling. I would never have thought of it. It is the word the CIA agent saw on the freighter in the Arabian Sea."

"Could it have been the previous name of the ship itself—before it was named THE EMPEROR?"

"No, it couldn't have been. If it was, Max would have told us. No! It had to be a word he saw on board the ship itself. Say like on the crates in the hold. The shipments were made in unmarked crates from Norfolk. Safer not to excite attention to anyone on the dock. Enemy agents that is. But when the ship rounded Aden, why, they painted the words on to the crates. Before reaching Bombay."

"Why?"

"Because, my guess is, that they are to be shipped to DOP. It must be the name of the importing company that will present papers for the unloading of the crates at the Bombay Port Trust Docks in the harbor. Oh, darling, you are clever!"

His admiration for her was undisguised. Almost as much as when he saw her undressed beside him. And though in the two weeks of marriage that had happened several times before, the admiration was just the same—undiminished and undisguised.

She blushed with the praise—and pulled him back into the bed with her.

"What are you going to do about it, Joshua?" Her concern was real. It was her problem too.

"The point is, darling, what are you going to do about it?"

"Yes, it is our problem."

"I wasn't quite honest with you, Julia," he said. "About the telephone call from Max. You're right. He did go on for some time, and it wasn't all about Indo-Pak relations either."

"Oh! Will you 'fess and tell? I promise to forgive you."

"May all wives be as loving and understanding. He was threatening to make a phone call—if I said 'no'."

"Who to?"

"To one of the directors of MI-6. Begging him to put some pressure on you to agree to his request."

This time she sat up in bed, pulling her bedclothes to her knees, hurting eyes flitting over his face.

"I'm sorry, Julia. They will use foul means. I can't see how Grandfather can refuse either, can he? They've helped him out often enough in the African arena—when he needed their help. And it's not as if there is any real danger. A simple investigation. You can probably make your own terms too—before you agree."

"Such as?"

"Such as fixing a time limit on the operation. Say one month?"

Julia shook her head firmly.

"I can't spare you for a month. I can't spare you for a week—or a day either! But you're right. I can make my own terms—and I will too."

Joshua looked at her apprehensively. He had not seen that look in her eyes before. The upward thrust of the chin, with the clamped lips—and the coldly, royal look in her eyes—that made the shy, sensitive, loving girl into the stubborn woman who would relentlessly hold her ground. It frightened him to see her that way. He kept forgetting, he told himself, that she was royalty, and they had their own way of dealing with commoners—like him!

"Come on, Julia. Out with it. What are you going to insist on having? Not a new husband, I trust?"

That caused her to soften.

"That too, perhaps," she said, with a chiding laugh. "But, for sure, I will insist that I go with you. Keep an eye on you. Make sure you don't get into trouble with all those beautiful Indian women. Either they get the both of us—or neither. That way we will always be together, darling, and if you say there is no danger, why, you should be happy to agree."

He frowned, throwing up his hands in despair at her logic—which was unassailable. He would have argued with her, and if that had not worked, tried other means as well—such as the use of sex as a loving inducement—but the matter was cut short.

The telephone rang.

Neither would answer it. She let it ring five times; then, with a sigh of resignation, pulled on a dressing gown, struggling with the cord of it, as she made her way into the living room of the suite.

It was, as Joshua had predicted, her grandfather, the eleventh Earl from Bromfield, England.

CHAPTER 3

They left next morning. Early. Catching a cab off the street outside the Inn; not calling for one. Their return flight was from Dulles. Instead they went to National Airport. The ticketing agent altered their tickets putting them on the shuttle to Kennedy. Then British Airways on a direct flight to London.

James met them at Heathrow with the Bentley. It was Julia's old Bentley and that pleased her enormously—as James knew it would. He had been with the eleventh Earl from the age of sixteen—a general handy-boy turned man, and though now both grown up and mature, with a steady girl of his own, he still worshipped her from afar. He was handsome in his own way, with long hair that he wore shoulder length, a strong chin and deep, dark eyelashes, that Julia suspected he touched up every day to accentuate their threatening nature.

Julia patted the bonnet of the Bentley as James put the luggage into the boot.

The drive from Heathrow to Bromfield took just over an hour. They did not stop at the lodge, but she did ask James to slow down to a crawl to allow old Crabtree to come out of it and come smartly to attention and salute, while she lowered the window and gave him a friendly wave of her hand—the free hand that wasn't nestling inside Joshua's.

James did not know that Old Crabtree had fed her, in childhood, many a muffin from his own high tea. Joshua knew about it, because Julia had filled him in with many details of her life at Bromfield, before she knew him, just so that he might feel more comfortable coming back with her to her old, ancestral home.

Joshua was not quite so certain. He did not know what was expected of him. This was the first time he was coming to Bromfield, to stay for a while. Certainly it was the very first time he was entering the gates as Lady Julia's husband and the Master of Bromfield. The Young Master, if distinction had to be made between him and the eleventh Earl who was still the real Master of the estate.

"Be yourself, darling," she whispered. "They'll like you, I promise! These are servants we've had since my early childhood—except James here—and even he's been with us over five years. Wave to them if you wish; they might rather like that."

Joshua declined. It was not his style, he said, with a smile. He was not royalty—as she was; had no wish to be. He was a commoner—and proud of it. Seducing royalty? Ah, now that was an entirely different matter. He'd enjoyed that last night. Had she enjoyed it too?

She blushed, and did not press the point. All she wanted was for him to be comfortable, and if he felt that was as a commoner, she had no wish to change it.

The old Earl met them at the front door. He could not restrain his impatience at the delay that would have occurred had he followed accepted procedures and received them in his study. So he was out on the front steps ahead of Tomkins, the butler, and Emma, the sixty-year old housekeeper, who had at one time been Julia's governess and had doubled as her mother as well.

The old Earl, sprightly as ever, tripped down the last few stone steps of the stately home to enfold Julia in his arms in a warm and tight embrace that would last forever. Neither had any other family in so many years past. Until Joshua.

He shook Joshua's hand warmly, pumping it with genuine pleasure, feeling the strong, young hand reciprocate.

"Welcome to Bromfield, my boy! And thank you for coming so promptly."

He took Joshua off to the study.

Not Julia. She had a reception line to meet first. All of the servants, in order of rank, with Tomkins and Emma leading the way, ending in a new scullery maid who curtseyed so low she nearly fell down, saving herself only by grabbing on to Julia's ungloved hand, and then died with embarrassment for years afterwards when she thought of it.

"I've put your ladyship in your old rooms, and Dr Samuelson—the Young Master, I mean—in the East Wing," Emma said.

Julia frowned.

"Why weren't we put together in the Blue Suite, Emma?" she asked quietly. "That would have been much more comfortable—and appropriate—for a married couple, that is."

"Yes, my Lady. But the Viscount Edward and his wife are visiting as well—they are with His Lordship in the study now—and we had no choice in the matter. His wife was adamant she wouldn't take separate rooms from her husband. Begging your pardon, Lady Julia, these foreigners don't always see things the way we do."

"Quite, Emma. Foreigner?"

"Yes, my Lady. The Viscountess comes from the Young Master's part of the world—Pakistan, I believe. Has a name that I've only just begun to master—Viscountess Begum Naseem Banu!" Emma ended triumphantly.

So Edward and the Begum were still together! Cecily had written that he had married a widow, whose husband, the Nawab, had been killed in a hunting accident. They had six children—four grown kids from the Nawab and two little ones of his own. That had been a surprise, but when she thought about it, she could see how, jilted by an English girl and the granddaughter of an Earl, he might turn to a foreigner for a wife. Not really jilted; it had never come to that. It had been the very first sexual experience for the both of them. They had both been sixteen years old. Cecily, Viscount Edward's sister, had set up the tryst in the shrubbery of the boarding school in Kent that Cecily and she attended. Except that the Viscount and she had both slightly differing concepts of what that first sexual experience would be. She had puckered up her lips for a kiss and closed her eyes. For a few seconds nothing happened. She opened her eyes to find his hands groping her breasts, markedly delineated even under the tight and sexless school uniform. So she slapped him hard, at which Viscount Edward burst into tears. After which she had spent the best part of half an hour in the shrubbery, begging him to restrain his tears, even passing his hands over her breasts to show him she was not offended—and in apology. That had been a disaster; the sooner forgotten the better.

What was he doing here in Bromfield, and with his wife too?

She would soon find out.

The more pressing problem was Joshua, when he'd find out he wasn't being put up in the same suite of rooms as her. True, it was an adjoining suite and there was a connecting door, which door would be kept permanently open, but would he still consider that as an affront? She knew so little about his cultural attitudes in such matters! But she did know Joshua, and knowing him, it reassured her that the matter would be satisfactorily resolved.

The men had already opened the sherry. The Begum declined. Too early for her, she said. She fondled a glass of lemonade in her jewelled fingers. That is what Julia noticed about her first—her jewellery. A filigree, 22-carat gold necklace adorned her neck, the delicate craftsmanship displayed in the finery of faceted surfaces that encased her throat in a lace of gold. And the long, hanging earrings that swayed with every movement of her head.

Why do I suffer from these feelings of inferiority, Julia thought, when I look at all these beautiful women from that part of the world? Because the Begum was extraordinarily and exotically beautiful, the slightly hooked semitic nose and the luscious lips bordering large cheeks; her charm enhanced by that agelessly mature look. Even the wrinkle or two in the eyes and the hint of double chin appeared becoming.

The eyes were fixed on Julia with that quizzical look of unrestrained curiosity, the eyelashes, long and languorous, ready to drop over the pretty, black eyes if the gaze seemed too searching.

Edward came towards Julia and held both her hands in his own, keeping her at a distance so that he might look at her full length; then drawing her close to kiss her on both cheeks.

Joshua watched from the sofa he was sharing with the eleventh Earl; the Begum watched Joshua.

"You're looking splendid, Julia!" Edward said. "You've matured a good deal since I saw you last—when was that? Twelve years ago?"

Julia nodded; freed her hands and walked over to where the Begum was sitting comfortably ensconced in a loveseat for two. Julia offered her hand, and the Begum, still seated, received it.

"I'm Julia," she said, "and I'm so very pleased to meet you. I've heard a great deal about you from my very good friend, Cecily, Edward's sister, who was at school with me. Welcome to Bromfield House."

The Begum patted the seat beside her. "Come, sit with me, Lady Julia," she said. "These men will talk shop and they bore me dreadfully. We may have more interesting things to talk about?"

"I'll be happy to sit with you," Julia said, "but on one small condition."

"Oh! And what is that?"

"That you call me 'Julia'. Otherwise I'll be forced to call you Viscountess Begum Nassem Banu."

"That would be dreadful. I do come from an old and aristocratic Indian family. My father was Maharaja of Cholistan in undivided British India. I was Princess of that kingdom. My upbringing, Julia, is not too different from yours. I go fox hunting with Edward and I am a better rider than he is—though I don't tell him that. I, too, was educated at a boarding school in England—in Sussex actually. When the British abandoned India, Father's kingdom went with it. It was fractured between India and Pakistan. We lost all our wealth, save a few rather valuable trinkets, and one loyal servant—our car-driver—who would not leave us. But you aren't interested in all this. I hear you and Colonel Samuelson have just returned from your honeymoon? From America? Tell me all about it."

The old Earl cleared his throat. Julia understood the signal and filled her glass with sherry, sitting beside the Begum, whose gold-embroidered sari pallav slipped off her ample bosom and trailed the hall floor. She made no effort to retrieve it.

"I'm sorry to be so abrupt about it," the eleventh Earl said, "but I have to go back to London in two days, and as we are having the banquet tomorrow, we will have no time—other than now—to discuss this rather important matter that our friends the Americans have thrust on us."

"Banquet! What banquet?" Julia interrupted with a renewed interest in the proceedings. "Are we having a banquet? When? Let's discuss it first—far more interesting than what our friends the Americans are foisting on us! And yes, Grandfather, that is the right word—'foisting'—because it is an imposition on my husband and me, and I have to tell you I take a very dim view of it."

"I know, dear, I know. And I am sorry to have brought you and Joshua back so quickly from the States; you will forgive me, won't you?"

"And so, Grandfather, you thought a banquet in honour of our marriage would placate me?"

"Well, I did think that it would be a good opportunity to bring together all your friends—and Joshua's too—in one banquet hall, right here in Bromfield House to celebrate—how do you put it, Joshua, in your country—this auspicious occasion?"

Julia burst out laughing. "Good try, Grandfather, but it still won't work. So you thought that bringing together a few friends—insignificant to you—would placate me? How little do you know me, dear?"

The eleventh Earl had a ghost of a smile in his eyes as he said: "Did you say the people I had invited to the banquet, to celebrate your wedding to Joshua, were insignificant to me—or to you? Would you say that Her Majesty the Queen was insignificant to us?"

"Really?" Julia looked into her sherry glass. "So you had to pull out all the stops, eh, Grandfather? Appeal to my loyalty to Queen and Country, so that if my husband of two weeks gets killed, it will make me feel better?"

"On the contrary, it is the Queen who wanted it! She's the one, who, on seeing the announcement of the marriage in the London Times, called me and suggested, in that Royal tone of hers, that a banquet would be in order for the young couple and how much she was looking forward to being there. I couldn't understand it, until the Queen's secretary called and explained. Apparently, Her Majesty has now collected her first editions of Jane Austen, and wishes to present one of them to Joshua and you as a wedding gift; more when your babies come along!"

Julia shook a finger accusingly at Joshua.

"You knew about this and you didn't tell me?"

"Darling, I had no idea, until twenty minutes ago, about any of this. I've been dying for a chance to fill you in on it, but you haven't been anywhere near me the time we've been here. I'm already missing you!"

"Their first marital quarrel," the Begum said delightedly. "How deliciously splendid! Go on Julia, don't spare him; tell him how you feel betrayed after all you've given him. The honeymoon is over!"

Julia laughed. "May all our marital quarrels be as easy as this one," she said. "Making up will be so-o-o enjoyable."

The old Earl rolled his eyes to the heavens.

"Please," he moaned, "may we get back to the business at hand—instead of being sidetracked on marital quarrels and how they may be healed? I am sorry to have interrupted your honeymoon in this way, Julia, but we had no choice in the matter. I have apologized to Joshua as well. He understands; he isn't quite sure you will."

"I don't," said Julia cheerfully. "And who's we?"

"Edward and I, of course. Didn't you know?"

"Know what? Nobody tells me anything. What should I know?"

"You poor dear," the Begum said. "Let me see if I can't fill you in, my dear. Your grandfather is the Director of the African Bureau—but you knew that already."

Julia nodded.

"Have you ever wondered who the directors of the other Bureaus are? Has Joshua never told you? Have you never asked him? He knows them all. I would have thought he would have shared some secrets with you—in bed."

Julia did not flinch. Joshua had to admire her for it. She might tease her grandfather in mock anger—and be teased by him—but a stranger like the Begum could never rile her up; upbringing forbade it.

Julia straightened her skirt over her knees—the slit had displayed a little bit more thigh than was appropriate in present company, and said: "He did offer once. The day we got engaged. In Paris. Sitting at a table on the sidewalk, in the warm sunshine, near the Place de La Republique, sharing a plate of Danish pastry and a glass of the finest French wine I have ever tasted. I told him, I didn't want to know."

"But have you never wondered who the Director of the South East Asian Bureau was? Well, you need to know now. It's Edward. My husband is a super-spy. I didn't find out until just a while ago, Julia, and I was devastated! Why could he not have told me before he married me?"

She felt betrayed and she showed it, in the way she put her head back and poured down her drink of lemonade.

"I will have a drink," she said. "Edward, darling, would you pour me out a small sherry? In my father's house, I have had the finest foreign liquor, but always in moderation."

Edward obliged.

"Well, the Begum is right," the Earl said. "Edward here has something he wants to tell us and we had to have you here for that. We need Joshua; it's as simple as that. And he tells me we can't have him because he's tied to your skirts—my words; not his. I never thought of you that way, Julia. You were the sort, I thought, who'd have let him have his own way—at least in the first few years of marriage, eh! Instead you have him tied in chains."

He looked at her approvingly. Men were meant to be tied in chains by the women they married. His wife, Julia's grandmother, now dead thirty years, had trained him well. He'd adored her.

"Don't you believe it," Julia said. "I'll show you the marks of the chains on me too. But I'm not going to allow my husband of two weeks—or fifty years—to be killed without at least knowing why?"

"Killed?" Edward interrupted. "There's no risk involved. No danger! It's just an investigation. A simple inquiry and he comes back right home to you."

"Are you sure?" Julia asked innocently.

"Oh, absolutely certain!" Edward said.

Joshua, who knew what was coming, broke into the broadest of smiles; put his hand across his mouth to conceal it.

"No risk at all? No danger, whatsoever?" Julia persisted.

"None! None at all."

"Then you'd have no objection, I presume, to me going along with him? There, Joshua, it's all settled. Edward tells us there is no risk whatsoever so neither he—nor Grandfather—can have any objection to our continuing our honeymoon in Bombay. There, dear, didn't I tell you, I'd sort it out?"

"Absurd!" Edward shouted. "Utterly impossible! He'll be travelling quite a bit; no place for a lady like you. You wouldn't want to be with him."

"Oh, I don't know. Joshua, this will give us a chance to see a little of India—his expenses paid, I presume?" This last question was addressed to Edward. "So now you know my conditions. Where he goes, I go. Or, quite simply, he doesn't go."

Edward slumped backward in his chair. He was beaten and he knew it.

"Well said, Julia," the Begum said, patting Julia's knee and raising her glass to Julia in admiration. "Lay down your conditions. Men—they should be led around on leashes. Child-bearing! That's all they think we're good for. Take me. Six children—through two husbands—and if they had their way, I'd bear them the entire cricket team!"

"Why don't you tell us what the problem is?" Julia said gently. "Then let us decide; not me alone—Joshua too."

She leaned back in complete control of them all. Except Joshua. He was leaning back too, enjoying the spin she'd thrown them into. He raised his glass to her too—as the Begum had done.

A pity she wasn't sitting next to him, Julia thought. What would he have done? Leaned over and whispered his admiration in her ear? The old Earl wouldn't have given it a second thought—might even have approved, at seeing his granddaughter glowing with Joshua tickling her ear. But, as she found out, Edward hated such public demonstrations of affection—bedroom stuff should be confined to the bedroom and forgotten everywhere else—as the Begum lamented to Julia later.

Edward began: "The problem started, as you know, with the Soviet invasion of Afghanistan. As far as we are concerned, it is a war. Brutal, savage, bloody. No holds barred, no mercy given. I was out there—that's when Naseem found out. About my connection with MI-6, that is. The mujahidin wanted arms; the Americans were only too willing to help; MI-6 with PMI worked out the arrangements for the transfer of arms. We're more familiar with that part of the world and the Americans were only too happy to have us deal with the routing and disposal of the arms after they reached Pakistan.'

'Well, the matter seemed simple enough. Ship them to Karachi, then move them by rail to Peshawar. But that part you know already; Colonel Roberts told us he filled you in on it—and on the sabotage that took place repeatedly. Almost as if they had a mole in the CIA. That sort of thing can be very frustrating. Hundreds of millions of dollars of arms wasted and the freedom fighters getting slaughtered by our own equipment malfunctioning. Didn't speak much for the arrangements we'd made. The General was bloody mad with the CIA and MI-6 and PMI and the whole setup. I can't say I blame him either. He's got a few million Afghan freedom fighters as refugees on his northern borders and within his northern borders. It is like a powder keg out there! They could easily turn on him, particularly if they are supplied faulty equipment. Slaughter breeds anguish, and anguish breeds hatred. And there is an awful lot of hatred out there."

The Viscount stopped. The clean-cut boyish face with the creamed and carefully parted blond hair on the thin, erect body, trembled as he spoke. The long, lean fingers clenched the sherry glass. The sharp eyes, piercingly blue, would not look up at them.

"To be fair to the General," he continued, "he didn't do anything behind our back. He called me in—remember I was in Pakistan at the time—and he told me. He was going to make other arrangements—and he did. He didn't tell me what they were."

The Viscount stopped again. He wasn't sure how much of all this he ought to be telling them. If he had his way, it would not have been any of it. Trust Julia to throw him into a bind!

"Well, he didn't tell me a thing, but everything was going smoothly. The arms were reaching the freedom fighters—and in pristine condition too—until two months ago, when two shipments of arms just vanished. That's when the General called me in again. I flew out from London—gave me a chance to be with Naseem who was already out there meeting with her family—and it was then that the General gave me the details, binding me to secrecy."

'The General went to the Prime Minister of India. A secret meeting was arranged in an abandoned Fort in the Thar Desert. On the border between India and Pakistan. An easy place to maintain security because nothing lives out there. Shallow sand dunes, unlike some of the deserts in other parts of the world. And lonely as hell! There they made a pact. The Prime Minister would find one person to work out a suitable arrangement to ship the arms, not through Pakistan but through India. His code name: Raja. The General would find another. Code name: Bahadur, who would arrange the route after the arms crossed the border. Raja and Bahadur met in that same disused Fort to hammer out the agreement; two handwritten copies—one with each. The documents had been named by the Prime Minister and the General, in their previous meeting, as THE THAR ARTICLES.'

'And it worked! For a while the mujahidin gave the Soviets bloody hell. They tumbled to it, of course, the Soviets I mean, but they couldn't very well do much about it. India had already advised them, through diplomatic channels, to get out of Afghanistan—and they had rejected that advice. After all India was their ally. They couldn't very well sabotage cargo in a friendly country. And the route that Raja and Bahadur had planned took the arms as close to the Afghan border as was practical—through the Punjab and into Lahore, where they entered Pakistan under stringent security. It seemed the two of them had solved the problem—until something went wrong."

"What went wrong?" Joshua prompted.

"Well, we don't quite know. That's what you're going to find out. All we do know is that the Indian then murdered the Pakistani."

"What?" Joshua said, quietly. "Are you sure?" The Begum showed surprise too. The old Earl, unflappable as ever, did not blink—or perhaps he already knew. Julia crossed her arms in surprise as well at Edward's remark that had shocked them all. Joshua waved his hands in disbelief too. Perhaps the aspersions being thrown on a top agent in the country—a choice personally made by the Prime Minister of India had to be one of his most trusted agents in the field—caused the incredulous look on his face.

"They'd made an arrangement—Raja and Bahadur—to meet, in that disused Fort, but only if either of them asked for it. Their very first meeting, to all accounts, had been a friendly one."

"How do you know?" Joshua asked.

"How do I know what?"

"That the meeting was a friendly one? Were you there?"

"No. Only the two of them would meet—that was the arrangement. But our man reported back to the General; filled him in on the visit, and his account of it was that the meeting was a very friendly one. He couldn't have been more pleased with the success of the encounter! 'Raja was a person he could respect; even love as a brother!'—his very words."

"What was his name?" the Begum asked.

"Whose?"

"The Pakistani agent?" Joshua said. "The one you say was murdered. Code name: Bahadur. Who was Bahadur?"

"Colonel Rashid Khan—a Pathan. A mountain of a man. Six foot four, and built as only a Pathan can be! Lean and strong—not an ounce of fat anywhere; built like a warrior of old. Wore a turban with a trailing edge, as most Pathan fighting men do, to wipe his face in the heat. To him it was personal. He came from the Northwest Frontier Provinces, and he would willingly have died to break the Soviets—but not at the hands of a 'friend' who turned out to be a traitor and a coward!"

"How can you say that?" Julia asked.

"One of them asked for an emergency meeting—we don't know who. It was set for July 23. What they discussed, we don't know. The meeting was over. But it was the hour for prayer. Rashid Khan knelt on the prayer mat, his eyes closed, and as he bent forward to touch his forehead to the ground, Raja shot him in the back of the head. Execution style! Cowardly, I would say, wouldn't you?"

"What was the name of the other agent?" the Begum asked. "The Indian agent—Raja—the one who murdered Bahadur?"

Edward thumped the fist of one hand into the palm of the other in sheer frustration. "We don't know! That is what is so annoying."

"How do you know the name of one agent and not the other?" Julia said, again in disbelief. She hated it, not being able to accept all she was told.

"Because our man didn't tell us. They made a pact, the two of them, in that deserted Fort in the Thar Desert. Each swore never to reveal the identity of the other. That was understandable. So that the system could not be monitored by third parties, and to prevent assassination. Little did Rashid Khan know that he was going to be assassinated by the very man he was so willing to trust."

"Are you sure, it was a man?" the Begum asked. "It could very well have been a woman, could it not? Women are pretty handy with revolvers these days."

Edward nodded, but in doubt. "The revolver, he was shot with, was left behind in the Fort. It was a woman's weapon, with a mother-of-pearl handle and only five chambers—not six. Light and delicate; the sort a woman might carry in her purse. Yet, I can't see the Prime Minister of India picking a woman to work out an arrangement with a Pakistani male agent in the middle of the Thar Desert—and if he did, she must be some woman!"

"What possible motive did the Indian agent have for murdering his counterpart?" Joshua asked.

"Ah! The motive. We come to that. They had hammered out the arrangement in about five hours, in that very first meeting in the Fort. They wrote it up in the form of a document called THE THAR ARTICLES. Two handwritten copies, four foolscap sheets of white paper, signed by the two of them, each as a representative of his government. Two copies, that is all. No other! Each had possession of one copy. As you can see the copies were dynamite—as far as documents go. A preamble that set the background, including reasons why the document was being drawn up—at the express command of both leaders; then the actual setup, giving the precise routes and internal arrangements in both countries that would see the arms safely from Norfolk, Virginia, through Bombay to Peshawar and the mujahidin, and their method of contacting each other. They signed both copies, the two of them. One copy with Rashid Khan; the other with Raja.'

'Just think what would happen if a copy of that document fell into the wrong hands? What would the repercussions be? Different for both countries—and for both leaders. Internal opposition to both these leaders—and their governments—runs high. If the document were to be made public by either side, the fallout would be catastrophic—but more so for India than for Pakistan. Pakistan has very little to lose by the document being made public. Some opposed to the General would grumble that it was not necessary to go to an old enemy for help, but the success of the venture would have stifled such criticism; he has the media reined in any way! It might do some good too, for Pakistan's relations with India.'

'But for India? Disastrous—there isn't a word strong enough to express it. The Soviets would protest this backstabbing by a friend, possibly cutting off their aid to India as well. The opposition, and the press, would clamor for the Prime Minister's head for making such an arrangement with the General without the approval of the government. India's neutrality would be compromised. He would be forced to resign. An already chaotic state of affairs, with the Sikhs in the Punjab, would degenerate into anarchy. The consequences of disclosure would be serious for India—and very real in that part of the world."

The old Earl had been silent until now, allowing Edward to recount MI-6's version of the state of affairs. He had seen Joshua's disbelief to the charge of murder being levelled against one of his countrymen. And he sympathised with the loyalty Joshua must feel, tinged as it must now be with the fear that it could, in fact, be true. With the evidence mounting up, Joshua would have to set aside his loyalties if he was to find the truth. Because they now had a motive for murder. He rose from the sofa.

Joshua smiled benignly at them all. "I still don't believe it. You have a very poor opinion of Indians! What would I do? I'd go to the PM and say: Sir, I cannot do this; find another to execute Bahadur. He is like a brother to me—if Bahadur thought of him as a brother, the feelings must have been mutual? Or, Julia, am I being naïve in thinking that one can love and the other can kill?"

Julia threw up her hands in despair. His logic was unassailable; the evidence pointed the other way.

"We are not discussing Indians or Pakistanis or Christians or Jews or Muslims—or Englishmen," the old Earl said. "We are talking about people. One man can turn traitor and execute his friend without universal condemnation. It is what we do. It must have been hard, but we have to admire his strength, that he was able to bring himself to carry out his orders! There are not many who are made that way. I have been Director of the African Bureau of MI-6 for some years now. Did I not give orders for Slagter to be killed? Fortunately, we got Slagter alive, but it could easily have gone the other way. Then, would not my hands have been just as bloody?"

Joshua motioned to Julia to come and sit with him, patting the sofa beside him. She obeyed. He reached for her free hand and held it unashamedly. She put her sherry on the side table and moved up close to afford him the warmth of her side. He massaged her arm lovingly. His face relaxed; the Joshua she knew and loved was beside her.

"When did all this occur? How did they find him? If you need my help, I need to know," Joshua said.

"They—Bahadur and Raja—had an arrangement to meet only if either asked for a meeting. They had a means to communicate with each other. They had a meal together. Potluck—Bahadur brought one dish; Raja, drinks for both of them. How do we know? Because that is how they found the set up when Rashid Khan did not return for three days. His wife got worried and contacted PMI. They sent two men with camels looking for him. The border is unpatrolled for most of that region. Particularly now that hostilities between the two countries have ended. Both sides may freely approach the Fort—no one lives out there in the blistering desert anyway! That is how they found him, Joshua. They cleaned the place up and brought him back on a camel."

"His copy of THE THAR ARTICLES was not on him."

"Perhaps he didn't take it there?" Joshua said.

"We searched his house. He has a small flat on the top of his wife's kabab shop, that also sells burkhas, in Meena Bazaar. The Bazaar is only for women. Women run the shops, provide the services, and only women may shop there. But the flat has a back stairs that leads directly out of the Bazaar—for Rashid Khan's use. We sent in the Begum with some female agents to question his wife. She was heartbroken—and very cooperative. They ransacked the place, taking it apart. Every floor tile, every loose chunk of plaster in the walls, every fitting and fixture behind which he might have tucked it away, all of his furniture, every book he owned, every chair had its seat slit, every sofa was cut—seat, back and sides—and we couldn't find it!"

"She allowed you to do all that?" Julia said. "His wife, I mean. She stood by and watched you wreck everything she owned?"

The Begum nodded. "She was more than willing, Julia. She egged us on! If it would have helped to find her husband's murderer she would have permitted us to slit her body! And all the time she kept beating her breasts and crying for vengeance. She was the wife of a Pathan. She knew how to handle both knife and gun. Tell me, she screamed, who the murderer is, and I will execute him for you! We found it difficult to restrain her. But I can tell you, for sure, and I was there Joshua, there was no document in that flat. Four pages, foolscap paper, in English, handwritten, called THE THAR ARTICLES—it was not there."

"So we can only presume," Edward said, "he took it with him to the Fort when he went to meet his counterpart. Look at the evidence, Joshua. There was motive. There was opportunity. The document is missing. Rashid Khan has been murdered. Who would you say did it?"

"It certainly seems to point to Raja," Joshua said. "The evidence is overwhelming. Find him and let the Pakistanis execute him. But that isn't why you need me, is it? You want me to find out where those arms went—and why? I'd say it now becomes clear I'll have to go there and poke around a little."

"Well said, Joshua. Good show!" the old Earl said. "I was wondering when you'd put your foot down and tell Julia she can't run your life—even if you did marry her. Two weeks flat! I have to tell you, to my eternal shame, I took a lot longer than that before I told Julia's grandmother she couldn't order me around."

"Oh, really?" Julia said. "I didn't know you ever did that, dear? Why haven't you told me this before? Emma has always said Grandma had you eating out of the palm of her hand until the day she died."

"Emma talks too much," the Earl grumbled, but he hadn't really expected anyone to believe him. He had adored his wife—and they knew it.

"Well then, that settled," Edward said, showing his relief at Joshua's acquiescence by raising his glass to him. He had been standing while he addressed them; he prepared to sit in the seat vacated by Julia, beside his wife.

"Not quite," Julia said. "I haven't said 'yes' yet."

"Oh, come on Julia! You can see the importance of it, can't you? We can't use anyone else. We don't have anyone else." Edward was about to leave his seat but Naseem restrained him.

"You did say there was no danger?" Julia said.

"Yes, I did. I assured you a few minutes ago."

"No risk at all?"

"None. Trust me."

"Oh, I do. Well, if you say there's no danger and no risk, whatsoever—and you've repeated it twice— why, then Joshua I'll come along with you. I can see you want those arms to reach the mujahidin. And as Edward says there's no risk and no danger in finding out where three ship loads of arms went, and who killed Rashid Khan, and recovering his copy of THE THAR ARTICLES—is there now? But, and I've said it before, I'm not going to allow my husband of two weeks—or fifty years—to go out there and get himself killed, without going with him, am I?"

"That's impossible!" the eleventh Earl shouted. "You will stay here in Bromfield with me. It's only for a month or so—and I could do with the company. Please, Julia?"

"I know that, dear, and I will come, with Joshua, and we'll spend more time with you, I promise. But not just now. Besides Joshua and I are on our honeymoon. It isn't over yet—and isn't likely to be for some time, is it Joshua? So that's my final word, and that's flat, and you can take it or leave it. Either you get the both of us in a package deal—or no Joshua."

Joshua had to admire her for it. It was a different Julia he was seeing before him. In all the time he had known her intimately—now for over a year since the engagement—she had never put her foot down to have her way, either with him or with anyone else. She had tried reason, and logic, and restrained argument, and sometimes—with him—cajoling and the use of her extensive charms. But she had never won a point by laying down the terms and refusing to budge. It was so unlike her. She was the most polite person he had known. She said 'thank you' and 'please' to bell boys and waiters and her servants too. He'd even heard her say 'thank you' to the dog when the golden retriever had brought in her morning paper, patting it on the head and surreptitiously feeding him a beef sausage under the table. Gentility was what set her apart from other people. Even from him. He was not a particularly aggressive person, but she was quite definitely the more kindly, accommodating half of them as a whole.

That is until now. When she had abandoned all that meekness he had almost taken for granted in her. She would risk her life to protect him; could he ask for any more from her in the marriage? Did he deserve her? Wouldn't she have been better off falling in love with someone nearer her station in life—say a Duke or a Prince of the realm? He shook his head to clear away the doubts that had crept in within two weeks of marriage. Julia saw the shake of his head and misunderstood him.

"Darling, you did say you would let me decide?"

"Julia," he said, as gently and persuasively as he could, "Grandfather is right. I will constantly be on the move. We may not be together. The monsoons in India are coming to a close; that will make India hot and humid—and very uncomfortable! Far better you wait for me here? I won't be long, I promise! And I will come back."

"Noble intentions. And well said. And the answer is still—No. You're not being very reasonable, Joshua. If this is to be our first real marital quarrel—and it shows every signs of being one—perhaps we ought to discuss it in the privacy of our bedroom? But if you wish to discuss it here, the answer is categorically 'No'!"

Julia leaned back, still hanging on to him, stretched her feet and looked at her toes, not daring to smile, though that is what she felt within her. The urge to be with him and near him and protect him had overridden all other emotions, but now that the day was won, she felt the need for reconciliation. Marriage, she decided, was almost a battleground. But when the war was over, the making up was even more important—and distinctly more pleasurable.

"Beside, darling," she continued, "you might even need me. For any inquiries to be carried out in Pakistan. You will not be very welcome there, being both Indian and Jewish. On the other hand, with a little help from the British High Commission in Islamabad—

and the Begum here—why, I could carry out your commands, obey your orders, be a Watson to you! Darling, think of it that way. Please!"

"What a splendid idea, Julia!" the Begum said. "Why, Edward and I will come with you two too. Did I get that right? The English I mean? I'll take you shopping in Meena Bazaar. Look up Rashid's widow. The kababs she sells in her food shop are out of this world. The finest! Cooks them herself with her own blend of spices. A little too spicy for you, perhaps, but we'll wash it down with lemonade. No beer, I'm afraid, though the men, surreptitiously, always seem to find some."

While she was speaking, Edward had stormed out of his seat, facing her menacingly. "You're not going anywhere, Naseem!" he yelled. "We've only just come back from there. And with the kids too. And I suppose you'll want to take them with you again?"

"Naturally, darling," the Begum said evenly. "Ever hear of a Muslim woman visiting family in Pakistan without taking her children with her? It just isn't the done thing. Julia will find that out too, real quick, when Joshua's mother will demolish her with disdain if she doesn't bring her children to visit their grandmother. Take my word, Julia. Never go alone to that part of the world without your children—all of them. They'll never let you hear the last of it if you do."

"It doesn't have to be that part of the world," Julia said. "I know one grandfather here who would demolish me with disdain if I visited without bringing my children to visit him."

"Well said, Julia," the Earl said. "And, please, will you make it quick? I'm not getting any younger and we need an heir. The twelfth Earl of Bromfield!"

They broke up after that. She had taken care of one problem, and it seemed to her satisfactorily, though what the consequences of her insistence on going with Joshua, she had no means of knowing. But it seemed to be the best of alternative solutions before her. She could not have prevented Joshua from taking the assignment—if she had, she would forever have been his jailor; not his wife—but at least she was with him. She cast a quick glance at Joshua. He seemed quieter; not his old exuberant self. His eyes looked wary, suspicious. She understood. That is how agents in the field stayed alive. Not trusting anyone—sometimes not even their wives. That is why she had been so insistent he resign from IMI, while she had severed her connections with MI-6. To build trust. And now it seemed her plans were being thwarted. If only they could have been left alone, their marriage would have had a fair chance of success—despite the differences between them. An Indian and a Jew married to a Church of England English girl! Could any pair be more poles apart? Except that his hand still nestled within her own, his fingers gently massaging hers.

Marriage, she decided, was like everything else; you took each day at a time and solved each problem along the way. Like finding out where three shiploads of arms had disappeared, or who killed Rashid Khan, and tracking down the Indian agent, Raja, and recovering the missing Pakistani copy of THE THAR ARTICLES.

But the very first problem facing her was Joshua being placed in the East Wing of the house. True it had a connecting door to her suite of rooms, but each suite had only a single bed in it. Growing up, with just her grandfather in Bromfield House, had not required much else. Her grandfather had his own elaborate suite of rooms with the study and the library and the meeting room. She had hers, with a sitting room and the bedroom—with the single bed—and the bathroom. An identical suite of rooms adjoining hers—called the East Wing—had been prepared for a second child. Except that her mother had died tragically young, when Julia was five years old, and there was no second child. There was one guest suite of rooms that had a large, double bed in it, but the Viscountess, arriving first, had already secured it for Edward and herself—and they could hardly be moved from it. Courtesy to guests was implicit in Bromfield House hospitality, though she wondered if rank had anything to do with it? The house itself was huge, but, other than the centrally placed massive dining room and banquet hall, with adjoining kitchens and servant's quarters, the remaining suites were empty of all furniture, and had been closed down.

She reached her rooms to find all their luggage—Joshua's bags and her own—at the foot of her bed. She had made a detour to the kitchens to have a word with Emma about the arrangements for breakfast. Joshua had wandered off by himself. She thought he might have got lost in the huge house, until she heard the shower on, the bathroom door closed, and the sound of fairly tolerable singing emanating from within.

He came out with a towel wrapped round his middle regions, dripping drops of water onto the bedroom carpet.

"Hello, darling," he said. "Tomkins made a mistake, putting my bags in the other room over there." He waved his hand in the direction of the door connecting the suites. "But I brought them in here. This is your room, isn't it?" He waved again at the photographs on the walls and childhood memories on the tables beside the bed. He pointed to the photograph of herself and Cecily in their school uniforms, before he said. "Tell me, dear, why do they make English schoolgirl uniforms so bloody sexless? Yet, even in that, and at that age—what was it, sixteen?—you would have captured my heart!"

Julia blushed. "Thank you, darling. But wouldn't you be more comfortable in a suite of rooms all to yourself? Instead of being cramped in here with me? The connecting door will always be open—night or day."

He didn't understand her—or perhaps he didn't want to—so he looked round the room once more.

"Cramped? This room is luxury compared to the tiny one we'll share in my flat in Bombay. And the bed isn't any bigger either. Best get used to it, darling," he said cheerfully. "Please, would you close that door," he said, pointing to the main door that led into the corridor. "I wouldn't want the maid coming in while I'm changing. There was a maid in here, but I asked her to leave."

Julia closed the door and locked it. "That must have been my personal maid," she said.

He whipped the towel off his mid-section, drying himself with it. "I'm sorry," he said. "Did I do wrong? Asking her to leave? Without permission from you?"

"No, of course not, Joshua. She's only a servant; you are the Young Master of this house."

"I don't think the servants quite think of me that way, Julia. Oh, she left immediately. And curtseyed too. But she seemed surprised at being asked to leave—and her surprise showed. Take Tomkins. He looks at me as if I wasn't there!"

Julia laughed to ease the tension. She walked over to Joshua, and taking the towel from him, dried his back with it.

"It's easy to see you don't know English butlers, darling. Their faces are expressionless and without emotion. That is part of their calling. You'll soon get used to his blank stare. He looks at all of us that way—including Grandfather. When you are dressed, would you like me to call him up and ask him a question or two, while you watch his expression—or lack of it?"

Joshua laughingly declined. But he did point to wet spots she'd missed on his chest, and stomach, and lower down, and she dried them all for him.

They slept well. Despite the bed being too small. Two could not live as cheaply as one, but two could certainly sleep on a bed designed for one, if they slept all entangled with each other. He fell asleep almost immediately; she took longer. His hand was thrown over her and inside her nightgown open at the top, his palm cupping her breast, his fingers almost in her armpit. His face was smothered by the pillows somewhere in the side of her neck. She had to check he was breathing. His leg was thrown over her thighs, the bones in his knee not hurting her only because of the softness of her. Thank God for what I have, she thought; he was all bone! When she turned over to the other side, sliding out from under his leg, he turned with her, his arm still inside her nightgown and around her breast, his thighs following the curve of her own, his groin pressed into her. That was equally arousing, though she told herself, sternly, she was trying to sleep—not be aroused. And when, finally, he fell into deep sleep and turned around, taking his hand and his leg off her, freeing her for the first time that night, she promptly turned around and held him in the precise same way—because she was afraid he'd fall off the bed!

I suppose, she thought philosophically, I'll get used to this—eventually. I will get to sleep too, at some unearthly hour, I suspect, but Grandfather will just have to invest in a bigger bed!

She did fall asleep, somewhere past midnight; he'd fallen asleep immediately. She had to admire that in him. As if without a care in the world. Her mind was not like that. She wasn't cut out to be an agent. One year with MI-6 was all she'd had. How many years had he had with IMI? How long did it take to make you that way? Able to drop off to sleep without worrying about what might lie in store? Hardened! That could be another way to put it. Did you become so hard nothing could move you anymore? No! Joshua wasn't hardened. Far from it. He felt as intensely as anyone else—more than most—if she knew him well.

She woke earlier than he did. Normally the maid would have drawn the curtains, bringing in her breakfast too, but Joshua had dismissed her when he'd gone for his bath in her bathroom. His hand was still around her, his head buried somewhere in her hair. It felt good to wake up near a warm body. Thank heavens he had a slim build. His arm, limp and bearing down on her and across her, didn't weigh much.

She heard the knock on the door. Must be the maid with breakfast, she thought. She propped herself up on the bed, his hand sliding down to circle her waist, his head now buried somewhere in her side. She made sure he was breathing. She'd heard of Sudden Infant Death Syndrome, but, if she wasn't careful, she ran the risk of his being the very first victim of Sudden Husband Death Syndrome. If he would keep burrowing into her!

It was Emma. Bringing up the breakfast trays. She saw the arm encircling Julia and stopped. Uncertain if she had intruded.

"Put the trays on the table, Emma."

"I've followed the instructions you gave me, my Lady. Regarding the breakfast trays. No bacon on either tray; eggs over-easy for the Young Master. Did I get that right?"

"Perfectly, Emma."

Emma placed the trays on the table by the window; stood hesitatingly beside it, unsure if she might speak. She approached the bed at Julia's bidding.

"Yes, Emma?"

Julia took the hand encircling her waist and holding it to her lips kissed it gently, looking Emma in the eyes.

"Perhaps you would prefer me to discuss it with you later, my Lady?"

"Discuss what, Emma?"

"The sleeping arrangements."

They seem to have sorted themselves out, as you can see. Perhaps you can move one of the larger beds in here? If you have one? But that is the only concession the Young Master is prepared to make—and I agree with him."

"Quite right too, my Lady, if your Ladyship wishes it."

"I do, Emma."

"Then that is as it will be, Lady Julia. What shall we do about the maid?"

"I'll manage without her."

"Oh, no, my Lady!" Emma said, almost in tears. "You will need a maid. Some of the formal dresses you have in the closet, they lace up or button up or zip up the back. How could you manage?"

"Then we do have a problem, Emma, don't we? I'll just have to give up formal wear and buy dresses that lace up or button up or zip up the front."

"Not if your Ladyship would give me permission to wait on you?"

"Oh, I couldn't ask you to do that, Emma. You have quite enough to do as it is, running the household. Besides we won't be here long."

"That is what I'm so afraid of, Lady Julia," Emma said, speaking fast. "This house, which is your home, will no longer be comfortable, to live in, for you and Dr. Samue—the Young Master—and you will avoid coming back to it, and I couldn't bear that. Not on account of us servants, my Lady."

She was almost on the verge of tears.

Joshua must have been listening in, or perhaps he always slept with one ear open, because he turned around propping himself up on the bed beside Julia. The bedclothes fell off; he wasn't wearing a pajama top. The rest of him was hidden beneath the bedclothes.

Emma stood her ground. Joshua put his hands through his unruly mop of black hair.

"Emma," he said, gently, "both Lady Julia and I would be pleased to have you attend Lady Julia as her maid, while we are at Bromfield House. And we can both reassure you I will take every care to see you are not offended."

Emma smiled in relief. "That does not bother me, Sir, that I might be offended. I would prefer you to be comfortable in this house. I was married for thirty-six years—and have five children—the eldest of them, my son, is about your age. Are you comfortable in this house, Sir?"

"Oh, I am, I am! Take last night, for instance. Best sleep I've had all week. Much more comfortable than the Inn in Washington DC, wouldn't you say so, darling? Must have something to do with the size of the bed? I like this bed."

"That will be all, Emma," Julia said. "You've heard what the Young Master has to say about it all? You will be my maid—and this bed stays."

While they were getting respectable for breakfast, Joshua said: "Darling, this lacing up and buttoning up and zipping up—isn't that what husbands are for? Or am I being old-fashioned?"

"Yes, dear, they are. But I thought you'd be more help lacing down or unbuttoning or zipping down, at the end of the day. Remind me to tell Emma not to wait up for me after the banquet tonight."

They had breakfast at the table by the window, with Tomkins sent up to wait on them. The old crusty lined face, expressionless, emotionless, hovered behind Julia's chair, napkin over his arm, saying nothing, replying very courteously when addressed, almost non-existent, except to carry out their wishes for a second cup of tea, a shining example of the English butler—efficient, stooping and deferential.

Joshua would have preferred to dismiss him from the room; not many breakfasts he was going to have with Frankenstein hovering behind her and facing him full in the face! It ruined his appetite. But Julia begged for his understanding.

As Tomkins cleared away the breakfast trays, he paused.

"May I have a word with the Young Master, my Lady?"

"Certainly, Tomkins. What is it you wish to say?"

"Am I right, Sir, you are Colonel Samuelson of the Indian Army?"

"That's right, Tomkins. The Rajputs. Stationed in Ajmer. Finest fighting infantry regiment in India. Incomparable, anywhere! Why do you ask?"

Joshua's tone was almost belligerent where his regiment was concerned.

"That was my regiment too, Sir, in the Great War. Before your time. I was only a Havaldar, Sir, but I couldn't agree with you more. The finest anywhere!"

Joshua turned to look at Tomkins with new interest. The face was flushed with pride, the stature was now erect; the soldier had taken the place of the butler before them.

"Well, Tomkins, this is a surprise. You fought very bravely in Burma, if I recall the history of the regiment."

"That we did, Sir. And it was commanded then by Major-General Sir Isaac Samuelson, who was killed in action in July 1944. Your grandfather, Sir, if I am right?"

"Yes."

"May I say, Sir, how very pleased I am that you are a member of this household and the Young Master of this house—if I don't presume, Sir, that is—and how honoured I am to be of service to you."

Tomkins turned to leave with the trays, bowed to them, then straightened himself erect and, like the soldier he was, left the room.

Joshua looked at Julia. He thought he'd see on her face that smile of triumph that he'd often had, when in war, he'd won the day on the battlefield. There was a smile in her eyes; not of triumph, but of relief that another of the problems facing her, in her marriage to him, had been overcome.

He felt so ashamed of himself that he rose from his seat and moved over to her. "Forgive me," he said.

"What for, darling? Anyone can misjudge someone he doesn't know. Tomkins, particularly."

"Not for that," he said, "but for misjudging you. I thought I'd see a smile of triumph—the sort of when I'd won the day in battle—but you had a wonderful smile of thankful relief, that my problems with Bromfield House had been resolved. Forgive me?"

She drew his head down and kissed him on the lips.

CHAPTER 4

Late that morning, it seemed as if a cyclone had whirled into Bromfield House for 'the banquet given by the Earl of Bromfield in honour of the marriage of his granddaughter, Lady Julia Rayburn-Spencer and Colonel (Dr) Joshua Samuelson of the Indian Army'. That is what the invitations read, sent out by the old Earl before the couple had even set foot in England. Julia assured Joshua that even she hadn't a clue who was invited and who was not; that the Queen had suggested the celebration to the Earl and then graciously accepted his invitation to her and her retinue—Joshua had actually been given that information twenty minutes ahead of her.

That was the reason for the cyclone. If the Queen was to attend—and she stubbornly resisted any limitations placed on her freedom—security was at the highest levels, with MI-5 agents descending on Bromfield House and inspecting every wall in the house and every crack in the floor. When the House had been made secure, they moved the agents to the gatehouse, where old Crabtree watched in horror as the lax and easy way in which he'd admitted visitors in the past was thrown out. Instead two MI-5 agents took over the inspection of any and all invitations, subjecting them to infrared devices, to discover forgeries that might let undesirables into the House.

The caterers and the food and drink were subject to the same rigid inspection, as were the musicians and their instruments. Finally, well before the first guests started to arrive, the agents, in plain clothes, took up their positions at all entrances and exits into and out of the banquet hall.

The East Indian gentleman driving a Ford Cortina parked his car not too close to the main gate—the plain-clothes men would have moved him on—but not so far away that he could not keep the main gate under surveillance. He was an elderly man, perhaps in his mid-seventies, with the retired look—tired kindly eyes behind large coral spectacles, no moustache, silvery hair thinning at the top, a determined chin, and rather largish ears and nose. Of medium height and slim build. Not an imposing figure; the sort of man easily lost in a crowd and easily forgotten. He wore a woollen, two-piece suit and a grey colour, easily-forgotten tie.

He sat in his car until the guests started to arrive, but it was only when a long line of cars were held up at the main gate—as each car and its occupants were vetted by the agents at the gatehouse—that he got out of it. He walked past the line of cars until he was abreast of a Jaguar driven by a young and very beautiful East Indian woman, wearing exquisite jewellery and dressed in a flaming red and gold sari. She was the only occupant of the car. He tapped on the passenger-side window, and she lowered it.

"Yes?"

"Devika Rani? Isn't it? I thought I recognised you. How are you, Devika?"

There was no recognition.

"You don't know me? But of course, you were so very young when I saw you last. Say, is your Father, General Rana Singh, still the military attaché to the Indian Embassy in Washington DC? I've known the General for some time now. Why isn't he here? I'd have thought they would have invited him with you? Or rather you with him."

The frown on her face cleared and she smiled at the older man peering in through the window. The line of cars had stalled.

"Oh, Daddy was invited; the invitation is in his name and mine, but he couldn't make it. I could, so I came over."

The line of cars inched forward. He would have been left behind, but she opened the passenger side door so that he could slip in. He buckled himself into his seat—as she was.

"Let me show you who I am," he said, reaching for his wallet in the inside pocket of his coat, and while he held out the identification, the car reached the gatehouse. She lowered the window, handed her invitation out to the agent at the gate, together with her driver's license. The policeman checked her license and the invitation; then came smartly to attention.

"Welcome General Rana Singh. And of course his beautiful daughter, Devika Rani. Please park on the left side of the driveway. The right side is reserved for the Queen and her cavalcade. And please, leave all weaponry, General, in the glove compartment of the car. All guests—except the Queen and her retinue—will pass through metal detectors; we even have male and female security staff for a pat-down search, if that is necessary. Wherever the Queen goes we are on full 'Red Alert'. Welcome to Bromfield House, and the banquet being held tonight in it."

He signalled them to proceed. Devika parked as best she could on the lawn on the left side of the driveway. The elderly gentleman put away his identification, and taking her by the arm, he steered her to the main entrance of Bromfield House.

She held onto his arm as they entered it. Rather than be a single woman without an escort, an elderly friend of her father—mistaken for her father—as escort, was very welcome. She would soon find out who he was, maybe even give him a ride back to London, if the poor dear had too much to drink and wasn't sober enough to drive himself home—as sometimes her father had been. She saw a butler, in full-serving regalia, carrying a tray of filled glasses, in the main banquet hall, and she stopped to get herself a glass of white wine. Other guests walked past her, separating her from her escort, who was swept along and disappeared from view. No matter, she would find him before the evening was over.

Joshua and Julia had no easier time getting into the banquet hall; their concerns were not security, but getting ready for the occasion. Joshua had to be dressed first—no mean task, for a man who would have worn an 'everyday' shirt and an 'everyday' tie to his own wedding. Julia promptly stripped him of his shirt and tie, and laid out the ones he ought to be wearing, and he meekly acceded to her wishes in the matter. When she produced a tuxedo, however, he put his foot down. He didn't wear anybody's hand-me-down clothes—not even for her! No, he didn't care if it had been dry-cleaned, or if it had never been worn before, or whatever. He didn't wear tuxedos; never had; never would! Julia relented and so Joshua was finally ready in his own woollen two-piece suit with his own pair of 'everyday' shoes—he assured her solemnly they had rarely been worn, but she knew better.

She had to get Joshua out of the room for Emma to do up her hair and dress her for the occasion.

"Darling," she said, kissing him on the lips, "why don't you go and find out what everybody else is doing—Grandfather, Edward, Naseem Banu—while I get dressed? I would like to surprise you for the occasion. I would like for me to be the most beautiful you have ever seen! Now, go, please?"

"You are always the most beautiful I have ever seen when you are sta.." but she put her hand across his mouth to cut him off in mid-sentence because she knew precisely what he was going to say—he had said it to her many times before, causing her to blush every time—and because Emma was at the door.

They met in the banquet hall, and he had to admit she was ravishingly beautiful with her hair piled up high, in one of Emma's creations, on the back of her head, the almost-Grecian aquiline nose, the faint touch of orange-red lipstick on full, sensitive lips, and the silken teal gown that hugged her body to perfection, from the slender neck over her generous form down to her toes. She wore open flat-heeled sandals, and the painted toes peeped out from underneath the dress. Emma had suggested the teal-coloured dress shoes with the high heels, but Julia declined. "I tower above Joshua, Emma, if I wear them. I've given up wearing heels, for over a year now; it has worked wonders for my posture. More comfortable too—if not very feminine."

The evening wore on. Guests were presented by the Earl to Julia and Joshua, who shook hands with acquaintances or strangers, hugged old friends or relatives, received bows and curtseys from those of lesser rank, and bowed and curtseyed only to the Queen and the Duke.

The Queen and the Duke came in last. The Old Earl tinkled a wine glass to draw attention from the guests, and then raised a toast to the Queen, followed by a toast to the married couple. There followed a few speeches from the principal characters in the show—the old Earl, Julia and then Joshua—each saying lovely things about the other two, inviting the guests to have a fine time. After that there followed mayhem; the musicians burst into dance music, the waiters, unobtrusively, served drinks and hors d'oeuvres, the bar was declared open, as was the sumptuous buffet that lined one wall of the hall. The old Earl leaned over to Joshua across Julia:

"Joshua, your guests may eat freely; there is no pork or ham on the menu. Julia insisted on it, and quite rightly so. This is your day as much as it is hers. I believe you have discussed children? I'm looking forward to seating my great-grandson as one of the very few Jewish Earls, past or present, in the House of Lords; it is high time we had some more."

Julia and Joshua danced together. Close. None of that modern dancing that left each partner a stranger to the other. Neither of them was very skilled at it anyway; as Joshua said: "In modern dancing, all I imagine is I'm out of the shower and rubbing my back with a towel—to music of course."

It was then that the Queen descended on him and he guided her to a secluded corner of the hall, where she gifted to him a first edition of Jane Austen's "Pride and Prejudice". He was loath to accept it, pointing out that while both he and Julia had an abiding interest in Jane Austen and would cherish her gifts forever, he hated to break up her precious collection.

"Colonel Samuelson," she said, "I would rather see my collection valued and cherished in Bromfield House than gather dust in my own, very extensive library. Please, would you accept this one for now? Why, one more will be forthcoming on the news of your first child, and then one more again for the next—until Lady Julia runs out of having babies or I run out of first editions! Julia's mother was one of my dearest friends; how she would have loved to be here today, Joshua. She would have adored you."

Joshua would have bowed low to her, but she opened her arms and hugged him. This display of genuine affection surprised him; pleased him too.

Julia was all alone as she looked down the hall, until Begum Naseem Banu joined her, looking at the same time for a glass of wine. She spotted her servant, the car-driver, who had been pressed by Tomkins into waiter service, and signalled him over. He was a tall, thin, spare gaunt man with hollow sunken eyes and a strong, sharply hooked, semitic nose, handsome for his age, dressed in full Eastern serving regalia—as might have been appropriate in her father's kingdom—with a magnificent turban, sporting a sheaf of feathers at the crown, and tight silver satin trousers with a silver satin long coat, buttoned in front, that reached from his neck to his knees.

"Hafez," she commanded, "Lady Julia and I are dying of thirst. What are you going to do about it?"

"My Ladies," Hafez said, bowing low, "your every wish is my command. What would you like to have?"

Julia opted for a glass of white wine; the Begum for a glass of sherry. Hafez disappeared promptly in the direction of the bar.

"Hafez was Father's favourite servant, hired first as his bodyguard; then he did everything we asked of him," the Begum explained. "He has dangled me on his knee, and told me stories that put me to sleep. He will die for me; such loyalty comes only between a servant and his master—never between equals."

Julia thought of Tomkins and Emma and had to agree.

Edward came to claim a dance from his wife. Though a little portly round the waist, the Begum was a good dancer, and amazingly flexible on the floor.

An elderly East Indian gentleman came up to Julia. She thought she recognised him; but couldn't quite place where she had seen him. He had to be a guest from Joshua's side of the family; quite obviously not of her grandfather's acquaintance. She held out her hand and he bowed low over it, holding it in both of his own.

"Lady Julia," he said, "You don't know me, but I know you—I met you when you were eleven years old, living here at Bromfield House with your grandfather, the eleventh Earl. May I say I've looked forward to meeting you again for a long time—a very long time.

Please accept my deepest, heartfelt wishes for a long and happy marriage. You are an elegant and a very beautiful woman; Colonel Samuelson is a very lucky man."

"Why, thank you, Sir," Julia replied. "That is very kind of you to say so. I'm sure Joshua will also appreciate your good wishes."

She pointed to the couples on the dance floor. The music had slowed to a waltz, and many of the older couples had dared to join in the dancing.

"But why aren't you dancing?"

He smiled shyly. "I'm afraid, I have no partner; women are hesitant to dance with strange men they do not know—particularly older men. I'm in my mid-seventies, you know."

"Really," Julia said. "I would never have guessed that—and I mean it! I'm not saying that just to be polite. Would you care to dance with me? I'd be honoured."

"I'm not a very good dancer," he warned her, laughingly. "If I can get through the dance without stepping on your toes, that will be an achievement."

"I'll let you into a secret that only my husband has found out; I'm a terrible dancer too!"

She took him by the hand and led him onto the dance floor. He held her close, but not so tight that she might misunderstand him. They were silent for a few minutes, concentrating on their feet. As Julia told Joshua later, she felt secure in his arms; he danced with her as if he cared for her.

The dance came to a close. They stopped on the floor for a few seconds; his arm was still around her waist; her hand in his.

"Lady Julia," he said, "may I make a prediction? Colonel Samuelson is with his brother Joe—who I haven't met before—enjoying a glass of beer and the fellowship of a brother. Soon he will look around for you and he will see you on the dance floor with me. Knowing Indian men, he will saunter over to us, claiming, quite rightly, the next dance with you. But what I have to say is important—and only for your ears."

She released his hand; he dropped his hand from around her waist.

"Please be very, very careful, when you leave for India, to find the shipments of arms and the missing copy of THE THAR ARTICLES. Please, we don't have much time, but I could not leave you without a word of advice—from one much older than you are. Don't trust anyone! In our business, we can trust no one. Why am I telling you all this and not Colonel Samuelson? Because, strangely, I feel I have more in common with you than with him. Odd isn't it?"

He felt Joshua's hand tap him on the shoulder.

"May I have the next dance with my wife?" Joshua said, smiling at the elderly Indian gentleman.

The old gentleman handed Julia over to Joshua—and before she could restrain him, he left them both on the dance floor.

Julia stared at his back as he disappeared from the banquet hall, and presumably from Bromfield House. She would have raced out after him, but Joshua—who had had a few beers with Joe—had an arm around her waist, and would have tipped over with her sudden disengagement, so she could only watch in dismay as the elderly Indian gentleman turned at the door, gave her a surreptitious wave of his hand and exited the hall.

"I don't even know what he looks like," Julia moaned to Joshua, after she'd related the incident to him. "I should have had a good look at him, but I didn't know then what I know now. Now wait, I do remember a look I had of him, as he was bending low over my outstretched hand; he has a shock of silvery white hair that is thinning at the top—an emerging bald spot!"

"He didn't say who he was? Who invited him?"

"No. And I didn't ask. I thought he was from your side of the family and I wanted to be especially nice to them. I wanted to dance with all of them. I had one dance with Joe; he's an excellent dancer, by the way, did you know?"

Joshua nodded emphatically. "Oh, yes! Joe used to win all the college dance competitions in Bombay in the days of our youth."

Julia had remembered to tell Emma not to wait up for her, which was just as well, because Emma, Tomkins, Hafez and the other servants were busy late into the night clearing up the banquet hall.

Joshua had no difficulty with the unlacing and the unbuttoning and the unzipping, but they were both too tired to do anything except lie together and talk—which is when Julia told him about the elderly Indian gentleman.

"So you don't know him either? He wasn't from your side of the family?" Julia asked.

"Mummy couldn't come because Susan is falling for some Indian Jewish, meteorology professor who, according to Mummy, is the most intelligent man she has ever met—and that includes me! His name is David Abrams. He, too, has fallen for her, though he is a few years older than her. They have no eyes but for each other, and as he had a field trip coming up he couldn't come, and if he cannot come, she will not come, and if she will not come, Mummy can't come either, and there you have the story of my family-boycott of our reception! If it hadn't been for Joe, I would have had no one," he wailed.

"You had me, darling," she comforted him, cuddling him tight, knowing fully well he was only fishing for comfort.

"I wonder who he was. He seemed so—nice." Julia suddenly sat bolt upright, the bedclothes falling off the both of them. "I know!" she shouted, shaking Joshua awake. "I know where I've seen him before!"

"You do? Where?"

"In the café in Georgetown. The one we entered in to shake off Devika Rani and Max. Don't you remember? He followed us in; stayed in the café while you dashed away; left it only minutes before I did. Almost as if he was keeping an eye over me—or you. I remember his smile."

"Well that is strange," Joshua said slowly. "We see him in Georgetown, then we see him in Bromfield House—how did he get in without an invitation?"

"I remember, Joshua, when he warned me not to trust anyone, he used the words 'in our business'. Perhaps he's high up in IMI, or even MI-6? How did he know about the missing arms shipments or THE THAR ARTICLES? Could he be Raja?"

Joshua pulled her down towards him. "Come to bed, dear. We'll keep a lookout for him. I doubt he has evil intentions, or he wouldn't have shown himself to you. Who was he warning you against, anyway?"

"How did you enjoy the banquet, darling," Julia asked, as she snuggled back into bed with him. "Any surprises?"

"Just one."

"Oh? Pleasant or unpleasant?"

"Very pleasant. And totally unexpected too!"

"Aren't you going to tell me? Or do I have to act like an ex-agent, and sell myself to my husband for this piece of information? Not that I'm unwilling. Name your price, dear."

He laughed. "How about one wildly passionate goodnight kiss? I think the information I'm selling to you is worth at least that much."

She kissed him passionately on the mouth. "Well?"

"The Queen hugged me, with genuine affection. Do you think she now accepts me as your husband?"

CHAPTER 5

Six days later they left for Bombay. James drove them to Heathrow in the Bentley. It had been an emotional farewell. Her grandfather held her tight. She felt the tear drop on her cheek; then he broke away abruptly and disappeared into the house. They checked in at the British Airways counter and got rid of the bags. Joshua slipped both their tickets, their passports and the boarding passes into his coat pocket. Julia had the traveller's checks and the cash in her large handbag. It seemed like a satisfactory way to distribute everything between them.

They'd come early—as was Joshua's custom. He'd been known to arrive at places even before they'd opened. With more than hour to kill, he had a few ideas on how they might spend their time.

First he sat them down against the wall of the Departure Lounge, with the concourse in front of them. Tired passengers, with handbags and little children, drifted in and out; he seemed oblivious to them, picking out the less straggling ones for his attention. The ones that were loitering as he was. He talked easily, but he wasn't there and she knew it.

Abruptly he closed his hand on her arm. He felt the urge to buy some duty-free liquor. Good stuff was hard to get in India! He bought a full bottle of Johnny Walker, Black Label; urged her to pick up a bottle of Bristol Cream Sherry, which she did.

Next he spent some time in the bookstore, picking out a magazine for reading on the plane; urging her to do the same. She declined. Then he felt the urge for a cup of tea, so they ended up in the cafeteria with two hot cups of tea and some Danish rolls.

The first call for passengers on British Airways Flight 972 to India came over the public address system. He made no move towards the departure gates, restraining her again by a light touch on the arm, as she knocked off her tea and reached for her handbag.

"Not yet, Julia," he whispered. "Go to the Women's Room, wait there exactly three minutes and come back. Please!"

She didn't argue. The Secret Service had taught her that much at least. He was the more skilled of the two in this game, which could easily turn deadly.

"Want to tell me?" she asked softly, when she returned.

"Third table to the right and one row behind me. The portly little woman in the orange dress and the large white hat. See her?"

Julia nodded carelessly.

"She hasn't left our side. Not in the concourse, or the duty-free shop, or the bookstore—except when she followed you into the Women's room. She came back before you did, so that must have been coincidental, because she's back behind me now. I wonder whose side she's on?"

"Why don't you ask her?" Julia said. "Best way to find out."

He looked at her approvingly.

"Good girl! I knew you'd come up with something brilliant. But not just yet, darling. We'll wait. We have to give her the slip so none can take any action."

They heard the last call for passengers on their flight to Bombay. They heard their names called. Julia looked anxiously at her watch; Joshua toyed with his polystyrene cup, half-filled with cold tea.

"Aren't you going to finish your tea, Joshua?" she asked, looking at her watch for the third time. "And shouldn't we be going?"

"In a minute, Julia. Don't panic, dear. Nothing comes of panicking."

He drew out the tickets and the boarding passes and the passports from the inner pocket of his coat and handed them over to Julia. For safekeeping, he said, winking at her.

When he moved, it was over so fast she had barely time to understand it. He walked rapidly past the table of the portly woman in the orange dress and the large white hat, and as he approached her, he stumbled, gave a cry and emptied his cup of cold tea into her lap. As she attempted to rise, he held her by the arm, apologizing profusely; then did what seemed to Julia to be the oddest thing—he leaned forward and whispered in her ear. She nodded, recovered herself, and hurried off to the Women's room.

Joshua grabbed Julia by the arm, this time gripping it firmly, racing her down the cafeteria exit towards the departure gates.

"Let's run for it," he said. "We'll make it in good time—before anyone else catches on, and acts."

She didn't ask what. She ran as fast as he did, down the long corridor that led to their gate. She actually beat him to it. She'd always been good at the sprints, even in boarding school. Her PE teacher had said she had the potential to be a great runner, if she trained for it. But though skill and the potential were there, the desire was missing. She wanted to be a writer, not a runner. Still it had come to good use!

This life is going to kill me, Julia thought, out of breath, as she slid into her seat and snapped on the safety belt. He slid into the seat beside her, smiling broadly.

"That was close," he said. "I really must give us more time to catch planes, darling. We nearly didn't make this one."

"Will you, please, tell me what this is all about? Or should it be obvious to me and am I just being dense?"

He shook his head in delight, caressing her arm, interlacing his fingers with hers.

"No, darling. There's no way you could have made this one out. I tumbled to it only at the very end."

"Tumbled to what?"

"That the dear old lady in the orange dress and the large white hat is one of Edward's people. She works for MI-6."

"How do you know that?"

"Simple. I took your advice and I asked her. When I dumped the tea in her lap, I leaned over and whispered in her ear: 'Did Viscount Edward send you here?' She nodded, so I apologised and sent her off to the Women's room to clean herself up. Very naughty of Edward to send her to tail us—without telling us. Just not the done thing! Maybe we should have a word with him about it?"

But Joshua didn't seem too upset.

"But why?" Julia persisted. "Why would Edward tail us? What could he possibly hope to learn that he doesn't already know? After all he made the travel arrangements. MI-6 is picking up the tab. It doesn't make sense, darling, to tail us."

Joshua looked out of the window, seeing the green English countryside and the rows and rows of small houses, neatly set in little English gardens, each isolated plot of land someone's estate, all receding fast beneath them.

"It wasn't exactly a tail, Julia. More like a bodyguard. Without the subject being aware of it. You. She was there to protect you."

"Me? Protect me? From who?"

"I don't know. An unknown elderly East Indian gentleman who eluded all of MI-5 and gate-crashed Bromfield House? I don't know."

"That's outrageous," Julia said. "I would have known him this time around."

"I tumbled to it when I sent you off to the Women's room; she followed you in. I thought she might be a handbag snatcher—which is why I kept all the important papers with me. Traveller's checks and money can be replaced easily; passports and boarding passes are not so instantly replaceable—and without them we wouldn't be on this flight!"

Joshua mused for a few seconds. When he spoke again it was almost to himself.

"If she wasn't a purse snatcher, she had to be either tailing you or protecting you. And as you said, MI-6 wouldn't put a tail on us. Who could she have been protecting you from? Me?"

"Joshua, that's absurd. Ridiculous! I'm married to you. How can they possibly protect me from you? Can they come into our bedroom to prevent you from doing all those nice things you do to me?"

He nodded in agreement. "Sorry, darling. You're quite right, of course. Are they nice things? But why would she follow you into the Women's room? She came out of it earlier than you did, though."

Julia could have told him—and didn't.

The woman in the orange dress and the large white hat had followed her into the Women's room. She came directly to the sink where Julia was killing Joshua's directive of staying there for three minutes. She stood alongside Julia, reached into her purse and drew out her identification.

MI-6.

Julia reached for the paper towels to dry her hands, comforted by the touch of the gold band around her wedding finger.

She was an older woman, Julia noted, the grey in her dark hair, untouched and uncoloured, carelessly merging with black wavy curls to give it a streaky look. Plump face, double chin, not unpleasing since it did not droop, tired eyes behind small spectacles peering out at Julia.

"You don't know me and you don't have to," she said, urgently. "But I have a name for you and an address in Bombay. One of our reliable agents there. In case you need help."

"I don't want it," Julia said.

"I'm afraid I have to insist," the woman said, not raising her voice, holding out a card to Julia, moving closer to her so there was no gap between them.

Julia tossed the paper towel into the trash can, hitting it dead centre.

"Viscount Edward insisted it be passed to you before you left London. On the clear understanding, Lady Julia, that you do not blow his cover. Because if you do, they will almost certainly kill him."

"Who? Who will kill him?"

"Paid KGB agents who are part of IMI. I can't discuss all that with you. Not a word to Colonel Samuelson about this, because he was with IMI. I'll be outside until you leave."

Two women entered the Women's room using the free sinks on Julia's side of the counter, effectively terminating the conversation. Julia took one last look at her face in the mirror. That was a mistake. The lady in the orange dress reached for Julia's handbag, snapped it open, slipped the card into the handbag, snapped it shut, and swiftly backed off into three young teenage girls, who parted to let her through. She turned around and fled through the double doors into the cafeteria.

When Julia returned to Joshua, the lady in the orange dress was sitting at her table exactly as before.

The card was in her handbag. She did not look at it, or even want to. Is this how treachery began? Yet, if the lady, and so Edward, had to be believed, the agent's life depended on his cover. Did she have the right to disclose it even to her own husband? Did his rights of survival outweigh her loyalties to her husband?

She leaned towards Joshua, holding him by the arm, pressing it into her breast, as when she felt guilty or confused. He mistook her advances and reciprocated by caressing her bare arm.

"You were clever, darling," she said, "to have spotted her in that huge concourse with all those people about. However did you do it? Like to tell me? Or is that an IMI secret too?"

He smiled with the glow of pleasure that her praise brought to him.

"Darling, I will have no secrets from you—except when I want to protect you! That I will not disclose. And this hardly qualifies for that exemption. As you say, the departure lounge has literally hundreds in it.'

'An impossible task to pick out a tail? Not true! First you sit against one wall, so that everyone is in front of you—and watch. Who are those sitting just waiting—as you are—as opposed to those coming and going, ready to move, with families, large amounts of luggage, or anxiously looking at the clock on the walls. Things like that. You look at their faces and their clothes so you can pick them out, in a different setting, if you see them again. All this takes time, at least half an hour. It can't be rushed in a few minutes; so you come early. Then you move your own location, to say the duty-free store—and there you watch only for a face or clothing you've seen before. And you will see some—not just one or two, because many want to buy duty-free liquor, as we did. So you move again. To the bookstore, and then again to the cafeteria. And you've spotted your tail! With an orange dress and her large white hat, she couldn't have been missed. You'd think a proper tail would have dressed more inconspicuously? Not this lady, which makes me think she wasn't a regular tail. She followed you into the Women's room, so she was keeping an eye on you; not on me. Why? I don't know. Do you?"

"Let's forget her, darling," Julia said, drawing him even closer, leaning her head against his shoulder and nuzzling him. He put an arm around her and closed his eyes.

Joshua had the tiniest of flats in Bombay. Housing was very scarce, almost impossible to get, he told her, and had it not been for his Father's foresight in building the Villa, many years before, they would not have had that much either. The Villa had four flats, but the two on one side had been let, leaving only two flats—one upstairs and one downstairs—for the Samuelsons. Joshua had the upper flat; his mother and Susan shared the lower one. Three rooms set in a line, with a balcony off the main living room overlooking the street in the Shivaji Park suburb of Central Bombay. About an hour by taxi from the business district and the main fashionable shopping centres of South Bombay.

The living room also doubled as the bedroom; it had a single bed in it—no wider than the one they'd shared in Bromfield House. The middle room was an elegant dining room with a built-in closet that held the crockery. The smallest of the three rooms had a raised concrete platform on which rested the kitchen appliances—none of them free-standing—and a small washing area for the dishes, with a water tap. The vertical wall of the concrete platform formed a natural enclosure for the washing area, and the area under the concrete platform—with a sliding wooden door—served for storage of the kitchen utensils. All very neat, compact and functional—and a far cry from the kitchens at Bromfield House. The bathroom was fairly large and opened on to a corridor that led directly to a secondary front door, through which the servant woman cleaning the bathroom had entrance and exit—without having to pollute the rest of the house? That is how Joshua explained it to Julia, while showing her around the tiny flat, half ashamed of the small rooms and the miniscule kitchen.

"Darling," Julia said, "if I was a great cook, I might be tempted to make comparisons to the kitchens in Bromfield House. Since I've only just barely learned how to feed both of us, with a simple recipe or two—for breakfast, lunch and dinner—this kitchen suits me just fine!"

The flat was only a minute from the sea, and the cool evening breezes caused the curtains to flap, bringing some measure of relief to Julia. She had dressed as comfortably as she could, with a white cotton blouse and a printed flared skirt, brought in at the waist. The heat was still oppressive; the monsoons were coming to a close; the steam rose from the concrete surface of the road in the afternoon heat. She could see the trembling vapours sizzle off the hot surface in perpetual agony.

They were two days in the flat recovering from jet lag. The flat was tastefully and expensively furnished, but there were neither cooking utensils nor dishes—as a bachelor, Joshua did not cook for himself—and until they stocked up on such items, she could hardly keep house for both of them. Besides, she was on her honeymoon! There would be plenty of time for such housework later; now they were here to 'live it up'—so Joshua said. In the meantime they had a standing invitation to eat with Joshua's mother and sister in the flat downstairs.

When she awoke the third morning, Joshua had left early. She went downstairs for breakfast with Joshua's mother—Susan had early classes at a nearby college—and after eggs, toast and hot tea, she was about to ascend the stairs to her flat upstairs—she already thought of it as her flat—when the old mother handed her a sealed envelope.

It was a note from Joshua. He apologised for leaving so early. He had to make a few inquiries and the sooner he got going, the sooner he'd be back. He couldn't say when, but certainly before lunch. Feel free, he said, to grab a taxi and go where she wished.

Perhaps she could visit the British Consulate and introduce herself? She would find several British staff in the consulate, he wrote, in case she felt the need sometimes to be with her own people? They would welcome someone of her rank.

It was a politely worded, loving note, but it did not camouflage his need to make some inquiries without her tagging along. Why? If he was going to be that protective of her all the time, she could hardly be of any help to him, if he needed her. He didn't seem to think she would. Was she a liability to him? Would it have been better if she had given him the month, and stayed behind in Bromfield or in her flat in London?

She opened her handbag—she'd opened it several times since coming to Bombay—but for the first time she searched in it for the card with the name and the address on it.

Major Vinod Patel, with an office on Veer Narriman Street. On the back of the card were brief handwritten directions and a hand-drawn map. From Churchgate Station, it said, go towards the sea. The building will be about halfway up Veer Narriman Street, on the right hand side of the road. Common enough name of 'Patel'—like Smith in England. Literally millions of them.

She dropped in before leaving, to say 'hello' to her mother-in-law, and to confirm she would be in before lunch. She chatted pleasantly for a few minutes while her mother-in-law cut onions and cried copiously at the same time.

"We must know each other better, Julia," the old Mother said. "I want to know you well. And for you to know us too. When you have more time, my love, why don't you come down and let me take you through the family album. I've some real cute photos of Joshua as a child. You'll just love them! Other bits of nostalgia too—the trophies he won in school and college, for oratory. Lots of other stuff too—some of it private, I guess, but then nothing can be private from you now, can it? You have more right to it than I have."

"I'd like that, Mother," Julia said, dropping a kiss on her head still bent over the onions, and reached for her hat—a large wide-brimmed sun-bonnet.

Julia hailed a taxi parked across the street. The turbaned, stalwart, Sikh taxi driver looked much younger than his sixty years. He had curling-away handlebars, any English colonel would have envied, and smiling eyes, as he politely held the door open for her. Not for any greasy customers, Madam, he assured her. He drove like a lunatic, weaving in and out of the slow-moving traffic with total unconcern, sometimes barely inches away from buses, military trucks, and loitering cows, cursing loudly at the rest of humanity occupying the road, in a language she did not understand, leaving her gripping the edge of the seat with fingers that seemed to be frozen. He kept looking at her in the rear view mirror, and while, normally, she would have been amused, she wished he'd keep his eyes on the road instead!

"You think we're going to have an accident any minute, don't you, my Lady?" he said cheerfully. "Relax, Madam. This taxi is like my wife. I have no other. She is sturdily built, and while she is getting on in years, she never fails me. Can one ask for any more from a wife? Would I allow any of the other filthy cars on the road to touch her? I say a prayer each morning to the Saint, for his protection over her. She has served me well; would I abuse her?"

He parked in a side street, at her request, while she paid him, offering him a generous tip, which he graciously declined. He came over and opened her door for her.

"Madam," he said dropping his voice. "Bombay is full of thieves and villains, who would not hesitate to take advantage of a beautiful foreign lady such as yourself. Please take care."

"Thank you, Mr Singh. I'll do that."

"Would you like me to wait for you here, around the corner? No waiting charge! It is just such a pleasure to drive you around. So much better than having those fat, oily, business men sitting behind me plotting to defraud each other and the government too. May I?"

"Perhaps, Mr. Singh, but would your wife agree?"

"She looks on you—as I do—as a daughter. She would welcome you!" He flashed her a smile, showing the pearliest of teeth, the trailing edge of his red turban, flapping with his exuberance. His laughter was infectious. The kind eyes that had looked into every type of face, sometimes villainous, still refused to see all men as villains. Women too! Some had abused him and insulted him, accusing him of deliberately tampering with the meter, or taking a circuitous route to their destination, to bump up his fares. And then there was this English lady who had called him 'Mr. Singh'. "I will wait for you at the corner, Madam," he said, "regardless of whether you need me or not. When you are ready to go home to Shivaji Park, I will be there for you."

The address was a flat—a luxury flat—in one of the most expensive areas of South Bombay. On the third floor. An elevator with a grilled sliding door took her up to it. The name on the door said: Major V. Patel.

She pressed the doorbell, hearing it peal within the flat. Then the silence as it faded away. No footsteps that might acknowledge her presence. She knocked lightly. The door was closed, but was it locked?

If it was locked, she was off the hook of decision-making. There was nothing she could do, except find his phone number and call him before she came again, to save herself a wasted trip. Perhaps, she should have taken Joshua's suggestion and gone to the British High Commissioner's office instead? Maybe, she could still do that on the return journey; Mr Singh would know where it was.

If it was unlocked, was it breaking and entering? And if she was caught......? The thought didn't even bear thinking about. Married three weeks—with a honeymoon in jail?

She tried the doorknob, pushing it ever so gently with her fingers, hoping it might be closed.

The door opened slightly, swinging noiselessly on well-oiled hinges.

She deliberated for a few seconds; then entered the flat and closed the door behind her. The lock on the door had been clicked in the open position. She left it as it was. Perhaps Major Patel had just stepped out, and not having his keys with him had made sure he could re-enter his flat.

It was a spacious flat; airy too, with the cool breezes off the Arabian Sea wafting out through the open door, wafting in from the balcony that looked down over Veer Narriman Street. The furniture was modern and expensive. The floor was marble mosaic tiles, with a large, expensive Persian rug in the living room. Indian-art paintings hung on the walls; a glass cupboard held delicate crystal from many parts of the world. Beautifully wood-carved and painted, full-size statues of Indian gods and goddesses graced every corner of the living room. Major Patel was an art lover—and lived well.

The living room was in spotless condition; not so the study which was in a shambles. The two filing cabinets were open, with the papers strewn all over the floor, as if someone had been searching in great haste through them. The study too had a balcony looking out over Veer Narriman Street; the door leading to it was open.

At the opposite end of the study, was the office desk, and behind it, facing the balcony to enjoy the sea breeze, was a swivel chair, and seated in the swivel chair, his head slumped over it was Major Patel, with a bullet hole in the back of his head, the blood dripping, from the single hole, over the back of the chair into a pool on the tiled floor.

He was dead. She was afraid to approach him, but she steeled herself to do it. She had to check if he was dead; if he was not, she would make the emergency call for the ambulance, and then wait there until it came. She checked his pulse with a light touch to the wrist that jutted out over the armrest towards her; there was none.

But the body was still very warm and the flow of blood down the back of his neck had not been stanched. He could not have been long dead—minutes perhaps? This brought on another wave of panic. Perhaps the murderer was still in the flat? She searched swiftly through the other rooms of the flat. They were all empty. A three-bedroom flat, each with its own private bathroom and its own balcony. Luxuriously decorated and furnished. The walls adorned with hanging-art and paintings. Major Patel had lived very well indeed.

She went back to Major Patel to have a closer look at him. The eyes were closed. The face of an older man, perhaps sixty-five years old. The head was almost bald, surrounded by a fringe of hair over the ears. He had been killed without his being aware of it; there was no fear in his face, no gut-wrenching twist of the lips and mouth, no horror in the open eyes. He had died not knowing he was about to die. Peaceful. He had died peacefully and instantly. A single bullet fired at very close range into the back of his head, by someone standing behind him, the bullet exiting the forehead, then through the open door leading to the balcony. No blood flowing down his face because his head had slumped backwards over the edge of the short office chair. He had not felt the horror of his own execution—but she did.

Don't panic, Julia, she told herself sternly, almost in a panic. There's no one in the flat—and he, poor chap, is dead. Now the only thing she had to do was what she could do; gather some information to give Joshua, and then get out of there as fast as she could. She was not concerned, she told herself firmly, with who he was, why he'd been killed, or who killed him? That was for the Indian police or IMI or MI-6 or whoever—but not her.

There seemed no point in going through the papers on the floor. The murderer had found what he wanted and taken it away, and if he hadn't found what he wanted, it wasn't there—so why waste time looking for it? She tried the office desk. It was locked. Major Patel's bunch of keys—his car keys, the flat keys, the filing cabinet keys—lay on the empty filing cabinets; she tried them on the office desk. Nothing worked.

She was about to turn around and leave the study, when she noticed the headed notepaper on the office desk. She was in the offices of DOP Import Company, whose logo stated they dealt in the import of heavy agricultural machinery and spare parts. They had a dealership for a foreign manufacturer in Virginia, USA. Now she had an interest in him!

Julia looked round for other files that might give some information on the method of transportation of such machinery from the USA to India, or on the route to be used in India, or on the destinations of the imported machinery, or the clients ordering such machinery—there was none.

Julia sat on a chair in the study opposite Major Patel to think things out. She didn't have much time, but she'd never get another chance to examine the papers in that office. She had to do it now—or never. It would be sheer bad luck if someone came.

She tried the office desk once again. Locked and no key anywhere. Perhaps the murderer had unlocked the office desk, removed the most important files, locked the desk, and taken the key with him? She was almost ready to admit defeat when she took one last look at poor Major Patel. He was dressed in an open neck tee-shirt, so comfortable in the warm weather, with the top two buttons open, showing a hairy chest with black hair. Strange the hair on his chest, she thought. There was a thick black hair that ran from his neck into his chest instead of growing out of his chest.

She walked over to him. Her hands were trembling as she touched his chest gingerly, half expecting him to wake up and glare at her with bloodshot eyes. But he was still dead and his eyes were closed. She tried very hard—and failed—to reach in without touching his chest. She felt as if she was desecrating a corpse, when her fingers slid over his nipple, as she traced the black thread in, to the weight at the end of it.

It was a small, single key. She drew it out, reached into her handbag to draw out her nail scissors, snipping the thread and sliding out the key into the palm of her hand.

The very first drawer—the long one beneath the desktop—gave her a DOP file marked ROUTING. There were other files, mainly bank files dealing with payments from unknown sources into several bank accounts belonging to Major Patel. She left them alone.

Where was the bullet that had killed him? He was sitting on a swivel chair. Had he been killed facing into the room, in which case the bullet would be embedded in the one of the side walls, depending on the direction of the swivel, or had he been killed facing the balcony door, in which case the bullet had exited the building. There was no evidence of cracked plaster or damaged ceiling. She went into the balcony to speculate on the angle of fire—and froze for the second time that morning.

The voices didn't reach up to the third floor, but she could see them clearly below her as they entered the drive leading from Veer Narriman Street to the main entrance of the building. Two figures, walking side by side. One was a man; the other a woman. The woman was wearing a sari, not too tall, tripping along, keeping pace with the Indian man striding purposefully towards the entrance. She'd know that head anywhere—even if seen only from above. The unruly mop of black hair, the large head with the straight forehead, and the spectacles sliding away from his eyes towards the bridge of the gently hooked nose. Even when seen from above, there was no mistaking him. Even the stride alone would have given him away. She had no problem keeping up with him because she was just that little bit taller than he was and had a stride that was close to his in length, if a little shorter, because he was a military man and, as a woman, she walked more daintily than he did. Besides, she always held onto his arm when they walked together, forcing him to cut down the length of his step, restraining the swinging action of the military walk by pressing his arm into the side of her breast. Devika could hardly walk that way with him, which accounted for the tripping steps she took.

Joshua and Devika turned into the building and disappeared beneath her.

For the first time that morning, Julia panicked. She grabbed the file, and in her haste dropped the handbag, and when she had both file and handbag clutched to her chest, she dropped the key. She fumbled on her knees for it, for a few seconds—wasted precious seconds—until she realised it didn't matter where the key was. She raced for the front door, closing the door behind her, but unlocked, to leave it as she'd found it.

She heard the voices come up the stairwell, that spiraled round the elevator shaft. No elevator; no whine of the electric motor. Someone had left the collapsible, sliding grill door open at one of the floors, and the elevator was stuck. They were coming up the stairs.

Julia pulled the sun-bonnet tight round her head and went halfway to the floor above. Not all the way; just around the landing at the bend in the stairs behind the elevator shaft. She hoped people weren't coming down the stairs, or they'd surely wonder what a foreign white woman was doing, hiding out on the stairs, clutching a file and a handbag in one hand and hiding her face behind a large, white sun-bonnet.

Their footsteps came to the third floor, opposite Major Patel's flat, and stopped. She heard the doorbell peal inside the flat with no response. A few moments wait for answering footsteps or a voice from within. None. Then the doorbell again.

"It's open," she heard Devika say, in surprise.

"That is odd," she heard Joshua's voice for the first time that morning. They entered the flat and the door closed behind them.

Julia raced down the stairs, two steps at a time. On the second floor she passed an elderly Indian gentleman, with a mop of silvery white hair, thinning to a bald spot at the top. She came from above him, slowed for a second abreast of him, then shot past him, turned the corner of the ground floor landing and raced along the corridor to exit the building.

The humid heat of the day caused the sweat to pour down her face and neck and into her armpits, spreading the rippling stains through the thin cotton blouse she wore. The shoes she wore weren't comfortable for running either, but at least they had no heels. She'd given up wearing heels so she wouldn't tower above Joshua. Thank God he was a little shorter than her!

The breeze from the sea threatened to lift up her sun-bonnet and fly it away, so she held it down with her hand above her head. That is when she heard the shouts from above. In a language she didn't understand, except that she knew perfectly well they meant her.

"Khuni! Chor! Pakdo!" It was Devika's voice from the balcony on the third floor. How she hated that woman! No doubt calling her a murderer and a thief and calling on passers-by to stop her and arrest her. No one did. They looked at her with curiosity, but none lay their hands on a white woman. Thank heavens for that!

And for Mr Singh, who was leaning against his taxi, philosophically chewing on a betel nut 'pan' leaf.

She threw her things into the backseat, and herself with them, holding onto her sun-bonnet so it wouldn't get knocked off by the roof of the car.

"Drive!" she shouted. "Quickly!"

"Where, Madam?"

"Oh, anywhere! Just get me out of here. Oh, please, Mr. Singh, don't waste time!"

He didn't waste time, lurching so fast round the corner into Marine Drive, the tires squealed on the hot pavement.

"Anywhere?"

"Home. To Shivaji Park. Only do hurry, please!"

He was about to ask why, pointing out that his old lady wasn't able to go much faster because of her age, when he heard the police siren of the car behind him. Then he knew. Julia was thrown against the back seat of the car, as he slammed the pedal to the ground, the car rattling and shuddering its protest at such brutal treatment.

When they had gone about a mile down Marine Drive, he began to see it wasn't going to work. The four lanes of highway in each direction, and no cows or bullock carts to slow you down, made for high speed driving. Even with a not-too-skilled driver at the wheel, the fast police car was gaining on them.

"This is no good, dear Lady," Mr. Singh said. "I think we better try some of the side streets, before my old lady falls dead on the both of us. There, I can lose them easily enough, but, here, if they get close enough to get my number, I am finished. A goner! My goose—as you say—is cooked. I have never been able to understand that phrase, my Lady. Perhaps you can explain it to me? If I am cooking a goose and it is cooked, I will eat it. One has to cook a goose to eat it. Does it mean that I am the goose, and if I am caught, I am ready for the pot?"

Julia burst out laughing.

"Mr Singh, you are priceless! I promise you that I will research the phrase for you, and one day I will explain it to you—but not now. Will you, please, get me out of here!"

Julia dare not look around to see if the police car was gaining on them. Joshua might see her through the rear window, and just as she could recognise him anywhere, so it might be with him too.

The taxi turned sharp right onto the Charni Road overpass, turned left again, ran a red light just in time, heading towards Bhendi Bazaar, where the flow of people, horse carriages, hand-pushed carts, cows, stray dogs, and more people, soon brought all traffic—not just them—to a crawling, halting, jerky pace.

But they could not hear the police sirens anymore.

Julia settled back and relaxed, grateful to all that teeming mass of humanity that surged everywhere round her. People, she thought, who had been so kind and helpful to her—just by being there. Never again would she ever pass critical judgment on the crowded streets of Bombay. She even spotted empty stretches of street, beside her, wherein she would have welcomed an extra cow or two.

She stopped the taxi some distance from the house.

She would walk the rest of the way. He understood.

"I will not ask what that was all about, my Lady," he said, "but I have to tell you that this has been the most exciting day of my life. I like to write," he confessed, "in my spare time. Poems, short stories in Punjabi—that sort of thing. Think of what a plot this might make? But if you tell me the reason why, it may all be so humdrum and ordinary, the mystery of it would be lost."

She sat back.

"You write?" she said. "Have you had any luck? Publishing, I mean?"

"No such luck, Madam. Where can a simple taxi driver like me have the contacts. Still, one day, perhaps?"

She handed him the fare, adding a generous tip, which he, again, graciously declined.

"I like to write too," she said, "and I haven't had much luck either. A poem—two actually—and a travel piece on Berlin. But we keep trying—always."

He turned around to face her. They looked at each other in a different light. The fellowship of writers. No longer was she an Englishwoman and the granddaughter of the eleventh Earl of Bromfield, and he a Sikh taxi driver in a Bombay street.

"I can see why you think of her as your wife," she said, patting the top of the front seat over which he leaned. "She is beautiful, and she has served us both very well today."

He glowed with pleasure.

"I would like to leave her a small gift, if I may. In appreciation of her splendid performance."

He did not understand. Julia walked to the front of the car, removed the sun-bonnet from her head, shaking her brown hair free, and placed the bonnet on the point of the hood, patting it down in affection.

This time Mr Singh burst out laughing, coming round to the front to retrieve it, turning it over in his hand with obvious pleasure at its possession.

Joshua had not yet reached home, so Julia dropped into the lower flat to see his mother, having a light lunch with her, before she went upstairs to examine the file she'd 'purloined' from Major Patel's flat. It was for a good cause, she told herself firmly. She put the file away in a brown paper envelope of somewhat larger proportions, curled up in bed and had a well-deserved nap.

Joshua returned several hours later. Distressed. She could see it in his face. The black eyes looked dejected; even angry. He played nervously with his keys, placing them first on the table, then slipping them into her handbag.

She watched him fumble around.

"Something the matter, darling?" she asked, propping herself up on the bed. "Anything you'd like to tell me? Talk to me about? I might be able to help you, you know. I did work for MI-6 for over a year. But, dear, not if you don't want to."

"Oh, I want to, I want to! A man was killed today. Someone I'd known for twenty years. Shot in the head. Murdered!"

"Really?"

"Yes, and we even saw the woman who did it, running away from….."

"Joshua," she interrupted him, "please, might I make a suggestion? Take me out to dinner tonight. Give me an hour or so to freshen up, while you go and spend some time with Mother downstairs. She has hardly seen anything of you since we came—and that hasn't been my fault either. You've just not been around. We'll eat and dance and, maybe, we'll see some of those frowns ease away?"

"I doubt it," he said moodily, but he went off to visit with his mother, while she got herself ready for their date.

He would have taken the taxi from across the street, but for once Julia insisted on a short walk halfway around the park, after which the suburb was named, and they hailed a taxi from the other side. The very last thing she wanted was to run into Mr. Singh. If he had a yearning for nostalgia, there would be a lot of explaining to give Joshua, and while she was prepared for that, it was decidedly better while dancing in Joshua's arms or cuddling up to him in a dimly lit elegant restaurant,, than in the back seat of a taxi.

Despite his initial resistance, he started to soften slowly. The food was heavily spiced, and though it was delightful, the Indian food she'd had in London paled in strength to the dishes piled in front of her. Despite her protests, he'd ordered a variety of dishes, both North Indian and South Indian—he wanted her to try all sorts of cooking so he could find out what she liked, thereby getting to know her better—until she finally leaned back, pushing her plate away as she did.

"Please, Joshua, no more! I can't eat a thing any more. This must be the finest meal I've ever had—I mean it, darling. Those gulab jamuns are out of this world!"

The band came on. Western music and western style dancing. Indian men holding their sari-clad women close to their chests, the hand encircling the bare back, between the blouse, high and tight under the breasts, and the sari tucked into the waist above the hip. In some of the younger women, the sari dipped dangerously low, in front, to well below the navel.

His hand, encircling her waist, held her close too, but, with the skirt and blouse that she had worn, he could not touch her bare flesh—as the other Indian men on the floor. Was he regretting her as a dancing partner? When he could have had so much closer intimacy with one of the other Indian women on the dance floor? She mentioned this to Joshua, and, for the first time that evening he laughed—almost at her.

"If I felt that way, darling, I'd be awful jealous of your bra and panty, wouldn't I? Always in such close and intimate contact with you. Like another husband! Keeping me away. Protecting you from prying eyes. Comforting you, supporting you. Leaving me on the outside. Having to be physically removed before I can reach you, for intimacy!"

She laughed. "Darling, you and Mr. Singh have a lot in common."

"Mr. Singh?"

"The taxi driver. The one who drove me around this morning."

"Where did you go, Julia? Did you see some of the sights in Bombay? I wish I could have taken you around and shown you some of them myself. And I will before long, I promise. After this mess is sorted out. Where did you go, darling?"

"Oh, towards the fashionable side. It was, I think, the Marine Drive? I certainly remember driving that way on the way back, though I can't say I had much time for the sights."

"That's odd. I drove by that way myself, this morning."

"Isn't that a coincidence?" Julia said, absently spooning another gulab jamun into her dessert bowl, despite her resolve to eat no more of them.

He watched her eat it. Thought it was odd she could be hungry again so soon.

"Where were you, darling?" she asked quietly. "Met anybody I know?"

He did not reply immediately. "Want to dance?" he said.

"No. I want to talk. I want you to tell me all you did today—where you went, who you met, and why—and I'll do the same. You did say a man was murdered?"

"Yes."

"Who?"

"A man named Vinod Patel. In a flat on Veer Narriman Street. Not too far from the Marine Drive. A retired major in the Indian Army."

"Was he the Indian agent who killed Rashid Khan?"

"No. At least I don't think so. He was the CEO of DOP. Remember the word, Julia? You said it might be part of Indo-Pak, and of course you were right. It is an import company set up, ostensibly, to import agricultural machinery from America and distribute to suppliers and dealerships in India."

"America? May I take a guess that the machinery came from Virginia?"

"You could. And you'd be right. Darling, you're quite the most intelligent woman I've ever met! How do you catch on so quick?"

Julia didn't reply. Better to play it a bit dumb—a dumb brunette—she thought, at least for now.

"Well, Joshua, wasn't it you who suggested it that night in Georgetown, that it could well be an Import/Export Corporation? Remember?"

He nodded. "You have a very good memory. I'd forgotten."

"I've had to use it," she said lightly, "memorizing French verbs. At school. All closed book exams too. You said you knew him? For twenty years? Who was he, our Major Patel? IMI? MI-6? CIA?"

"IMI, until he resigned to go into business. A poor sort of guy. Financially, I mean. Came from a poor family in Gujarat. Had a deprived childhood; father was a tailor, mother worked as a servant in my grandfather's household—cook I believe. I gave him the job in IMI, and he was very trustworthy, as far as I knew, until I left IMI."

"He certainly had a change in his circumstances, I'd say," Julia said, and immediately regretted it.

"Why? Why do you say that, Julia?"

"Darling, if, as you say, he was living in a flat on Veer Narriman Street—just off the Marine Drive, as you tell me—he couldn't possibly have been very poor, could he?"

"You're right. You haven't seen his flat, but he certainly seems to have come into a lot of money. The flat itself is not significant. Our Indian agent—what's his name, Raja?—could have set him up in it to handle the Bombay end of the setup, but the décor inside, the furnishings, the crystal and the Persian rugs must have cost him a fortune!"

Joshua fell silent; Julia too. They both knew how treacherous this business could be—even when money was not involved. And when it was, as in Major Patel's case, loyalty amounted to nothing more than a signed check or a bundle of bills.

"He got greedy, Julia," Joshua said. "Such men are easily bought. What they sell is honour and finally—in his case—himself."

"We're making progress," Julia said. "We know what the scheme was—importing arms meant for Afghanistan into India using DOP as the importing agency. We know who ran it at this end—even if he's dead. Now all we have to do is to find out where they're being sent."

Julia drained her glass; refilled it. It was coming to that time of the evening when she would have to talk a little more freely—and she wasn't too keen on it. In fact, the idea was causing butterflies to flutter in her stomach.

"That's just it!" Joshua said. "The ROUTING file is missing. The murderer was after that and she got it."

"She?"

"Yes. Definitely a woman. Devika saw her from the balcony above. Running away. And it was a woman. I was too late reaching the balcony; I was examining the body."

"Devika? You didn't tell me Devika was with you."

"Didn't I, darling? Must have slipped my mind. I need IMI's help in the matter, and they've deputed Devika to help me. She knew about DOP and Major Patel. So we went along together to question him. You don't mind, do you?"

"Why should I?" Julia said lightly. "Strictly business from what you've told me. And you told it to me quite honourably. I mean I didn't have to worm it out of you now, did I?"

He flashed her a grateful look, caressing her arm that lay alongside, kissing her on the cheek near the eye, nuzzling her neck, until she smiled in return. He took it as forgiveness.

"So Devika is sure it was a woman?"

"Absolutely! Wearing a skirt and a blouse and a large white sun-bonnet that covered her head and face. I was a fool, Julia. I could have nabbed her easily enough. She was in the flat when we entered the building—because the door to the flat was open. And instead of checking the stairs to the floor above—where she had to be hiding out—I entered the flat. The open door should have alerted me. I'm slipping, darling. I must be getting old."

"Don't blame yourself, Joshua. She probably made quite a few mistakes herself, I'll bet. Well, go on. Then what happened?"

"We saw immediately he was dead. He was seated at his office desk. Shot in the back of the head, facing the balcony; the bullet exited his forehead into the open air—we'll never find it. The place was a shambles. She'd gone through the lot. We found a lot of other material that confirmed he ran DOP—and inventories of every shipment through Bombay, including THE EMPEROR which docked two days ago—but no ROUTING file. How was he routing those railway wagons out of Bombay?"

"You searched everywhere?"

"Yes."

"The drawers of the table—you did say he was seated at the office desk, didn't you?"

"She got to it first. The key was on the floor where she'd dropped it, while taking off. In the top drawer is where we found all the inventories of all the shipments—but no ROUTING file. What were the routes he was using to hijack those wagons instead of sending them to Amritsar."

"Amritsar? Why Amritsar?"

"Because the only rail line to Pakistan that goes to Lahore, and from there to the Afghan border, from India, is out of Amritsar. A railway map tells us that. But the wagons—two shiploads of them—didn't make it to Amritsar. So where are they?"

Julia licked the froth off her beer, in a most unladylike manner, had another long draw; then leaned over and pressed herself into Joshua. He caressed her bare arm, absent-mindedly, his fingers plunging into the side of her breast, caressing it too. In the dim light they were unobserved.

"Then what did Devika and you do, darling?"

"Wasted time. Precious seconds while she was getting away—stealing the file—the bitch! That's what we did. Devika went onto the balcony and shouted for someone to stop her, but of course no one did. No one wants to interfere these days. I called the IMI police number in the Churchgate area for a fast car with a siren, and they had one at the door within two minutes. She must have had an accomplice in a taxi waiting at the corner—the conniving woman—and she beat us. Oh, I could wring her pretty neck!"

"Was she pretty, Joshua?"

"I don't know. I didn't see her at all; neither did Devika. All Devika saw from above was a large sun-bonnet she was clutching to her head. We gave chase down the Marine Drive, and we were gaining on them too. At one time we could not have been more than a hundred yards behind—too far to get the registration number of the taxi. I was hoping she'd turn around to see how far back we were, but no such luck."

Joshua looked so dejected, she felt sorry for him.

"Never mind, darling. She'll soon turn up; I know it. You'll find out who she is before long. Do you think she is a bitch and a conniving woman, Joshua? Couldn't she have, sort of, just blundered into it?"

"I don't know what you mean."

"Well, couldn't she have walked into the flat for different reasons altogether—and found your Major Patel lying dead in there? Then panicked when she heard the two of you coming into the building?"

"Not likely! Why would an innocent woman run like a murderer and a common thief? If only I'd caught her in the act, wouldn't she have been surprised?"

"Not as surprised as you might have been, Joshua. I mean, she might have had a gun! She would have had the element of surprise—as you army men put it? Oh, Joshua, I'm so glad you didn't surprise her—not in front of Devika."

"Julia, what are you talking about? You've lost your capacity for beer—not enough practice in India—of the sort we had at the Evening Star in Hampstead, on our very first 'date'? Go easy on the stuff, my darling, or I might have to carry you home."

Julia laughed. Feeling perfectly sober. Beginning to enjoy the evening more than she'd anticipated. Even looking forward to watching him as she told him. But not just yet. A little longer? To enjoy the mood of the evening?

"Does it matter, darling, if I have a drop too much? Who better than you to take me home safely, undress me; then tuck me into bed? If I can't trust you to do that—without ravishing me—who can I trust?"

"Have another beer," he said. "Here I am stumped by the lack of any progress at all in this case, my principal contact murdered by a bullet through the head, the file on the routing of the wagons gone missing—and all you can think about, my wonderful wife, is me putting you to bed? I hope you've packed a few thin, see-through negligees. It is awful hot at night, and we don't have air-conditioning. Those English nightgowns of yours will never do in this climate. Perhaps we ought to try sleeping in the raw?"

"Darling," Julia said. "I'm in the mood for giving. Put out your hands."

He did as he was told, laughingly.

"Now close your eyes."

He did that too.

"Now wish for what you'd want most lying in your hands."

He thought about it for a few moments.

"Does that include parts of your body, darling?"

"Oh, Joshua, do be serious! Just when I was about to grant you a wish. I have half a mind not to give it to you—but I will grant all wishes today. The ones you just asked for you can have—but only at home and in bed. But here, I'll give you what I know you've been longing for."

"You have a present for me?"

"You could say so. Will you forgive me for springing it on you in this way?"

"I love surprises!" Joshua said, closing his eyes and holding out his hands for the second time.

"Not this one you won't," Julia muttered under her breath. She turned to the large handbag lying beside her, and placed the ROUTING file in his hands.

He opened his eyes. The smile faded, slowly. He put the file down on the table in front of them, sweeping aside empty dishes like inconsequential fluff. The dirty dishes piled up in front of her. Trust the dirty dishes to land in front of me, she thought. Ah well, for once some else would be washing them.

He didn't have to open the file to know its contents.

The title on it gave it away. ROUTING. A thin, brown folding file, with pockets to hold the papers inside. No clips or binders.

Then he understood. Not what the file contained—that he already knew—but how she'd obtained it. He leaned away from her so that he could turn to face her. With accusing eyes. No smile on mouth or lips or in his eyes.

"Julia!"

"I didn't do it, darling," she said quietly. "You have my word on it."

"Julia!"

"He was dead when I found him. Just as you did. Don't you believe me, Joshua? I didn't do it."

"Julia!"

"Darling, if all you are going to do is to sit there with your mouth open and accusingly shout my name, I have nothing more to say."

"I'm not shouting your name!" he said shouting. "God! What if we'd caught you. Geez! The very thought of it makes my blood curdle. For murder! What did you say? You didn't do it?"

"That's what I've been trying to tell you—if you'll only listen! He was dead before I got there. The door was unlocked so I walked in—as you did. When I saw you and her come into the building, I ran for it. Now aren't you glad I did? Instead of being caught by you and—her!"

He had to admit she was right. He took a little time over it—most husbands took their time admitting their wives were right, he told her when she upbraided him for his delay—but he put his arm around her and hugged her sideways.

He felt like a new person, he told her, and to prove it he ordered another round of another exotic Indian sweet—rasgullas—specially for her, he said, and another pot of tea.

Then he opened the file.

It told them what they wanted to know. The route the railway wagons would take to the Pakistan border, where an export permit classified them as non-strategic items of common trade between the two countries.

The route itself was laid out on a map of West and Central India. From Bombay they were to be moved by Western Railway to Ahmedabad in Gujarat, then without diversion to Marwar Junction in Rajasthan. At Marwar they were to be moved through Ajmer to

Delhi; then a mere two hundred miles away, through Ambala to Amritsar in the Punjab. It was one of the very few points where the railway line ran, through the town of Atari, into Pakistan. There an import permit classified them as non-strategic materials of common trade between the two countries, the wagons being routed to Lahore barely forty miles away.

Simple and direct. Except that something had gone dreadfully wrong and the wagons weren't reaching Amritsar. Somewhere along more than one thousand miles of track they had disappeared. Where?

Joshua unfolded the map, from the file, on the table in front of them, now cleared of all dishes by an obliging waiter, and traced the intended route for Julia. She leaned over his shoulder to peer at it in the weak light. Geography had always been her weak subject in boarding school. Drawing a map of the British Isles with all its inlets and coves, particularly Cornwall and Scotland, had been a headache in the extreme. This was a foreign country.

"Where, darling, can they hide two shiploads of heavy arms?" It was a rhetorical question. They both knew the answer to the question.

Only in the Thar Desert.

Except that the Thar Desert was five hundred miles long and two hundred fifty miles wide. As Joshua explained it to Julia, with his head in his hands, one could fit the entire British Isles in it and have room left over for a small European kingdom or two!

"Why don't we examine the rest of the file?" Julia suggested.

There were bills of lading for the three shipments; the latest was for THE EMPEROR that had docked in Bombay Port two days before, the cargo awaiting unloading onto flatbed railway wagons for dispatch into the hinterland. Nothing else in the file except one handwritten memo addressed to Major Patel, source unknown, reminding him that all three shipments had to be completed before the deadline on October 25—if he wished to be paid. No signature. A neat, cultured handwriting, even if it carried a pointed threat.

Joshua kissed Julia again.

"You're not mad at me, are you Joshua?" she pleaded, knowing fully well that he was not.

He put on the air of the injured husband—as if she'd been caught in an adulterous affair.

"You still have some explaining to do, Julia. To clear those lingering doubts that will keep cropping up in my mind after this 'episode'—shall we say?"

"Explanations! Explanations! That is all husbands want from their wives. Fire away."

"Why did you go to see our dead friend—Major Patel?"

She hesitated for just a few seconds before she answered him.

"Because he was my MI-6 contact in Bombay."

"What!"

"You seem surprised, darling."

"Why didn't you tell me?"

"Do you tell me everything about your IMI contacts? Did you tell me you were going to see Devika this morning? Besides, I was specifically asked by Edward not to reveal his identity to you, since it would mean blowing his cover—and now he's dead, I'm so very glad I didn't."

"Oh, why?"

"Because I—we—would have thought that it was the cause of his death. Now at least we can both be assured that neither you nor I had anything to do with a blown cover for his murder."

Joshua nodded in agreement. A blown cover in their line of business was pretty close to committing suicide. In Major Patel's case, keeping his cover hadn't helped.

"And how did Edward pass on his name to you? You can tell me now, can't you? Seeing he's dead and we can't hurt him anymore."

She nodded. "The tail at Heathrow. The older lady in the orange dress? Remember? She followed me into the Women's room, while you waited for me outside in the cafeteria."

He slammed his napkin onto the table in triumph.

"I knew it! I knew it! I told you that in the plane, didn't I?"

"Yes, you did, darling. That was very clever of you. I was ever so proud of you, even if my lips were sealed."

That mollified him a great deal, because he became quite himself again, stroking her bare arm causing sensations within her that could easily threaten to boil over if he continued that way.

Strange as it was, that is how they'd fallen in love. In a crowded tube train in London, traveling from South Kensington to Baker Street on the Circle Line. She had been assigned by Farnsworth to protect him while tracking Slagter, the South African hit-man. The train was packed, but she could hardly travel apart from him! She hadn't been quite prepared for how closely they would travel those few stations together, thrown against each other by crowds of friendly strangers hemming them in from all sides except the front where they hemmed each other in. Joshua had raised his hand—to protect himself from a burly stranger whose elbow was digging him in the ribs—and found it cupping her, on the fullness of her breast. The rocking of the train swayed them from two independent strangers into two warm bodies that fought, at first, the emotions that arose within them, and then, later, abandoned themselves, to each other, in surrender. His hand pummeled her breast as the train took a particularly sharp turn and she was slammed into him, the nipple retreating into the breast that bore it, emerging into the palm of his hand on the straight runs. Until the tracks curved the other way and he was slammed into her, his thigh between hers; hers between his. She was in his arms.

There was a warmth of feeling here that she had missed before, even in her own bedroom, with the only other man who had made love to her. Neither Joshua and Julia had planned it that way; yet neither was going to discard such warmth if they could possibly help it. It did not arise easily between two people, and when it did, she had said to herself, she wasn't going to let it go. And he had felt the same way too.

"Did you know that our Major Patel worked for MI-6, Joshua?"

"No, my darling. I wish I had. I might have saved him."

"Who else was he working for? Raja?"

"We'll find out. What did you do with the bonnet?"

"The bonnet?"

"Yes, Julia, the sun-bonnet? The one you were wearing this morning. We'll have to get rid of it."

"I gave it away," she said.

"Who to?"

"Mr Singh's wife."

"Who's Mr. Singh?"

"The taxi driver. The one who saved me from a cruel Indian Army Colonel and a beastly Indian woman. An absolute gem of a man! Writes poetry too. In Punjabi."

"How did you meet his wife?"

"She was there with us, darling, all the time."

"He takes his wife along when he drives his taxi?" Joshua said in disbelief. "That is odd for a Sikh taxi driver—for any taxi driver, anywhere."

"Not in this case, darling," Julia said. "He drives her around all the time. So, as my thanks, I gave his wife my sun-bonnet. He was so very pleased. I had to get rid of it, and it seemed like a nice way of saying 'thanks'. You don't mind, do you, darling?"

Joshua threw up his hands in despair. He put it down to the drinks she'd had—though he knew, from their first 'date' in the Evening Star, that her capacity was a lot more than the beers she'd had—or perhaps to her imagination as a writer, in which case he wasn't too far from the truth.

The meal had come to an end—though not the evening. Julia stretched herself luxuriously, stifling a yawn. He took the hint, helping her from the booth, acknowledging the thanks of the tall waiter, for the very generous tip he'd left behind, by a slight nod of the head, moving her in the direction of the car he'd taken on loan from IMI.

"Darling," he said, as he drove home, "we're being very foolish—like a pair of immature, insecure lovebirds—not trusting each other completely. My fault too. What say we make a pact tonight? No matter how damaging the evidence might seem to be against either of us—and you must admit when you produced that file, I had every reason to believe you killed him for it—the other will still believe it can't be true! Yes?"

She leaned against him in the car, head on his shoulder. Fortunately traffic was light at that late hour, and so he could pay attention to her, kissing her hair, and honking at an errant cow on the road at the same time.

"I think that's a wonderful idea, Joshua. And why don't we make this a memorable night to seal that trust? I did make you some promises in the restaurant, I'd like to keep. And besides, there's the promise I gave to Grandfather as well."

"Grandfather! What's he got to do with this?"

"I did promise Grandfather, I would deliver the twelfth Earl of Bromfield, Joshua. Why do you think I married you? It's your children I want."

"You know what I'd pray for?" he said.

"What?"

"That we have three—no maybe four—daughters first, before we have a son—so that I can have you around me perpetually barefoot and pregnant."

"Joshua, do you know, as a child, what I envied most that other children had?"

"No, tell me."

"That they had brothers and sisters. That they could laugh and play, and yes, even squabble with their loving siblings. I was an only child; I had no one, except Grandfather, until you came into my life. Do you think I'm going to inflict that longing on our children? I'm in a generous mood tonight. Give me a number and they will be ours. Four did you say? Or was it five?"

They had never discussed the projected size of their family before. After they were married, twice, the honeymoon had been their only concern—and even that had been fractured beyond belief. It had been her one fear that, when they came to discussing children, Joshua might say: "One boy, one girl, that's it, dear; we can't afford an entire brood!"

In the darkness of the car, he did not see her smile, as he kissed her again on the head.

CHAPTER 6

Joshua left early the next morning. Force of habit woke him up at four o'clock, and rather than disturb Julia who took longer to fall asleep and so slept later than he did, he had breakfast with his mother downstairs.

There were one or two things that needed his urgent attention. Matters where Julia's presence could be positively uncomfortable. Such as having a friendly word with the police inspector handling the Vinod Patel murder case that the presence of a large number of an unknown woman's fingerprints in the flat were better left unexplained since they involved IMI. No further explanations were necessary and Joshua gave none. That she'd been working, for MI-6, as she'd been in the act of contacting one of their agents, had better be left unsaid.

Having done the needful, he swung the car round and headed for the Bombay Port Trust docks where THE EMPEROR was being unloaded. He carried a dock pass, and dressed as he was, in a suit with a tie in such hot weather, clearly marked him out as a bureaucrat, and hence not to be questioned.

The men unloading the huge crates onto the flat-bed railway wagons paid no attention to him. The crates had 'DOP' stenciled in huge letters on all four sides, providing instant identification and hence precluding inquiry or inspection.

So far it was all he had expected it to be. Nothing unusual. The line of flatbed wagons stood on the tracks running alongside the pier. The cranes towering above both ship and dock picked up the crates, weightless and insignificant, depositing them directly onto the wagons. For transport into the hinterland of India.

Where? Where were they being sent to? The destination? It was not marked on the crates. He examined several of them. Not even tucked away on some little railway tag attached to the wagons themselves.

The operation was being supervised by a clerk of the Bombay Port Trust, responsible for the cargo while it lay within the dock area; after that it became the responsibility of Western Railways.

Joshua went up to him. A thin, old, wizened man, with the many years of experience that made him indispensable; so underpaid he could hardly hope to retire from it. He had on a white shirt and white trousers—the best dress in the heat—but without a tie; that would have been part of his attire in the days of the Raj. He was only too pleased to have the company of the young man while he checked off the crates on his cargo list. The bright eyes beamed with self-assurance at being asked for help by the handsome young colonel with the military bearing—even if he was in civilian clothes. He, too, had served in the army at one time. A lowly private, but he had seen some action in Burma. He came smartly to attention to show the colonel he hadn't forgotten the respect an officer deserved.

"Tell me, Kantilal," Joshua said, after inquiring his name, "what is the final destination of these flat-beds? The ones with the DOP crates on them?"

Kantilal referred to his manifest.

"Marwar Junction," he said. "That is what I will put on the tags attached to the wagons when they are all loaded. Sort of routing tickets, attached by stiff wire to the flatbeds. Why do you ask, Sir?"

"And that is their final destination?"

The old man shook his head slowly.

"No," he said. "No, Sir. Most unusual, but in this case I don't know the final destination of these crates until the flatbeds reach Marwar Junction."

"Oh, and why is that?"

The old man beckoned to Joshua, to come with him as he led the way to his little cabin, against a stone wall at the back, that could survey the docks in front of it. He invited Joshua to sit; then offered him a cup of tea that was gratefully accepted. Nothing like a good cup of hot tea, Kantilal said, to bring out the sweat and provide for automatic air-conditioning to the body!

He hailed a tea-boy with his tea pot and cups, roaming the dock area in search of customers, chastising him for his unclean cups—washed, from customer to customer, by the simple expedient of dipping the cups into a bucket of unclean water—refusing Joshua's offer of payment. Joshua thanked the good Lord for having the foresight to not bring Julia along on this part of the inquiry. He loved her dearly, but there were times when a well-bred English girl—who was his wife—was better off not being around to see the dirty cup he was drinking his tea from.

"Well now, Sir. Let me see if I can't explain to you the tagging system we use here. It's all tied up with shunting."

"Shunting?"

"Yes, shunting. Putting together a freight train needs skill. Sure you can send wagons all over the country, haphazardly, and they will eventually reach their destinations—but at what expense! If you want the whole operation to run smoothly, why then, Sir, the wagons have to be put together in the line-up that allows them to be removed, at intermediate stops, quickly from either the front or the back of the train—without having to dismantle the whole damn train. You see what I mean, Sir?"

Joshua feigned ignorance. With good cause. Far better to keep the old man talking, slipping in the right questions when the need arose. Pretend you know too much, and he might leave out what you were really after.

"Take these DOP flatbeds, for instance. They will all be sent to the Central Marshalling Yards in Bombay—the largest in the world, barring none. Thousands of wagons come into the yards every single day. Let's say a freight train is to be assembled for Marwar Junction—since that seems to interest you. The train goes through Surat, Baroda and Ahmedabad in Gujarat to Marwar in Rajasthan. Wagons going to Marwar—these—will form the body of the train. All wagons going to Ahmedabad will come on the outside of them; wagons to Baroda still more outside; finally wagons going only to Surat will come at the very front and the very back of the train. When the train reaches Surat, the main diesels will be uncoupled. Lineman will uncouple the Surat-bound wagons, and the shunting locomotives will pull the Surat-bound wagons off the train. If wagons are to be added in Surat for Baroda—the next stop—they will go to the new front and back of the train. However, if there are wagons from Surat to Ahmedabad, the Baroda-bound wagons will have to be uncoupled and shunted off first, so that the new wagons for Ahmedabad can be shunted in and coupled. See what I mean, Sir?"

"It's all very simple," Joshua said, "the way you've explained it. But you still haven't told me why these haven't a final destination. What happens at Marwar Junction?"

The old man sipped his tea with relish. When he spoke again, it was with considerable hesitation.

"That's what so odd, Sir. Normally the entire route of the wagon, or flatbed, is listed on the tag, so that there is no delay during shunting. We use ink markers, like this one here, on the tags."

Kantilal handed a marker to Joshua, and an unmarked tag. "See, there are several lines on the tag. The final destination is on the uppermost line; intermediate junctions come on the lower lines in descending order, with the nearest junction on the lowest line. When a wagon has cleared the nearest junction—say Marwar—the line above would give the next junction to which the wagon has to be sent. And so on to the final destination. But sometimes, as in this case, the dispatching party—in this case, DOP—can't say for sure where the shipment is to be sent. Then they just give us the first junction to which the wagons have to be sent, and arrange with that junction to have the other lines on this tag filled in, but at their end. I don't mind; saves me having to route them the entire way. But it is odd."

"So what is so odd?" Joshua persisted.

"Because this happens in the case of isolated pieces or single wagons, where the supplier wants to move some inventory to a particular main junction—say Marwar—awaiting a final destination as the need arises. Never in the case of entire shiploads—as this one or the two shiploads previous to this one!"

Joshua thanked him and prepared to leave.

"Why don't you ask the DOP people?" Kantilal said. "They'd be able to tell you for sure where they go after Marwar Junction. They can go in only one of three directions after that."

"Three?"

"Well, after Marwar, they can go to Ajmer, and then on to Delhi. Or they could be routed to Jaisalmer. Or, finally, they could be tagged and routed to Barmer. But that is highly unlikely, Sir."

"Oh, and why?"

The old man rose from his high stool, in front of the cabin window, where he had been keeping an eye on the cranes unloading DOP crates on to the flatbeds. He picked up his clipboard, with the sheets of inventory clipped in at the top, flipping the first four pages over, to reach the crate he'd checked off before Joshua had engaged him in conversation.

"Quite unlikely, Sir. Why would anyone be sending heavy agricultural machinery into the Thar Desert?"

Kantilal waited until Joshua was out of sight, and then fully ten minutes more, before he went back into his little cabin with the huge glass window that looked out onto the ships being unloaded in the harbor. He waited another ten minutes before he reached for the telephone. Unsure of what he ought to confide in the voice at the other end.

"He was here! Colonel Samuelson was here. Making inquiries about DOP shipments."

There was a silence.

"I didn't tell him anything he wouldn't have found out anyway!" Kantilal whined. "Marwar Junction. That's all he knows. He'll be headed that way. Perhaps you can take care of him at that end?"

Another long silence as the voice at the other end berated him.

"I didn't tell him anything. I didn't! You have to believe me. Please! Perhaps, we ought to let this shipment go through?"

His protestations must have been in vain, because the party at the other end hung up, and the line went dead.

The old man put his head between his arms, on the counter, and sobbed in fear that convulsed his body.

When Joshua reached home, he found Julia helping his mother set the table for the noon meal. Better get some expertise on these spices, Julia thought, by assisting the old mother, asking the names of the spices that went in, and the proportions of them. Joshua's mother didn't weigh out a thing. She used experience for weights, but that made the job a little more complex. Four sprinkles, two dashes, one scoop between five fingers; then taste and add two more sprinkles of this and a dash more of that!

Cook at Bromfield House would throw a fit if she was instructed to cook in that way. It might take longer, but she'd eventually work it out in ounces and cups, Julia thought. At least she'd made a start into the subtle mysteries of Indian cooking. Never again would the exotic aromas outside the Indian restaurant on Finchley Road in Hampstead be exotic to her. Why, she might be even able to pick out the individual dishes—the biryanis or the kababs—that were wafting the aromas into the street?

The servant woman washed the dishes, and while Joshua's mother went off for her afternoon nap, Joshua and Julia went up to their flat, where Joshua filled Julia in on his visit to the docks and his morning with Kantilal.

"Doesn't seem right," Julia said, making them both a cup of tea, English style—that was also Indian style—with milk and sugar. Iced tea might have been more sensible in the hot weather, but no one seemed to care for it in India; neither did they.

"What doesn't, darling?"

"The routing. Did you see the tags on the wagons?"

"No."

"Why not?"

"There weren't any on them. The crates were just being unloaded. Kantilal was going to do them this afternoon. About now."

Julia shook her head. "Doesn't seem right," she said, again. "The old man being so helpful. Oh, I know, Indians are the friendliest people in the world—but to even buy you a cup of tea? Almost as if he was buying time? Put it down to woman's intuition, darling, but our Mr Kantilal rates a big question mark."

He scoffed at her, wrinkling up his nose at her logic. Woman's intuition! She saw the grimace, and told him he looked cute, and could he, please, do it again? So he did.

"Come on, Julia. Next you'll be telling me he's an agent, working for the other side?"

"Could be."

"Only one way to find out," Joshua said, putting aside his tea cup and reaching for her arm. She would have spent some time touching up her makeup, but Joshua hurried her downstairs and out of the house. The morning shift would soon be coming to an end, and Mr Kantilal would be off work. The evening shift clerk might not be so obliging.

Joshua drove. He drove as fast as he could—one could not make haste with slow moving bullock carts and horse drawn carriages—but he used the horn so often, Julia remarked he must have a repressed desire to be in an orchestra?

"I don't have a dock pass," she pointed out.

"Not to worry. The security guard at the gate is one of my old men. From my regiment. I gave him the reference that got him this job. If he doesn't come to attention and salute, I'll boot him into the sea! Besides I do have a pass."

"For the both of us?"

"It's in English. He doesn't read English well. Nearly cost me a battery position in the fighting round Lahore."

The security guard stopped the car at the gate. Joshua lowered the window drawing instant recognition. The soldier drew himself to his full height, and saluted smartly.

"And how are you, Pratap Singh, these days?"

"Doing fine, Sir—thanks to you! What a pleasure to see you. After a long time."

"I was in this morning," Joshua said. "But I used the Lion Gate. Thought I'd show my wife round the docks."

Pratap Singh folded his hands to Julia in a namaste.

She responded likewise. It had been difficult at first, folding the hands together instead of extending the right hand. Avoiding the touch of strange hands, Joshua explained. So husbands might not be jealous there was undue pressure or emotional messages being passed between the clasping palms. Hygenic too! Some of the hands could be very dirty. And in the hot weather certainly very sweaty.

The morning shift was almost at an end. Those who could leave early without being reprimanded had already done so. Others were waiting for the steam whistle that would announce the end of the shift. It did—a welcome sound to them that worked there; ear-splitting to Julia.

Kantilal's cabin, at the far back wall, overlooking the area appeared deserted. THE EMPEROR was still moored against the dock, but the cranes were silent. The door of the cabin was half open.

"Perhaps, he's left," Joshua said, as they walked towards it.

Nobody paid them any attention.

He was sitting at the counter, on the high stool, his head between his arms, facing them. The coral handle, glinting in the sunlight that streamed in through the window, of a steel-bladed long knife jutted out from between his shoulders.

Joshua stopped in the doorway and backed out, stepping on Julia's toes as he pushed her backwards. She saw Kantilal over Joshua's shoulder and backed out hurriedly as well. He took her hand and without speaking headed for the DOP flatbeds on the railway tracks running the length of the pier. Trying not to hurry, walking casually, without attracting attention. The morning shift had ended; the second shift clerk would walk into the cabin any minute now and raise the alarm, calling out for help.

Julia looked at the cabin, now bathed in sunlight coming off the water. It looked so serene, unrushed by the workers streaming off the loading sheds and warehouses that lined the wharf.

The first wagon had the tag tied on with stout wire. The tag itself was of white cloth and stiff paper, reinforced with fine wires, that would not tear even over thousands of miles of travel. They went to the next wagon, and then the next. They all carried the same single destination, written with the thick black ink marker that Kantilal had shown Joshua in the cabin. There were other markings that would make sense only to railway employees, but the destination, so important to the routing of the wagons, was clear to anyone that saw it.

'Marwar Junction'.

"Let's get out of here," Joshua whispered, "before they find our friend Kantilal in there. We'll go out by the Lion Gate. They never check dock passes of workers—or anyone—leaving the docks, but I'd rather Pratap Singh didn't see us leaving so soon."

She nodded, and walking with quick unhurried steps they made their way back to the car.

CHAPTER 7

Julia always maintained it was the nicest part of any assignment—sitting in a café, in a private booth of a rather tucked-away nature, sipping hot tea and digging into some of those fabulous Indian sweets that Joshua had taken upon himself to make sure she enjoyed. While he picked at a little here and there, he sat there watching her face light up at the first taste of some sweet culinary delight.

She saw him watch her eat.

"Aren't you going to have some more?" she asked. "This is absolutely delightful, Joshua, but oh, so rich! I'll get fat, darling, and that would never do."

He laughed. "You will always be perfect, my love. So eat what you wish. Whatever pleases you."

"That is what all husbands say—at first. Then when their wives put on a few pounds of fat—a double chin or a tire or two round the waist—all they have eyes for are the thin, lissome models they never seemed to care much for before."

Joshua laughed again, but his mind was not there, and she knew it. She felt guilty. She was still carrying on as if they were on their honeymoon—as if nothing of importance had occurred—while he was struggling with the shrouded deaths of Major Patel and now Kantilal. She'd asked—no insisted—on coming out here with him, so she could be of help to him, and she hadn't been much of that. True she had obtained the ROUTING file, but that had been pure chance, and she'd complicated matters no end by leaving her fingerprints all over the flat. How was she to know she was going to meet a dead body? That, she decided, was what was wrong with her.

She wasn't cut out to be a professional agent. It had been the same way when they'd been trailing Slagter, the South African hit-man. Until she'd been overcome by the brutality of his killings; then she'd changed.

"Want to share some of those thoughts with me, darling?" she asked.

He was only too willing to unburden himself to her. At times, she felt, he'd been secretive—but not today.

"Why did Kantilal tag those flatbeds for Marwar Junction? When he'd told me that was, precisely, what he was going to do."

"I see." She didn't, but it was better to keep him talking, unburdening himself.

"He had been tagging those wagons; he knew about the last two shipments because he mentioned them That is precisely what an innocent man would do; tag them for Marwar Junction and express surprise at why the wagons weren't being tagged to their final destination. Yet he was murdered! So he must have been involved in some way. But he told me all about it. Why?"

"Could it have been," Julia said, "that he knew who you were, and why you were asking questions, and rather than sink deeper into the mess he was in, he decided to back out of it—to save himself. That would account for the correct tags, the information he provided—and his murder! When a link in the chain decides it wants out, neither the power crane nor the hook have much choice—but to kill."

"Darling," Joshua said, putting his arm round her and squeezing her tight. "You are brilliant! What would I do without you? He told me all I needed to know—just in case he ended up in a real dock. I would have been his defense. Unfortunately, perhaps, he decided to play it both ways, and the other side wasn't buying his story. That is sad."

"So what else did he tell you, that helps us?"

"Marwar Junction is on the route to Amritsar—so, technically, he hadn't routed them incorrectly. But, as he mentioned, it is also the route for two other destinations—Jaisalmer and Barmer. And both are in the Thar Desert. And at one of those two small towns, my love, is where those arms are!"

He threw up his hands in triumph, the military moustache parting with his lips as he smiled broadly, the black eyes abandoning despair and coming to life again. They could communicate, Julia thought. His triumph did not leave her feeling inadequate; it elated her. His joy was also, unreservedly, hers too. Unlike many marriages she'd known in England where the success of one was humiliation for the other.

"Well, then you've found them," she said.

"Not quite, my darling, not quite. Jaisalmer or Barmer? Which one? But they're there somewhere, and I'll be damned if I don't find them. This has become something personal. I can hardly ask you to ride a camel with me in the Thar Desert, hunting for lost flatbeds, but I will have to go out there, darling. You know that, don't you? And alone."

She nodded miserably.

"Cheer up, Julia. I'll tell you what you can do."

"Keep Mother company, learn Indian cuisine, and wait for you to come back?"

"You could do that. But it's not what I was going to say. We've still got the problem of who killed Rashid Khan. And the answer to that lies not here but in Pakistan. I remember you telling me I was persona non-grata? Could you go instead?"

She brightened instantly.

"Edward and the Begum are there. Stay with them. They'll look after you. Introduce you to people you might want to meet. Such as Rashid Khan's widow—if he is dead, that is?"

"Isn't he?"

"I don't know. That's what PMI says. But if IMI is riddled with KGB agents, PMI is probably riddled by the CIA. They may well have motives, we're unaware of, for having him thought of as dead."

"Raja killed him," she said. "While at prayer. Kneeling towards Mecca. With a hole in the back of the head. At a meeting that had been prearranged between them, so he could steal Rashid Khan's copy of THE THAR ARTICLES. Why can't you accept it?"

"Is that what you believe?"

"Makes sense to me, darling. The documents are a serious liability to India, and the Prime Minister. They don't imperil Pakistan or the General—if they are made public. But that would play hell this side of the border. And you know it. I do understand—believe me, I do—how you just cannot believe one of your countrymen could murder his partner, and possibly a friend, in cold blood. Men have been known to do that when the stakes are high, and, believe me, Joshua, they couldn't be higher."

He was silent, letting her talk on, avoiding her eyes, while she continued, with ruthless logic.

"Raja had the opportunity and he had the motive.'

'A strong overriding cause to kill. Why will you not accept it, Joshua? The logic is inescapable."

"I will accept it," he said quietly, weighing his words with what seemed, to her, infinite care, "if you will accept by the same logic that you murdered Major Patel."

"What!" Julia shot up from her seat, turning sideways to face him, the surprise, in her widened brown eyes, turning to incredulous dismay.

"Well, darling, you were the last person to see him. Opportunity. You came away with the ROUTING file—motive. I'd say the circumstances were at least as close to the ones we've been discussing for Raja murdering Rashid Khan, wouldn't you? Possibly closer, because we do know that Major Patel is dead, but we aren't a hundred per cent certain that Rashid Khan hasn't been put out of commission—maybe against his wishes—but is still very much alive."

"But Major Patel was dead when I found him!"

"Ah! But that is what you say."

"And I didn't go there to steal the file. I picked it up as an afterthought. To help you!"

"Ah! But that is what you say."

"Don't you believe me?" she said, bitterly. "I wish to heavens I'd never gone near that bloody flat in the first place!"

"Ah! But that is what you say."

"If you say that once more, I'm walking straight out of here and taking a taxi home. And then the next flight back to London—even a red eye!"

He put out both his arms to her, circling her waist, drawing her back gently into her seat beside him, passing his hand over her bare arm, soothing back the curls of brown hair on her face and neck, kissing her gently, first on the cheek and the lobe of her ear, then down the side of her neck, moving pleadingly to her lips, his eyes apologetic for having stirred her anger up this way. The café was empty. The waiter had withdrawn discreetly.

"I believe you, darling. I'll always believe you—and I'll always love you. But you do see how an observer, given the same facts, could conceivably come to the conclusion that you had done in our Major Patel? And you didn't! Perhaps that's the way it is too with our Mr Raja?"

"His code name is 'Raja'. No title before it," she said, not fully at peace with him. Not kissing him back.

"Well, whatever. But you've raised interesting questions, Julia. If Raja killed him, we've got to find him, and hand him over to the Pakistanis—both for justice to be served and to mollify them. If Raja didn't kill Rashid Khan, then who did? That is assuming Rashid Khan is dead. If he isn't, then why are PMI and the CIA playing such a dangerous game, by making out that he is? Will you go to Pakistan, darling, and find out—while I ride a camel in the Thar Desert looking for lost flatbeds?"

She was trembling with the thoughts he had put in her mind. He was right! Third parties, such as the CID branch of the Bombay Police, investigating Major Patel's murder could well ask some very nasty questions—if it weren't for Joshua. What would she have done without Joshua? Her fingerprints all over the place, the evidence of a taxi driver, however friendly he had been; he would have to speak the truth in a court of law: 'She was panicked, Sir, when she came running out of the flat.' And Devika Rani—how she hated that woman! She would identify the sun-bonnet, even if she could not identify the face it concealed. What would the sentence be? In an Indian women's prison? Would they have the same justice for her as a white woman—or would they extract even greater retribution because she came from the old Raj?

Stop it, Julia! Stop it this very instant! No one is after you.

Would Joshua stand up for her?

After all I did marry him. Even if he is an Indian!

This last thought made her feel so ashamed of herself, she turned towards him and smothered his lips with kisses, the passion of which he had not aroused even in bed with her. That surprised him too. He put it down to the general insecurity she must feel, as his wife, coming out to a strange land, surrounded by strange people and an even stranger culture. He was all she had, to keep her sense of balance with what was going on around her. So she had clung to him—and instead of being supportive of her, he had accused her of murder! He ought to have his head examined. Here she was, the granddaughter of an English Earl, who had married him—a commoner—when she could have had a Duke or a Prince of the realm! She had married him despite insurmountable differences—to others, but not to her—in culture and religion between them, and he'd had no kind words for her—just accusations. What the hell did it matter if she believed Raja had killed Bahadur?

He felt so ashamed of himself, he turned towards her and responded to her kisses with a fervour of his own that filled her with delight.

"Will you forgive me," she whispered, as she nestled in his arms, "for some of the shameful thoughts I've had?"

"That's exactly what I was going to ask of you—forgiveness for some of my shameful ones too. Please, will you forgive me?"

She stood up and took his hand, to leave the café.

"Come with me," she said. "I know of a nicer place, and a nicer way, to forgive each other."

CHAPTER 8

Julia insisted on a time limit. Ten days, no more, for either of them. For him to locate the missing arms shipments in the Thar Desert; for her to find out what she could about Rashid Khan's death—and his killer.

Karachi was only a two-hour flight from Bombay by Air India. Marwar Junction took longer, because there wasn't a straight flight from Bombay. It had no airport of its own, lying on the railway line between Udaipur and Jodhpur in Rajasthan, both of which were well-served by Indian Airlines. Joshua chose Jodhpur, which was further away, opting to come backwards to Marwar Junction.

They both left the same day; neither saw the other off. His flight to Jodhpur left early. She opted for a later flight to Karachi, because the Begum was to pick her up at Karachi Airport, and the Begum was a late riser. With Edward forbidding her to go to the shops, there was nothing much she could do, she moaned to Julia on the telephone, so what was the point in rising early? They would be delighted to have her stay with them for the ten days she was in Karachi. Only ten days? She would dearly love to show Julia around Karachi, especially the shopping district. Julia smiled, even on the telephone. She could well imagine Naseem going raving berserk in the shops with all their wares—especially the jewellery stores—and the Viscount's distress at the results of her excursions.

Julia called the Begum, with Joshua standing alongside her, to confirm the travel arrangements.

She noticed Mr Singh parked a little way up the street, awaiting a customer. Joshua hailed him, waving to Julia standing on the balcony, who waved goodbye.

The taxi passed slowly, almost under her, turning the corner to disappear from view. And as it did, the silence set in. Not the silence of the street—that was just as noisy as before—but the silence within. She wandered from one room to another, not quite understanding her disquiet, until she realised it was the first time she had been apart from Joshua since they were married, not quite four weeks ago!

Stop behaving like a silly schoolgirl, she told herself sternly, and do something useful—like visiting her mother-in-law in the flat below. Susan, Joshua's teenage sister, had gone off on a college trip organised by one of her professors—who was a meteorologist, and Indian-Jewish too. He was a little older than she was, but she was hopelessly in love with him, and he with her; Joshua's mother hoped something would come of it.

"A brilliant man! Professor David Abrams. World renowned in his field. We don't know the family; they're originally from Delhi. Oh! I do hope David and Susan find each other."

And shaking her head, as if not quite sure and in partial despair, Joshua's mother took Julia into the room at the front end of the flat where Joshua's childhood memories had been stored.

It was the old Mother's favourite room in her flat.

It was the living room, well lit, with a niche in one corner that had a rocking chair. Facing the chair, and within easy reach of it, were three cupboards, all closed and all locked, that held her priceless treasures. One for each of her children. Joshua—who was the eldest—had his in the corner. Joe, who was in England, and Susan, the youngest, had theirs along the walls on either side of Joshua's cupboard. His was the largest, possibly because as the oldest the old mother had collected more, with more to store.

She led Julia to Joshua's cupboard, throwing open the doors, unlocking the drawers, burrowing under stacks of photographs of fading hues to fish out an award or a certificate of prized value—to her. The one he'd won in an oratory competition in High School. Joshua a Speaker? She hadn't known that! Would he have been able to hold his own at Hyde Park Corner? Without much doubt. How much did she know about him, even though she was married to him? It was all there before her—the hidden talents, the childhood successes, captured by documents or photographs—for an old lady's viewing pleasure.

The old Mother left Julia to explore the contents of the cupboard; she had to put lunch on—Julia must have something to eat before she caught that plane to Karachi. She didn't understand any of this! Married four weeks and her son was off to Marwar Junction in Rajasthan, and his wife was off to Karachi in Pakistan! Julia assured her and reassured her that their marriage was not unraveling—she was still deeply in love with her son, and he with her—but before Joshua and she could settle back to married life in London, he had some loose ends to tie up, while she had a long-standing social obligation to visit Viscount Edward Andrew and his wife, Begum Naseem Banu. The last statement was not an untruth—Julia did have a social obligation to visit Edward and Naseem Banu, but in England. As that was not possible, Julia firmly told herself, this would just have to do instead.

Julia sat in the rocking chair, looking idly through the albums, seeing photographs of Joshua's dead ancestors. They weren't her ancestors, and she had to admit that were she to see any of them walking down the street, she would have been hard pressed to identify any of them. But they would be the ancestors of her children, and for their sake and their heritage, she had better get to know them a little better. All that would have been much easier with Joshua leaning over her shoulder and fixing the relationships for her. Now all she could say with any degree of certainty was that they were dead.

She closed the album, looked at her watch and decided that looking through Joshua's things would be more pleasurable—and meaningful—with Joshua.

She closed the drawers she had opened. They slid in easily, the ledges at the sides gliding in between wooden guides. No rollers; just good workmanship.

Except one drawer. The very bottom one. It slid in easily enough until the very end of the guides and then ran into a soft obstruction. Soft because it didn't come to an absolute full stop, as it might if the obstruction was wood or metal. Cardboard, perhaps, or a piece of rag cloth, that had slipped in behind, she thought, as she pressed it in and clicked it shut.

Almost tea time. She took out the single key that locked all the drawers in the cupboard, when the thought struck her that she wasn't being as good a wife as she could be if she didn't treat Joshua's things as if they were her own.

She unlocked the bottom drawer and it slid open a few inches. She removed it and placed it on the ground, reaching into the back for the obstruction. Her hands touched paper. An envelope of some sort containing sheets of paper. She drew it out.

It was sealed. No address on the outside. No writing of any sort, front or back. Brown, manila. She turned it over in her hands; closed the drawer that now slid in easily to its full depth. She locked it.

She sat on the rocking chair and rocked. The squeak of the chair could not be heard in the fierce arguments that raged within her. Those were all she heard.

What rights did a wife have? He had never concealed anything from her. If one of them was away, the other opened all the mail—to whoever it was addressed. They had both agreed on that even when they were first engaged. A practical necessity. Some action might be necessary—an urgent request or a bill to be paid? Even if it was marked 'personal' or 'confidential', each would open the other's mail.

The envelope she held on her lap had no such markings. No markings of any sort.

But did she want to open it? That was an entirely different question. In all probability it contained innocuous material—perhaps a letter from an irate patient, written ten years ago, complaining about Dr Samuelson's non-availability when he'd come in with a cold. Or perhaps letters from a friend?

What if the letters were from an old lover? Then did she really have the right to read them? Did she want to? What if it were even worse? What if they were his letters to an old lover that she'd returned, out of her generosity, because he was getting married to an English girl?

Would she be able to read his passionate yearnings for another woman—who might have even yielded to them—and still stay the same Julia? It might change her; she might never see Joshua in the same light again. And all because she'd read a few pages she should well have left alone.

That is where strength arose. Nobody was perfect. Like her, and everyone else, her husband was frail and human and searching. If before he'd found her, he'd been led into the arms of another woman for comfort, wouldn't it be better just not to know?

Some other woman like Devika Rani?

She slit open the envelope. She held in her hand handwritten sheets of paper. Two identical sets of four pages each on foolscap-sized paper. Written in real ink on fine, lined bond paper. They weren't identical.

One set had been written in a handwriting she recognised easily—a doctor's hurried scrawl, modified by deliberate attempts to write legibly, out of a concern for other people's reading problems, by going back over the lines to straighten out the curve in an 'I' or the twist in an 'r', the lines disintegrating towards the end of the sentence, as space ran short.

The other handwriting was much more measured in its strokes; the writing of a man who valued his writing, because he treated it as an accomplishment—his ability to read and write. Neatly written, well-spaced, so that others might find the same joy in reading his work as he'd found in writing it. Straight lines, every letter of the alphabet, every word, every sentence, easy on the eye.

Yet, they were identical because they both conveyed exactly the same message in identical words and sentences. It was as if the two authors had sat together and framed their thoughts, and then, when they'd argued about it and the wording was perfect—or at least satisfactory to the both of them—they'd dipped into a common pot of black ink and set the words down on paper. Each sentence at a time. Identical in every respect, even to the punctuation.

She did not need to read into the document—there was no time here, where Joshua's mother could come in any minute; it was after all her flat—to know what it was she was holding.

She held in her hand THE THAR ARTICLES.

Both copies of them.

Julia got up hurriedly from the rocking chair and made for the door. Her mother-in-law in the kitchen called out if she'd like a cup of tea, and Julia, while acknowledging the inquiry, saying she'd be down in a minute for it, bounded up the stairs, two at time, to her flat upstairs—almost as fast as she'd run down the stairs on finding dead Major Patel.

There was no doubt. She had both copies of THE THAR ARTICLES. So Joshua was Raja! She flipped to the last page, as if unwilling to accept it, but the two signatures at the end of the document mocked her.

Colonel Joshua Samuelson for India

Colonel Rashid Khan for Pakistan.

The date was October 23, of the previous year.

The doorbell rang. Julia stashed the documents away in her handbag.

It was the old Mother with a tray of tea and savory snacks. Julia helped her in.

"Oh, Mother! You shouldn't have. I would have been down in a minute."

"No problem, Julia. I thought I'd have tea with you up here in your flat for a change. My! But you've put up some nice curtains. Were they expensive?" She went over to the window to feel the fabric, turning the edges over to see the print on the other side.

"Yes," Julia admitted, "but they were on sale. Would you like me to buy you some, Mother, for your flat downstairs? As a gift from Joshua and me for all the care and trouble you've taken over us these past few days? We'd love to! May we, please?"

Joshua's mother blushed with the praise being heaped on her. She hadn't been thrilled when she'd been given the news by her eldest son that he was planning to bring home a foreign bride. Could he not have found a suitable Indian-Jewish girl in their Bene Israel community? Was there a shortage of well-bred girls in Bombay that he'd felt the need to go prancing off to England for a wife? And how would she fit in with their way of living? The granddaughter of an English Earl no less! Did he think she was going to live happily in three poky rooms after having lived on an estate all her life? In a house—Joshua himself had told her, and so couldn't deny it—that had forty rooms, half of which had been shut up because there wasn't anyone to live in them. He was a fool! But then Joshua had always been that way. Even the times they'd lived in South Africa—in Durban—all he'd had eyes for were the white girls who were out of his reach. Why couldn't he have been happy living with his own people?

That is, until she'd actually met Julia. Then she hadn't been able to do enough for her daughter-in-law-to-be, and the love had been mutual. So now she went around to her relatives humbly confessing that Joshua had more sense than she had—and she wasn't ashamed to admit it.

Julia washed the tea dishes. She had to insist on it.

She had learnt a great deal about Indian attitudes just watching the old Mother. Sometimes, she'd found, you just had to insist, or you'd never have your own way. Even in little things, the firmness had to be unequivocally stated, or you ran the risk of being swept aside like driftwood on a beach.

Like who would do the dishes!

Julia waited until she heard the old Mother close the door to the flat below, before she retrieved THE THAR ARTICLES. Now there was more time to study them carefully. To read them line by line and then over and over again. She had to admire the minds that had put the scheme together. Because that is what they did—unfold their plans to transport American arms through India to Pakistan and the mujahidin. Handwritten on paper in a disused Fort in the Thar Desert.

No wonder Joshua had known about DOP! It was his brainchild. Oh, he could pretend all he wanted that she'd discovered what DOP meant, when all the time he was laughing at her? He had set it up with three trusted agents. Major Patel had been one of them handling the Bombay end of it. Arranging for the shipments to be unloaded and sent on their way to Marwar Junction. There he had an agent named Mansingh to route the flatbeds to Amritsar. Why was the name Mansingh familiar? Wasn't he the IMI agent whose unidentifiable body was found burnt to a cinder at the bottom of a ravine on the Bombay-Poona Road? And at the far end of the line was an agent named Abdul, a Muslim. Wasn't he the one who had disappeared with not even a body to show for it?

Rashid Khan had set up an identical company in Pakistan, called INAK Import and Export Co., that had a government license to import non-strategic agricultural machinery, textiles and other goods from India. The Karachi end was to be managed by Rashid Khan himself, with an agent for the company, named Moussa, stationed in Lahore to receive the goods and an agent, named Ali, in Peshawar to supervise the distribution into Afghanistan. Single names were all that were used. There was a written explanation of why Raja was permitted three agents and Bahadur only two. The route through India was considerably longer than the one through Pakistan—1200 miles through India; only 200 miles through Pakistan.

There was another reason why Joshua had been permitted by THE THAR ARTICLES to have an extra agent in the field. He was engaged to be married—the name of the girl was not mentioned—and so he was unable to look after the Bombay office of DOP, as Rashid Khan could do for INAK in Karachi.

The documents were specific on other matters too. Either Bahadur or Raja could call the other for an emergency meeting, at the disused Fort in the Thar Desert, if necessary. Their very first meeting had been on October 23 of the previous year. Only one emergency meeting had been called by Bahadur on July 23—nine months later—but the reason had not been given. Both documents had the date on it, but neither was initialed by either of them.

It was the last time they had met. There would be no further meetings because Bahadur was dead.

The manner in which Bahadur and Raja would communicate with each other was also specified in the document. The code to be used was simple, devious, and explicit. Finally, the Prime Minister and the General would meet on October 25, where each would produce his copy of THE THAR ARTICLES, to decide on retention for the next year—or immediate burning! Each had veto powers; if they could not agree, the documents would be burnt.

She had both copies of THE THAR ARTICLES.

Dear God, what should I think? What must I feel? Should I admire the brilliance of the two minds that had set up the scheme? It had worked for nine months, with pristine arms getting through, untouched, to the mujahidin in Afghanistan.

Or should I feel revulsion at the treachery with which it had ended? When Raja had turned upon Bahadur while he was kneeling at prayer, and put a hole in the back of his head. What was it? Treachery to a friend? Loyalty to a leader? Patriotism to the nation? How should I look on it, when they are the same? Depending on the point of view. One side would call it murder; the other would pin medals on its hero.

Medals for a murderer. For her husband.

Julia dressed rapidly. Packing her bags with lightning speed, not because she was rushed for time—the plane was not due to leave Santa Cruz Airport for another three hours—but because she wanted to get out of the house as quickly as possible.

Why could he not have told her? That would have made it so much more bearable, his eyes pleading for understanding of his actions. Done for a noble cause? Done when ordered to do so by his Commander-in-Chief—and he was a soldier! What excuse would he have given her? Could she not understand?

Were there any compelling reasons at all, ever, under which a man might be permitted to execute a friend?

Never! Her mind cried out the answer to her question even before she asked it.

Did Indians think differently? Did agents think differently? Did soldiers think differently? Her father had been in the British Army. Had he killed enemy soldiers in his short life? Her grandfather was a Director of MI-6. He'd admitted to having given the order for a mission that could have ended in death? Does that too cause revulsion in you?

What had Joshua said?

'He would always confide in her except to protect her!'

Good excuse, Joshua! Nice try. She didn't want his protection, thank you! Not that sort anyway.

Didn't they have some statement in THE THAR ARTICLES to protect each other? She searched through the document while putting on her high-heel shoes. She'd brought a pair for use when she wasn't with Joshua—and this was certainly that occasion.

'Raja and Bahadur will make every effort to each protect the identity of the other'.

That was what was wrong with legal documents. Only the legality mattered; not the common values common people applied to the same words. Such as: 'You cannot execute me while you are protecting my identity'!

She sat on the bed unsure of herself, the dress she was about to pack in her suitcase lying across her lap.

Could she have been thinking such thoughts about her husband? Did she know him so little? Wasn't it treachery on her part, as well, to believe he was capable of murder—even under the most grotesque of circumstances; even under compelling reasons of Indian National Security?

He had lain beside her. They had lain together. With each other and on top of each other and entangled with each other, their bodies warm and naked, feeling the flesh that must belong to each other and no one else, thinking she knew mind and body and soul—when all she had known was his love. Isn't that enough, she heard herself scream to herself. What more do you want from marriage? Does he have to strip his soul naked too, so that you can feel the power of possession? Do you want him that way? Must he always think the way you do? And if, in your profession, which is a brutal one, he had felt the need to kill, did he have to ask your permission to do so? Did he not kill in the army? Did your Father not kill in the British Army?

But this was different. Killing men you didn't know was one thing. Was it?

Rashid Khan had sat with Joshua. They must have had food and drink together. Rashid Khan must have had a soft drink—lemonade, perhaps—because he was a religious Muslim. Joshua would most certainly have had hard liquor to fortify himself for the deed that was to come. Drinking in courage for a cowardly act? How had it ended? With them shaking hands, celebrating their careful planning and the success of their mission? Calling the session to a close as Rashid Khan took off his shoes and his turban for prayer, kneeling on the floor of the disused Fort—for his execution.

Stop it, Julia, she told herself sternly. Stop it this very minute, I tell you! These are rabid thoughts—of a rabid mind. Thoughts like these had led to all that bloodshed and slaughter on that sub-continent in 1947. A rumor, word of mouth, sketchy evidence, a private vengeance, inflamed into religious hatred and the murderous slaughter of innocents. Escalating to even more rabid revenge, until there was no escape from the bloodbath that had ensued.

It had all started with thoughts just as these. She had to get out of the house, quickly.

The old Mother did not understand the tight embrace Julia gave her, or the shaking girl in her arms. She put it down to a longing and a crying need that Julia must feel for Joshua.

"There, there, child. He'll be back soon. Trust Joshua to keep his word. He always keeps his word. If he said ten days, that's all he'll need to finish up whatever he has to do in Marwar—and he'll be back to you. Though why a man on his honeymoon would want to go to Marwar all alone—leaving his wife of four weeks behind—I'll never understand? No consideration; men have no sense at all!"

And the old lady fumed in her disgust at such behaviour—even from her son.

Julia was grateful to see Mr Singh parked as usual across the street. She would welcome his company for the ride to the airport. It wasn't healthy to be left alone, with her thoughts. They had acquired a mind of their own and they could overpower her. She had never thought of herself as being unable to control them, but then, as she reflected back, she'd never been in such a state before. Danger, yes. Several times. Even when she'd faced Slagter, the South

African agent, there had been no panic because there had been no sense of fear. So what was she afraid of now? It could not be Joshua. She could never be afraid of him. She was afraid of the truth—that's what it was. And the consequences of it.

She could never live again with Joshua, if it were the truth. That is what was tearing her up. Her life with Joshua was at an end. It was over.

She closed her eyes for part of the journey. It didn't help with the thoughts, but it did help with the tears. The old Mother had said Joshua would be back within ten days. Julia had heard her clearly; the old Mother had not heard Julia's unspoken reply: "But Mother, will I be back within ten days?"

That too was cowardice. Running away from Joshua without an explanation of some sort? She owed that much to Joshua, even if it were all true.

She sat upright in the taxi and opened her eyes.

Would that account for Joshua's resentment at her for the accusations against Raja in the café the evening before? His consistent refusal to accept the evidence that Raja had murdered Rashid Khan. Who would know better than he? Had he been trying to tell her something? That he had not killed Rashid Khan despite the evidence against Raja? No matter what the evidence was, Joshua had denied it! That is why he had drawn the parallel with her finding Major Patel dead in his Marine Drive flat—and her possession of the ROUTING file. So she could see how it had happened. That would also account for his securing temporary possession of Rashid Khan's copy of THE THAR ARTICLES—would it not?

Because Rashid Khan was already dead when Joshua had reached the Fort!

Knowing she had not killed Major Patel, but being accused of it by him, had riled her up into such a state, she'd threatened to leave him and take the next redeye flight back to London. How deep must his own anger be at having her, his wife, repeatedly call Raja a killer? He had shown remarkable self-control—much more than she had.

What were his words, the evening previous, as they drove home from the elegant restaurant in which she had put the ROUTING file in his hands?

"What say we make a pact tonight? No matter how damaging the evidence might seem to be against either of us, the other will still believe it can't be true! Yes?"

She had broken their pact.

"Forgive me, Joshua, forgive me." She whispered under her breath, not just thinking it but saying it softly because she wanted the words actually spoken.

She took out her vanity mirror and opened the little powder box underneath it, powdering her nose and cheeks. Mr Singh looked at her in the rear view mirror, and she gave him a tremulous smile.

He'd never understand women, he decided. Not if he lived to be a hundred! One moment they looked to be on the verge of tears—when they hailed you and got in—and the next minute they were smiling, and were cheerfully powdering their noses, applying lipstick to their lips, and even giving their hair a few strokes of the brush that came out of their cavernous handbag. He was glad he hadn't married. He didn't think he could take all these changes of mood without ending up a lunatic! Or at least with some sort of palsy. Give him his old lady any day. At least if she was going to breakdown she gave some warning signals—like a whining noise, or a rattle somewhere, or a red light on the dashboard. Did women do that? No, Sir! They just led you on a merry-go-round, being miserable one minute and completely recovered the next.

And that is when Julia went into a panic for the second time that day. After she had looked at herself in the mirror and satisfied herself she looked presentable, before putting it away.

If she knew who Raja was and had believed he'd killed Bahadur for THE THAR ARTICLES, other agents—PMI or KGB—might also know who he was and would also be looking for him. To extract revenge! For Bahadur's death, and for the return of their copy of THE THAR ARTICLES. And if Major Patel, who had been one of Raja's agents before he sold himself and was killed, had squealed that Raja was Joshua, others almost certainly knew who he was, if not where he was.

It wouldn't be long before they got to him. She had to find out who killed Rashid Khan—and quickly! Joshua wasn't too concerned about that part of the problem and had downplayed any danger to himself. He would be more concerned with finding out why his and Bahadur's plans, so meticulously detailed in THE THAR ARTICLES, had gone awry? And who was responsible for it? And where were the missing shipments?

She didn't care one bit for all of that now. Now she had only one question she wanted answered.

Who killed Rashid Khan? Not even why? That question would eventually answer itself. But who? She had to reach the killer before they reached Joshua. Suddenly there was purpose in her visit to Karachi. No longer was it just a way of keeping her occupied while he poked around in Marwar, or a courtesy visit to Edward and the Begum, and to see a little of that beautiful country. Now there was haste and urgency to the visit—while Joshua had his back turned to his assassins.

"Won't she go any faster, Mr Singh?" she pleaded.

"What is the rush, dear Lady? Your flight does not leave for another two hours, and we are nearly there."

"And if I know all airlines, it'll be another two hours late taking off—no reasons given! To where is this flight bound, if I might be so bold as to ask?"

"Karachi."

"Ah! Never been there. It's a big city. Take care, dear Lady."

"I will. You've never been to Pakistan?"

"No, but I lived there as a child in a small village the other side of Lahore. Until the bloodbath came. An uncle and I were the only two to make it alive to Amritsar."

"I'm sorry," Julia said. "I should not have invoked such memories."

"On the contrary, dear Lady. All that happened a long time ago. We committed atrocities, I would be ashamed to recount—so did they. One has to forgive, or we are less than human. I have forgiven. It took time—almost twenty years—for me to see that history inflicted such horrors on Hindus, Muslims and Sikhs. But it is left to people, simple people, to undo the wrongs that history inflicts on them. Will you be coming back? To Bombay, I mean."

"I hope so," Julia said. "I certainly hope so."

"You're not sure?"

"Yes! I'm sure. I will be returning to this city. I'm learning to love it. All the filth and the dirt and the noise and the squalor and the misery and the heat and the traffic and the crowds—I am beginning to feel at home in it. Tell me, Mr Singh, is there something wrong with me?"

Mr Singh laughed at her description of Bombay. Because she had described it so aptly. That is what the tourist saw on his way from the airport to the first-class hotels in South Bombay. But then, they weren't in love. That is what made all the difference.

Without it, even the most beautiful city in the world would have been desolate.

He helped her with her bags to the main entrance to the airport building. He could go no further into the lobby. In the past, the crowds of relatives and friends, who had come to see a single passenger off, had so inundated the terminal building, that regulations had been enforced that barred everyone—except the passenger—from entering it.

She paid him, offering him, for the third time, a handsome tip, which was graciously declined.

He lingered, as if loath to leave her. Perhaps he expected her to fold her hands in a gesture of farewell—a namaste?

She folded her hands to him; he did likewise, but would not move. Almost as if he was bent on seeing the back of her disappear into the terminal building, all the way to the check-in counters.

He came two steps towards her, dropping his voice. She held her ground. He was not uncomfortably close—perhaps a foot away—

but closer than would have been appropriate for a taxi driver and a beautiful woman customer. Particularly a woman travelling alone.

"Perhaps, I will see you on your return to Bombay?" he said softly. "Perhaps, my Lady, I can give you a ride back from the airport, when you come?"

"I would appreciate that, Mr Singh. There isn't a taxi in Bombay I'd rather travel in than your wife. But I do not know when I'll be coming back—the day, I mean. Or the flight. And when I do know, there is no way I can inform you so that you can be here to await my arrival. But the thought is appreciated."

She smiled and reached for her suitcase; her handbag was across her shoulder.

"That is a minor matter, Lady Julia," Mr Singh said, dropping his voice almost to a whisper. "When your travel plans are finalised, please ask Viscount Edward to convey the message to me in the usual way. He knows how—and I'll be here to receive you."

And without delay, he looked her in the eyes, giving her a warm smile and a wave of his hand, as he turned away, mingling with the crowd of incoming passengers and their guests, saying tearful goodbyes, around the main entrance to the terminal building.

CHAPTER 9

Joshua flew into Jodhpur, and while the red-sandstone buildings and the old palace would have been attractive to visit with Julia, it would have to be at some other time. He hired a taxi for the run to Marwar about a hundred miles away. But first he had a slight detour to make to Luni, some thirty miles from Jodhpur.

To the railway station.

It was almost deserted at that time in the afternoon. No trains were due for another hour, and even the porters, in their red uniforms, were sheltering from the heat by lying on the platforms under the shade of the overhanging roof. No ticket collectors, no station master, no passengers either; just the silence of the afternoon sun that hit the tracks and glinted in his eyes.

Three platforms. One for the UP trains, one for the DOWN trains, but it was the third platform, set a little distance away that interested him. Luni was a minor railway junction, and the third platform was for freight trains serving the line that ran from Marwar to Jaisalmer, in the Thar Desert.

On the flat ground round him, he could see for miles in every direction, and there were only three closed wagons—not sixty-seven flatbeds. His shipments were not at Luni.

Not much he could do until he'd had a little chat with Mansingh in Marwar.

Mansingh was the second of the three agents permitted to him. Stationed at Marwar Junction to monitor the progress of the arms on their way to Amritsar. Except they hadn't been reaching Amritsar. And for two months there had been no word from Mansingh, advising him that something had gone wrong. He, Colonel Joshua Samuelson, had to find that out from others—Max and Devika Rani! From the CIA. The anger within him threatened to boil over, but he calmed himself. No point in getting agitated here; there would be plenty of time for that in Marwar.

The man had been one of his most reliable soldiers. Just a Havaldar. Poor, underpaid, brave beyond belief, and a soldier through and through. His ancestors had fought for Rajput kings, where dishonour was more shameful than death. But the generations had changed too; no longer was death an acceptable alternative to the one facing it. Dishonour could be lived down—by staying alive.

He'd find out. Mansingh had better come up with some better explanation than Major Patel had. His only explanation had been greed. But then Patel hadn't been in battle with him, where his courage might be tested; Mansingh had.

It had been easy to arrange for Mansingh's quick disappearance by borrowing an old military truck from Poona, and a cadaver from the streets. Some nameless, faceless beggar who had been found dead in the street at night, and who faced being cut up by first-year medical students at the local medical college. A cremation at the bottom of a gorge on the Bombay-Poona Road seemed, to Joshua, at least an acceptable alternative. He was serving his nation.

Mansingh had been happy to be stationed in Marwar. It was his home town. He had a small mud house, in one of the crowded poorer areas of town, where such mud houses stood only by virtue of leaning against each other. Cheek and jowl—literally. Tiled roofs of local, half round red tiles, floors of cow dung dried hard to form a resilient surface, overlaid in some areas—where a colonel might be welcomed—by stone flagging, for a cool touch to bare feet.

Joshua decided to go late. Better to wait until it was dark. He had dinner in one of the restaurants in the richer areas of the city, away from where Mansingh lived. It would never do to have Mansingh, accidentally, bump into him in the city. The man was resourceful—Joshua had to give him that. He had fought two wars under Joshua's command—and was still alive.

He could easily disappear, if the need arose.

Fine man, Mansingh, at one time, Joshua reminded himself. Tall, built like a Rajput, with a bristling moustache and a full beard, that military regulations made him keep in order. Fiery eyes. Turbaned, as most Rajput soldiers preferred, the trailing edge hanging past the shoulder, so that he could wipe his face in the heat of battle. Very sensible—it kept the sweat from getting into his eyes. Joshua often wondered how he'd look like in a turban—or Julia's reaction to seeing him in one. She'd suggested he shave off the little goatee beard he'd had, when they'd been tracking Slagter in London—and he'd agreed. It made him look years younger, she'd said. She had that way of making it seem as if he'd always wanted to take it off, but had just never got round to it. He smiled when he thought of Julia. She must be getting into Karachi about now. She was safe! Not much trouble she could get into in Pakistan, with Edward and the Begum looking after her. The rounds of parties. Social evenings; playing cards or dancing. Back to being Lady Julia again—granddaughter of the eleventh Earl of Bromfield. The life she was so comfortable in. He wished she'd keep quiet, though, about her marriage to an Indian colonel. That wouldn't go down too well with the military in Karachi. Maybe he'd misjudged them. Maybe the wounds of war had healed after all these years, and they were as willing to forget as he was.

He'd lost quite a few men in the attack on Lahore; they had too, in their probe of Amritsar. Senseless! War between people who at one time had been brothers.

The sun set rapidly over the region. Twilight had started to take over from the setting sun, leaving everything visible but shadowless. Darkness started to take over from the twilight, leaving a single deep shadow over the entire street, punctured in places by the weak lights of the street lamps.

The owner of the restaurant threw an inquiring look or two in his direction. The military-looking gentleman had certainly been generous in the meal he had ordered and the tip he'd left, but did he need any other service? Or was he planning to just sit there, looking out into the street until closing time?

Which is precisely what Joshua did. It was a few minutes before ten-thirty—closing time—that Joshua strode into the street. He knew

Marwar well. He'd passed through it often enough, from Bombay, when the regiment had been stationed in Ajmer, or on his way to the front. He knew that he would see Marwar again. He'd never imagined it would be under these circumstances—at night, and feeling the comfort of his service revolver in the inside pocket of his coat. Being left-handed, it was the right pocket. Despite the weather he had elected to wear a coat. No tie though. A shirt with an open collar.

It was eleven o'clock when Joshua knocked lightly on the door. Old and poor houses such as Mansingh's had no doorbell. It saved waking up the household and, if the doorbell was particularly hearty, the neighbourhood as well. His wife and three children would be asleep; the youngest was only a baby. He hadn't seen them in a long time. Beautiful woman, his wife had been. A village girl, illiterate, schooled only in her duties as a cook and maid. Jet black hair, combed back and usually tied up carelessly in a bun at the back of the head to be out of the way when she worked, the long skirt with the multitude of flares reaching from her navel to the floor, a bodice above the skirt, covering her breasts in front but leaving her back bare, tied to her body by two thin cords, one around her neck, the other around her waist. And when in front of strangers, a long piece of thin muslin she pulled around her head so that men might not look into her eyes.

But he had seen her face. It would have been impossible for a working, servant woman in his household, coming in each day to do his cooking and cleaning, to be perpetually under a muslin shroud. Beautiful large black eyes, with strong eyebrows; a face that disdained make-up of any sort, oval face with a strong chin, and small, delicate ears with dangling real gold earrings that he'd given her on her birthday.

There was no response, no shuffling of feet, no half-smothered grumbling—half-smothered because the visitor at that time of night could well be his mother or someone demanding equal respect.

Like his old Colonel. Joshua knocked again; this time he heard the feet come to the door. He drew out his gun, stepped back into the shadows and said: "Mansingh it is I, Colonel Samuelson. Turn around, and with your back to me take three steps into the room, so that you are in the centre of it. Three steps, no more, you understand?"

The figure, whose outline had been barely visible, obeyed promptly. Always a soldier, Joshua thought as he followed him into the ill-lit room. That was Mansingh. Schooled in military obedience. Never questioning—the perfect soldier! Dependable, trust-worthy, always loyal. But then, that is what he'd thought about Major Patel too. Men could be bought; what had been Mansingh's price?

"Turn around."

Mansingh turned around and saw the gun. He raised his hands; a soldier does not argue with a gun. But his eyebrows came together questioningly.

"I don't understand, Sir," he said. "Is there really a need for you to have come this way—with that in your hand?"

The Rajput in him was offended. Joshua lowered the revolver, put it away in his coat pocket.

They stood opposite each other, not saying anything at first, looking at each other with suspicion and not wanting to believe.

"Is there anyone else in the house?" Joshua asked. "Other than Rupa Devi and the children?"

"No, Sir, and they are asleep. Though it will not be long before my wife wakes up and finds me missing from her side. She will, then, come into this room to find me, because the light is on. What shall I tell her?" Mansingh sat on the ground before Joshua.

"She can wait. First there are a few things you have to tell me! Where are those bloody flatbeds, Mansingh?"

"What flatbeds?"

"Don't play games with me, Mansingh! The DOP crates. Two shipments of them. Where the bloody hell are they?"

"In Barmer, Sir. About two hundred miles from here. In the Thar Desert."

"I know where Barmer is! But what the hell are they doing there?"

"Your orders, Sir."

"My orders? You must be out of your mind. You were stationed here, in Marwar, to make sure those flatbeds were sent on to Abdul in Amritsar. But they aren't reaching him. Why?"

"And with good reason, Sir. Because you ordered them to Barmer. A change of route your message said. The one sent to me—and Abdul too—by Major Patel from Bombay. Abdul was surprised too, but orders are orders! I have Major Patel's explicit instructions here telling me that the route had been changed, and to route the flatbeds to Barmer."

"And you didn't question that? Neither did Abdul?"

"I have never questioned a superior officer's orders," Mansingh said quietly. "Did I ever question yours on the field? Why would I start now?"

Joshua put his head in his hands. There was a lot he could still learn in this business. One never stopped learning, and sometimes the learning could be fatal. Never appoint three men, with one of them a rank above the others. He could go rotten and control the chain without the others even raising questions. They weren't to blame either. He had not been around for them to have voiced their doubts on the change in the route. He'd been having a fine time with Julia in England.

"But didn't it strike you as odd? Routing the flatbeds to Barmer?"

"No, Sir. Not at all. There is an old line that runs from Barmer into Pakistan. To Mirpur Khas in Sind. Abdul and I both talked it over the telephone, and we decided that is what it must be. You wanted the crates shipped to Mirpur Khas, not Lahore."

"But that line is not operational. So if they weren't shipped to Mirpur Khas, where the devil are they?"

"May I ask a question, Sir?"

"You may."

"Why would Major Patel send us these instructions if they were not your orders, Sir?"

"Major Patel is dead. Shot by a single bullet in the back of his head. By his masters who controlled him until he became a liability to them. Money, a lot of money, Mansingh! He was bought with a lot of money."

Mansingh stood up, towering above his commanding officer, without permission to rise.

"And you thought, that I, a Rajput, one of your most trusted and loyal soldiers—twice in war with you on the battlefield—had been bought too?"

"I didn't know what to believe, Mansingh. I'm sorry. I apologise."

"That is not necessary, Sir," Mansingh said, giving the broadest of smiles. "You have restored my faith in you! As a commander of men, you are without equal—if I might be permitted to say so, Sir."

"Mansingh, Mansingh. I have just come into your home, confronting you with a gun, and—what did you say?—I have restored your faith in me?"

Mansingh sat down on the ground again near Joshua's feet. He invited his Colonel to take the only chair in his house.

"Do you remember, Sir, in our last battle, when I, young and impetuous as I was, offered to take out a battery defending Lahore with just two hundred men? I begged you, I pleaded, to let me try—you said no! For me it would have meant a promotion, and yes, more money too. But you said—No! Not until the advance scouts had come in with a report. You were always cautious as far as the safety of your men was concerned—though I didn't appreciate it that day. I sulked; even thought of you as lacking in courage! Do you remember, Sir?"

"Actually, Mansingh, I do."

"The advance scouts you'd sent out to evaluate the enemy came back next morning. And what did they tell you? That the enemy had brought in heavy artillery during the night. We would have been decimated! So instead you sent in the tanks the next day, and we conquered that outpost without a single life being lost. Mine was saved too."

Joshua was silent.

"Because you were cautious then—as you were tonight. You had no means of knowing I had not also gone over to the enemy. I am alive today because you are a careful commander—and not only I, but my wife, thanks you for it. I know she prays for your safety every single night; to her you are like a god who decreed life for me. I know it is late, but she would never forgive me if I let you go back to your hotel in Marwar without a cup of tea. Please, Sir, do I have your permission to awaken her? She will never forgive me, otherwise."

There was no need for Joshua to nod, because Rupa Devi had awakened, and, still sleepy-eyed, she entered the room. The cloth she wore to shield her face from other men was not around her; she did not sleep with it. Her face beamed in surprised delight as she saw her former Master, and she folded her hands in front of her chest in a namaste. He responded likewise.

"And how are you, Rupa Devi?" he said. "How are the children?"

"Very well, Sir. I will not ask Mansingh what brings you here, Sir, except to say how happy I am that you are here! Did I hear Mansingh say something about a cup of tea for you, Sir? You remember the pakoras you loved so much when I served you before my marriage? Well, as it turns out, I fried a batch of onion pakoras—your favourite, I recall—just today. They could not be more fresh! I will be back with them, and the tea. Forgive me for having intruded, Sir."

She left the room. So did Mansingh. He returned a few minutes later carrying a tattered file.

"I did my job, Sir. I would like you to know that. I kept track of every DOP crate that came through Marwar Junction. Most times it was one large DOP crate per flatbed; but then sometimes the crates were small and they fitted two crates on a single flatbed. So while there are only sixty-seven flatbeds, there are seventy-five crates. I have complete information including identification numbers, date of shipment from Bombay, date of arrival at Marwar Junction, and trans-shipment to Barmer. The hours and hours I've spent at Marwar Junction with railway officials hunting through the marshalling yards for DOP flatbeds. I have them all. Not one missing. I've made sure of that. All awaiting release to DOP—on payment of demurrage charges, of course."

"Demurrage charges?"

"Well, Sir, they've been sitting for varying lengths of time in the marshalling yards at Barmer. Some for a month; others for two. Shunted into an unused siding that links up with the unused line to Mirpur Khas in Sind."

Joshua breathed a sigh of relief. His face seemed to shed the tensions that had been overcrowding it these last three days.

He had located the missing arms! He knew what had gone wrong, and it could be set right. He had completed his part of the mission. Joshua patted the check book in his upper pocket. The side that did not hold the gun.

"No problem, Mansingh. I have the DOP check book with me and I'm authorised to use it. Tomorrow we release those flatbeds."

"And ship them off to Mirpur Khas, Sir, across the border? Shortest possible way into Pakistan, and we'll be rid of the bloody arms—if you'll forgive me saying so, Sir."

Joshua dissented. It was a tempting enough idea. Get the crates across the border; then let the Pakistani authorities worry about the large shipment of sophisticated arms on their hands and about their delivery to the mujahidin. But that was not his way. That is how it had started in the first place. Sabotage in the lower reaches of Pakistan. That is why he and Rashid Khan had been entrusted with the job of setting up a safe and secure route for the arms. By no less than the leaders of three countries. It would be an admission of defeat—even failure—if he were to have the arms enter Pakistan in Sind, instead of the Punjab. Besides, he didn't have the export permits for the flatbeds at this end of the line, and neither did the Pakistani authorities have the import permits in Mirpur Khas. Abdul, up in Amritsar, had the paperwork to ship them as manufactured textiles and non-strategic materials into Lahore.

"We have to bring them back to Marwar," Joshua said, "and activate the old arrangement to move them to Amritsar, where Abdul will see them across into Lahore. It is the only way we can keep the route open as before, without questions being asked."

Rupa Devi entered the room with a tray. On it were two cups of tea and a plate of onion pakoras. In addition there was a plate that had sweet padas on it. A guest—particularly her old Master and her husband's Colonel—could not be allowed to leave their home without having eaten something sweet in it. The cloth was drawn low over her face in front of their guest—as was their custom. She seated herself on the floor beside her husband.

"You have been a long time visiting us, Colonel Saheb," she said. It was almost a gentle reprimand.

"I know, I know. But Mansingh must have told you I was recently married—only four weeks ago—and, as you know, so soon after marriage, time seems to desert you! When was the last time, I met you?"

"When I was not married, Sir, and worked as a servant woman—cooking and cleaning for you—in your military bungalow at Ajmer."

He remembered too. Then she was not married and did not cover her face. Their eyes had met, sometimes laughingly, over the antics of a local donkey that insisted on straying into the open yard of the Colonel's bungalow, and braying, until Mansingh drove the animal away. The eyes had flashed then, with the strength of the full woman in her, almost flaunting, behind the impenetrable wall that kept them both secure. Between a master and his servant. All emotions under strict control. The same that must exist—he reminded himself—between James and Julia.

She had been very safe then; as safe as she was now. She had not, however, been safe from the attentions of his Havaldar, who, Joshua found, was visiting his Colonel more often than was strictly necessary. Until one day, his Havaldar had blurted out his desire to be wed to Rupa Devi. She was an orphan and under his care, and so Joshua had taken his proposal to her, and arranged the match. Quietly underwriting all of the marriage expenses between a poor Havaldar in the Indian Army and an even poorer servant woman.

He congratulated himself, when it was over, that they'd never discovered who their benefactor was—and though Mansingh and Rupa Devi often talked about it in bed—they never gave him any indication that they knew.

She collected the tray from the table beside him, and left the room. It was the last he saw of her that night.

The railway clerk in Barmer, half hidden behind the stacks of files that littered his table in full bureaucratic glory, looked over his reading glasses at Joshua and Mansingh, in front of him and protested:

"But, dear Sir, they were released yesterday! I can hardly release them twice. What will my superior officer say if I take your check too?"

Joshua who had been sitting comfortably in the wooden chair, noticed how hard it was and sat up; Mansingh, beside him, who had been standing, stiffened.

"You released them?"

"Yes."

"Who to?"

"Why to DOP, of course. They had identification letter-heads, a DOP checkbook—like you have here, Sir. So I released the flatbeds to them. Let me see I have a huge file on DOP shipments. Earlier in the year they were routed to Amritsar; the last two shipments were to Barmer."

He dug through the stacks of files until he found the one he was looking for. It was thick; almost an inch thick, because of all the delay in the release of the shipments from the marshalling yards and the constant reminders to DOP head office in Bombay to pay demurrage charges and arrange for the release of the flatbeds.

"I remember those shipments from Bombay and Marwar Junction very well. Agricultural machinery in the middle of the Thar Desert, Sir, I ask you? And then no one to accept them. Gave me a severe headache each time the shipments came. No space to put them. Our yards in Barmer are not large. Where could we keep them? So we finally opened up a stretch of old, unused line leading to Mirpur Khas into Pakistan. Just to park them there, Sir," he said hastily, so as not to confuse the military gentleman and the stalwart soldier standing beside him.

"Did DOP release them through an agent who came here personally or was it through the mail?"

"Personally, Sir. Sat across me, just as you are sitting now. I could never forget him, Short man. Rotund, bald, sweating profusely, using his large handkerchief to continuously wipe his face and eyes. Stocky; barely fitting into that chair. And wearing a suit with a tie, in this weather—I ask you?"

"Did you find out where the DOP offices are? In Marwar? In Barmer? Where!"

The railway clerk registered a pained expression. What did these military types think about civilians, such as him? Inefficient? Operating without regard to the rules of the railway?

"Of course, Sir. How could I have released the flatbeds without having their office address? In case the check bounced, I would be in serious trouble, if I could not locate them? Let me see; I have it here."

Joshua noted it down. A house on the outskirts of Barmer, in the rich residential area that skirted the desert. He showed it to Mansingh leaning over his shoulder. Their eyes met; Mansingh nodded. He knew where it was.

The old man thought about it for a moment.

"Strange you should ask for their office address. There was another gentleman in here yesterday asking for that same piece of information."

"Another gentleman?"

An elderly, very refined gentleman. Looked to me like a military man too—like you, Sir—and I'm a good judge of people. No moustache, largish ears and nose. Kindly eyes behind coral-frame glasses, shock of silver hair, thinning at the top. Was the very model of courtesy; a real pleasure to deal with, Sir—as you are too!"

"Where are the flatbeds now?"Joshua asked.

"They are being tagged. On the line, I mentioned to Mirpur Khas. They are about a mile from here. Come to the window, good Sir, There you can see the tops of the crates from where we are standing."

"Where are they being tagged for?"

The clerk looked at his files.

"Strange," he said, "most odd. But they are being tagged, not for Mirpur Khas, but a little town this side of the border. Why would anyone be sending heavy agricultural machinery there, unless the powers that be in the government have some sort of plan to develop the Thar Desert? Maybe, I should buy some land there? Its value is bound to escalate."

"I wouldn't advise it," Joshua said dourly. "This side of the border? You're sure?"

"Absolutely! And that is their final destination. Because a few miles further and they will be in Sind in Pakistan."

"And they have already been tagged?"

"I think the linesman must have finished by now. It doesn't take long. Wire tags. Sixty-seven flatbeds. A few minutes each—and then onto the next. It's easy enough if all the flatbeds are coupled together and in one place—as these DOP flatbeds now are. Quite different when the foreign gentleman wanted it released yesterday. Immediately, he said! But, good Sir, they have to be coupled into a train—and that takes time, I said. But I scheduled a pair of powerful diesels for the job. One wouldn't have been enough, but by working both ends, we had them coupled yesterday, for the lineman to tag them today, and for them to be on their way tomorrow!"

"What did you say?" Joshua asked.

"They will be on their way tomorrow."

"No! No! About the man being a foreigner?"

"Why, yes. Didn't I mention it? A white sahib, we might have said in the early days. Not now. We aren't given to such servitude. But yes. He came from England or America? He didn't say and I didn't ask. None of my business where he came from. All men—

Indians or foreigners—are to be given the same treatment; those are the instructions of the government. So I helped him as best I could. Said he owned DOP when I showed some hesitation. No, not quite. He said DOP was some sort of a subsidiary of his government."

"One last question," Joshua said, feigning pure ignorance. "How do the diesel engine drivers know where they have to take the train? Do they check with you?"

"No, Sir!" the clerk said firmly. "I would go crazy if every engine driver was to ask where a particular coupled set of wagons was headed. That's what tags are for! Every diesel has two men—a driver and a guard. So the two guards, of the front and rear diesels, check the tags on each wagon or flatbed. One goes down one side of the train; the other goes down the other. They meet and compare notes. If there is no discrepancy in the tagging—all tags are for the same place, or on the same route, and the same on every wagon or flatbed—they inform the Station Master they are ready to leave. The Station Master then informs the signal man, by telephone, and the train is on its way. The Station Master then also informs the next stop on the line to expect the freight train—and it is finally, finally out of my hands and out of my hair!"

He would have talked on for some more. He'd just seen the tea-boy serving tea three tables down, and he was about to offer the military man, and his man, a cup of hot tea, but Joshua thanked him profusely, graciously declined the offer, and hurriedly backed out of the room. Once outside the railway office building, and inside the marshalling yard, Joshua dug into the inside pocket of his coat and came up with two broad felt-tip marker pens. Kantilal had shown him how it was done—the tagging of the flatbeds.

"You know where they are," he said softly. "Change the destination on all of the tags. Cross it out with broad strokes that obliterate it. Make sure it cannot be read! Then on the next line up, put DELHI and for final destination, put AMRITSAR. Check whether it is front and back, or only one side. Both sides of the train! The coupled flatbeds are, at best, half a mile long. How good a shape are you in?"

Mansingh smiled, showing his anticipation of the work ahead.

"I'm a soldier, Sir. I'm always in shape."

"Good! Then start at one end. When you have tagged a wagon, run—don't walk—to the next. And so on to the end; then cross the tracks and do the same for the other side. Remember, you run! That's an order, Mansingh."

"Sir, yes Sir!"

"When you have finished, and it will take you at least two hours, meet me at the address given by our friend—the bald-headed foreigner—to the railway clerk. I know who he is, but it will be quite a surprise to him when he sees us. Oh, and Mansingh, don't forget to come armed. I'm going back to the hotel for a while, but I'll meet you at that address in, say, three hours?"

The house was a brick and concrete bungalow in one of the richer suburbs of the town, with marble tile floors and barred windows, with shutters. One story high, with a terrace for sleeping out under the stars on hot, sultry nights. The house was designed to keep the house cool in the desert summer heat. The barred windows kept burglars out; the shutters, if opened, let in the cool night air. Three bedrooms, each with an attached bathroom, a large living room, separate dining and kitchen areas; even a small room attached to the kitchen where a live-in servant—cook or maid—could unroll a mattress and sleep at night.

Joshua had spent the three hours—while waiting for Mansingh to retag the flatbeds—usefully. He had perused town records, and chatted with the town clerk—an elderly widow, without children, who had taken a motherly interest in him, and who willingly divulged any information he needed for his inquiries.

That house in the rich part of town? It had been unoccupied for a long time. But the taxes were paid up-to-date, and the owners came and stayed during the winter months to escape the freezing temperatures up north. The owners? A general in the army—who lived abroad, she didn't know where—and his only daughter.

The house was in darkness. Except for two rooms at the back. One he surmised was a bedroom; the other could be the attached bathroom, because the only window to that room was of opaque glass and was barred and shuttered. The shutters were closed.

He went silently round the side of the house to the bedroom. The shutters were open. Joshua peeped in. It was an elegant bedroom; a woman's bedroom with a dressing table and mirror directly opposite the very small window, a matching dresser alongside it, and a large bed with a matching carved headboard against one wall. Someone was sleeping in the bed, covered by the bedclothes, but, from where he was standing, he couldn't say whether it was a man or a woman.

Now he had to get in. There were three doors into the house. He dare not try the front door; besides he was sure it would be locked. The back door might be open. He went around the back. It, too, was locked. That left the last door in from the roof terrace. Even though it was only a single story house, it had an accessible flat roof, and so a staircase that went from inside the front lobby to the roof. Normally the door into the roof terrace would also be locked, but if it was used for hanging clothes out to dry, the servant woman might just leave it open for the several trips she might be required to make during the day, leaving the door to be locked only once at night.

He put the safety catch on his revolver, and tested the drain pipe for firmness. It seemed solid enough, anchored as it was to the brick wall, and—unlike Mansingh—he wasn't too heavy.

He scaled the parapet wall of the roof terrace and made for the door to the stairs. It was closed, but unlocked.

He left the revolver in his pocket with the safety catch on; it was a mistake, he bitterly regretted later. He crept down the stairs into lobby, and thence into the living room. It was in darkness, but the light from the master bedroom helped him see; it would never do to bump into a chair or knock over a vase.

It was a man on the bed in the bedroom, and he was dead. Poor Max! He looked so peaceful lying there with his eyes open, facing the wall and with a bullet hole through the back of his head. A brief look under the bedclothes told Joshua all he wanted to know. He knew of some instances in the animal kingdom where the female enticed the male to make love; then devoured it after the act—never had he, in all the years he had been in IMI, ever seen it performed that way between a woman and a man.

"Yes, Joshua," the voice said from behind him. "I gave him a good time before I shot him. Look at his face. Does it show any terror? Or is it the face of a man entirely satisfied and at peace? But it won't be that way with you, Joshua. You will die screaming, begging for mercy—and, yes, I will kill you, for all the pain you have given me. For my suffering! Turn around slowly and keep your hands out of your coat pocket, and move away from the bed. I am an excellent shot; you ought to know, you trained me."

Joshua turned around slowly, and moved away from the bed. His back was to the small window, his arms to his sides. Devika Rani sat on the dressing table stool, directly opposite to him. In her hand was a service revolver—standard issue to IMI agents.

She was fully dressed in a red and gold sari over a red, braless, blouse, with a clasp in front that held tight the two sides over her large breasts. Her toes peeped out from underneath the sari. The toenails had been painted a matching red colour too. She had elegance—he reminded himself she was the daughter of a general—and it showed.

"I loved you, Joshua. What would I not have done for you? Look at me! Am I not every bit as beautiful and desirable as your English woman? Why could you not have married me? Would I have been a disappointment to you in marriage? Tell me, Joshua. Because you have made me what I am. They say a woman becomes a widow when her love dies. If that is true, you will make two widows—not one—when I kill you. And I will kill you. Why don't you say something—or do you want to die in silence?"

"I didn't marry you because I didn't love you. It's as simple as that. And the reason I couldn't love you is because of what you are—look at him!" Joshua waved his hand at the body on the bed. "Why, Max? What did he ever do to hurt you? What is he doing in India anyway? And in Barmer of all places!"

"I had to get him down here to clear the flatbeds. It was easy. I told him the truth. I told him I'd located the arms in Barmer, and for a payment we could release them and ship them off to Mirpur Khas. I told him Major Patel had turned traitor—and so had Raja! It was so easy. So much easier for a foreigner to wangle the release of sixty-seven flatbeds, using the check book I'd stolen from Major Patel. Not so easy for an Indian woman—alas, I'm sorry to say. Max bought it—and he came. I'm sorry I had to kill him, but I did give him a nice time before I did it."

"And did you give Major Patel a nice time too, before you killed him? You did kill him?"

"Oh, yes. We bought him for money. And then, when he found out you were coming down, he turned difficult and threatened to squeal on us. I got there about fifteen minutes before your wife did. He thought I was bringing him more money. One shot through the back of the head and exit Major Patel. He died peacefully. I searched through the filing cabinets but I couldn't find the key to his office desk—which your wife did."

"But you made one little mini-mistake which told me, later, that it had to be you. Who's 'us'?"

"Oh, the KGB in India. You can ask anything you wish, because you aren't going to be able to repeat it to anyone. In about ten minutes, Joshua, you'll be quite dead. As dead as he is, though you won't have quite the pleasure he did, before he died. So ask."

"Does your father, General Rana Singh know?"

"No!"

"Well then, at least he has his honour left intact."

"Don't talk to me about honour, Joshua," she said quietly. "You have made me what I am."

"It is all very well to say: 'you did this to me!' or 'you have made me what I am'. The only daughter of a general—you thought you owned us all, me included. Well, Julia is the only granddaughter of an English Earl, and she doesn't think the way you do. Never has! So now you know why I love her and married her. She is a fine person, of class elegance; you, on the other hand, are a ruthless killer!"

"I don't have to take this from you, Joshua. I think I'll shorten your lifespan to five minutes. Do you want to say your prayers? Do you want to die standing, or are you going to grovel at my feet for mercy? I rather think I'd like to see you grovel. Down on your knees!"

Joshua remained standing. "You're not even a woman of your word. You said ten minutes. You said I could ask you anything I wished. Do you think I could have married a bitch like you?"

She fired a warning shot that sizzled past his left ear. He tried not to flinch and failed. She laughed.

"Not the brave colonel are you? The one your wife thinks she married? Oh, after I kill you, I won't kill her. See you united up there? Never! No let her suffer—as I have. But I will talk to her and tell her you died a coward, on your knees—not a soldier!"

Joshua looked in the dressing table mirror behind her and thought he saw a shadow flit past. Just wishful thinking he decided. Was there someone out there? Where the hell was Mansingh? It was well past the three hours, he'd allowed for retagging of the flatbeds, but no sign of Mansingh. Must keep her talking.

"Why did you have to kill Kantilal?"

"Oh, him? An insignificant little cog, who lost courage and wanted to route the last shipment to Amritsar. He knew who you were, and instead of putting you off the scent, he gave it all away. I must confess, though, that I prefer a gun to a knife. Much more impersonal. I didn't like to be near the little drip when I killed him, but I had no choice. I didn't have a silencer and a gun might have made too much noise. Ah, well, have I answered all your stupid little questions, Colonel Samuelson?"

She dipped the gun. "Down on your knees, Joshua!"

He remained standing. "I knew it was you, because of one little mistake you made that day when Major Patel was killed."

"Oh?"

"All those years of training, Devika, and you failed your mentor when the test came!" Joshua clicked his lips in scorn.

"Mistake? What mistake? No one can pin Major Patel's murder on me. What mistake?"

"Well, maybe not a full blown mistake. Say a mini-mistake, because it told me it had to be you."

"Why do I get the impression, Joshua, that you are being condescending? I can kill you at any moment, like this!"

She fired a second shot across his right ear, and again he flinched. She laughed delightedly. She knew how a cat felt when it played with a mouse—and it pleased her.

How long did a black tip marker take to obliterate one word; then write two other words? He would write them in the language in which the original was written—either in Hindi or English; Mansingh was fluent in both. Then he had to run to the next flatbed. Run, not walk! Those were his orders, and Mansingh always obeyed the orders of a superior officer. Sixty-seven one way and then sixty-seven the other way.

He looked into the dressing table mirror behind Devika. Her body hid most of it, and his body, also reflected in the mirror, hid most of the small window behind him. Just the edges of darkness, but he saw a shadow move. It could be the branch of a tree in the yard, swaying gently with the night breeze off the desert. It was dark now—and almost eight o'clock. He'd left Mansingh at four-thirty in the evening. The coupled flatbeds could not have been more than half a mile long—each way.

"What mistake? Or mini-mistake as you've put it. Are you going to tell me or do I have to send a bullet through your thigh to elicit a response?"

"You saw my wife run out the front entrance, underneath you, while you were standing in the balcony of Major Patel's flat?"

"Yes."

"She was wearing a sun-bonnet; so you could not see her face—so you told me."

"Yes! Yes! So what? Lots of women wear sun-bonnets in our blistering sun."

"True. But the wind was blowing off the Arabian Sea. Blowing rather hard, wasn't it?"

"Perhaps. So what if it was?"

"Julia told me that evening when I took her for dinner and dancing at Berry's. She had her hand on the top of her head, clutching her bonnet, fearful it would fly away. And you were above her."

"So, I saw her hand."

"Why didn't you tell me it was a white hand? The hand of a foreign, white woman? Because you didn't want her to be caught. Allow the police to search for her—her fingerprints were all over the place; you'd wiped yours away—drawing all suspicion away from you. If she had been caught, she would have been able to explain, easily enough, why she was there, and though Major Patel's connections to MI-6 would have been out in the open, it would hardly have been evidence to arrest her for it. Far better she get away, and but for you and a resourceful taxi driver, I would have nabbed her. Then they'd start looking for the real killer—and that was you."

The talk between them had come to an end. She had made sure he knew why he was being killed—for having scorned her. He had asked all the questions—except one. She got up from the stool, standing in front of him, her feet slightly apart, for balance when she fired. The sari slipped off her shoulders.

"How did you kill Rashid Khan?"

For the very first time that evening he seemed to have stopped her. The hand that held the gun tightened on the trigger, but she looked inquiringly at him.

"Rashid Khan?" she repeated as if unable to comprehend who he was. "Oh, you mean 'Bahadur'? Your Pakistani counterpart? You killed him. Every-one knows that. So you see, even if I don't kill you—and I will—PMI will execute you, as soon as they catch up with you. Raja killed him. And you are Raja. Major Patel sold us that piece of information too; I can tell you it wasn't cheap! So you can't pin that one on me, Joshua. That was your doing."

"You're mad," Joshua said without emotion. "I didn't kill Rashid Khan; I had no cause to."

"Oh, I've heard differently," she said. "Quite differently. His copy of THE THAR ARTICLES has gone missing. Do you have it? The truth, Joshua!"

"Yes."

"Well then you killed him for it. Have I proved my point?"

"No. But no matter what I say you will not believe me, so why should I bother?"

"Because I have the gun. If you will go down on your knees, grovel at my feet, like a dog, I will unclasp this blouse in front. It is so tight on my breasts, the sides will fly apart. I've nothing on underneath. You've always wondered about them—now be honest—before you met your English girl? I will kill you with a single bullet to the head. If you do not grovel, I will kill you anyway. Standing. No breasts for you! You will be holding your own gun, with a few bullets in Colonel Roberts, and he will be holding this gun that has executed you. No, don't move away from that window! I don't know who is outside. They can kill me, but I will kill you first!"

Joshua slid to his knees and bent over. She laughed a diabolical laugh and moved her left hand to the clasp in front of her blouse underneath her breasts.

It was not entirely Mansingh fault for the delay in his reaching the bungalow. He had gone straight to the flatbeds, after receiving his orders from his Colonel. But as he reached the first flatbed and had drawn out the felt tip marker, he saw the linesman who had marked the original tags walking up to him. He put away the marker; introduced himself as a security guard for DOP, who was going to keep watch over the DOP shipments until the next morning, when the diesels would move them, where?

Where was it they were to be moved?

"A little town this side of Mirpur Khas," the linesman replied. "Strange, but that's where they want the flatbeds sent, so that's where they will go."

The linesman took out a native cigarette—a bidi—and offered Mansingh one, but it was graciously declined. The linesman then squatted on the grass beside the tracks and invited the stranger to take a seat beside him. It was a boring job, he confessed, with no one to talk to; perhaps Mansingh could give him some company until his shift came to an end, and he clocked out.

That wasn't until five o'clock.

Mansingh sat beside him and they chatted desultorily about the weather in Barmer and the price of good rice, and the rich getting richer and the poor getting poorer.

At five o'clock, the siren in the marshalling yards, a mile away, wailed the end of the shift. The linesman made no move to rise. Mansingh reminded him that his work day had come to an end.

"What do I have to go home to?" the linesman said. "My wife ran away some years ago with another man. I have forgiven her. I have no children. I will listen to the depressing news on the radio, have my dinner, and go to bed—and be here tomorrow morning for the same to be repeated all over again."

Would Mansingh like to come and share his dinner with him, at his humble home?

Mansingh thought fast. That is why they had colonels—like Colonel Samuelson—to do thinking for him. If he had ever bemoaned the inequality in pay and status between him and the officers, that instant he realised what a fool he had been! What would he not give to have Colonel Samuelson get him out of this situation? Mansingh yanked the linesman to his feet. Perhaps, his Colonel's thinking had entered into him?

"I'd be delighted to share your meal with you," Mansingh said, "but, you can see, I am now on duty here. Why don't you go to your house, cook us both a simple meal—a little plain rice and some lentil and one vegetable; vegetables are good for health; no meat, because I am a strict vegetarian—and bring it back here and then we can spend some time together. Maybe play cards? It can get pretty boring for me too, but a job is a job."

It was five-fifteen before he saw the back of the linesman and set about the retagging of the flatbeds. He'd lost forty-five minutes. He raced from flatbed to flatbed, up one side and down the other, breaking every speed record he'd ever aspired to. But it was not until past eight that he'd finally finished.

How long would it take the linesman to cook the meal and reappear?

There was no danger of the retagging being discovered, because it was now pitch dark. Mansingh thanked his God for denying India much of a twilight. There were faint lights in the marshalling yards, about a mile away, but the flatbeds had been moved to an unused line linking to Mirpur Khas, and the entire area was in total darkness.

Then he had to reach the residential area, another mile away. He raced down side streets, using every short cut he'd known in Barmer, praying he would not lose the way. He almost made it.

He was twenty yards from the bungalow, sprinting down the last stretch, when he heard the two shots come from the direction of the house.

CHAPTER 10

Julia was met at Karachi International Airport by the Begum. Edward was up in Islamabad discussing important matters with some of his military counterparts up there, and couldn't be there to receive her. He sent his apologies through the Begum. But the Begum privately confided to Julia, it was just as well. He was always so demanding when he was around—everything had to be just right—it hardly gave her time to herself. It wasn't that way when he'd married her. Then, she'd treated him like her eldest son—and he'd loved it! Julia believed her. She had received exactly the same report from Cecily—Edward's sister and Julia's lifelong friend from their days of boarding school in Kent—after Edward had been married.

Men changed, the Begum wailed, while their wives were expected to be just the same as on the day they were married. Was that fair? She was not loath to tell Julia that it would be the same with her and Joshua, and she'd better beware and prepare for it. Julia laughed; she would welcome some changes in Joshua she confided to the Begum—such as his agreeing to a wider bed? On second thoughts, she'd gotten so used to sleeping in a cuddle with him—to prevent him falling off the bed—maybe she might not get good sleep in a wider bed? Besides, Julia said, smiling deliciously, how could a couple go to bed mad at each other if they had to cuddle up to go to sleep? Could anyone explain to her, Julia, why married couples weren't prohibited—absolutely forbidden!—by their marriage vows to sleep in any bed that was designed for more than one? Julia would have carried on for another good five minutes more on her idea of incorporating the 'bed-designed-for-one' condition in all marriage vows—not just Judeo-Christian ones—but the Begum laughing so hard, her scarf fell off her head and her dupatta off her ample bosom, put her hand across Julia's mouth and promised never to rail against all men—only Edward—if Julia would only stop!

But today she had Julia all to herself and they would go shopping. Where else? Shopping on Zebun Nisa Street. And a visit to the All-Women's Meena Bazaar. A must, Naseem Banu said, as she took Julia by the arm, shooing away the beggar children who crowded round the foreign Madam begging for alms. A coin or two? Street urchins and orphans; Julia would willingly have emptied her purse out for them, but the Begum firmly restrained her.

"Do you want to be mobbed by them?" she asked. "Give one a coin, and they'll hang onto your skirts until they've torn it to shreds! I've had it happen to me—trust me."

Julia freed herself from Naseem Banu. "Stand in line, and hold out one hand," she said in a firmness of voice she did not really feel, but they understood. Twelve of them. She counted them. There were fourteen hands but she gently patted away the two extra hands. Each outstretched hand had a single silver fifty-paisa coin placed in it. Before the urchins could spread the word to other friends that a foreign woman, soft in the head, was giving away half-rupee coins, Naseem Banu swept Julia into the car and drove away.

Edward had rented a bungalow for them for the short time they were to be in Karachi. The Begum's family came from Cholistan near the border, and at one time, all the land in that area had been part of her father's kingdom. Her widowed mother had moved to Rawalpindi after the kingdom had been absorbed, partly into India and partly into Pakistan.

Julia felt miserable, homesick for Joshua and worried about his whereabouts. She had not heard from him, nor did she expect to. The Begum did what she could, but wasn't entirely successful. So she did what she did best—she threw a party in Julia's honour, inviting everyone who was anybody to meet Lady Julia, granddaughter of the eleventh Earl of Bromfield, who was visiting from England.

No mention was made, on the invitations that were sent out, of Colonel or Dr Joshua Samuelson.

Julia wasn't aware of it until the Begum mentioned it casually while they were at Meena Bazaar.

"I've just heard from Edward," she said. "They're coming down for the party—and rightly so! You a guest here, and he's out there gallivanting in Islamabad? He ought to be ashamed of himself. But he's going to make up for it."

"Oh, and how is he going to make up for not being here to receive me?"

"By bringing the General down here, of course. You'll get a chance to meet him, Julia. He's really a very fine man. The old school. Sandhurst, actually. A military man through and through. Sadly, they're the only ones who believe in honour any more. You'll like him."

"I'm sure I will," Julia said.

They were now in the heart of Mena Bazaar. Women—and only women—everywhere. The veils of the burkhas had been lifted, so she saw their faces as they sipped tea in teashops served by women or ate Pakistani sweets made by women. No fear here of men casting eyes of lust, or making sexual advances, or even being aroused by the act of seeing a beautiful face or a full body. Male jealousy had devised Meena Bazaar, and the more orthodox women, grateful for the crumbs of freedom being thrown their way, were loath to protest what had been their real loss of freedom, demanded by their orthodox men and sanctioned by the State.

Julia decided she wasn't going to take it up with the General, however tempting an issue it might be; she had problems of her own.

They stopped outside the front of a shop selling Pakistani savories, the aroma of which had attracted a crowd of women clamouring for the hot pakoras coming out of the deep frying oil.

'Begum Rashid Khan for kababs, pakoras and burkhas', the sign said, above the shop.

Julia looked around to see Naseem Banu disappear into the store next door, selling women's jewellery. She would not be missed.

She entered the shop. The older lady, sitting on a low stool in front of the deep fryer, paid no attention to her. The clamouring crowd, wrapping the pakoras in wax paper, and the money changing hands, kept her busy. Besides, at the rear of the room Julia saw the burkhas for sale, and women were encouraged to touch the cloth and examine the texture before purchase. All sales final!

There was a curtain of coloured beads, in the door at the far end of the room. She passed through. Coming in from the daylight into the darkened room left her temporarily sightless. She put her hand out to steady herself—and felt herself holding on to a woman's soft hand. She instinctively recoiled from the unexpected touch, and the hand let her slide away.

"What is it you want, my child?" an older voice, gently spoken, asked of Julia. "We do not sell savories in this room, nor burkhas. Only in the room outside."

Her eyes were now accustomed to the darkness. There were no windows; just the light streaming in from the beaded curtain behind her, throwing rainbow coloured raylets into the room. A sitting room of some sort, with a desk and a chair. And a sofa, adjacent to the door, in which Julia saw the shadowy figure looking up at her. Another door at the back of the room was closed.

"I wish to speak to Begum Rashid Khan," Julia said, using the word 'wish' instead of 'want'. Much more polite and respectful, in keeping with Pakistani culture, when addressing an older woman.

"And who might you be, child?"

"I am Mrs. Joshua Samuelson. My husband knew your husband—very well, I believe."

She saw the figure rise gracefully from the sofa. She was not wearing a burkha. Begum Rashid Khan beckoned to Julia.

"Come with me," she said, "into the living room at the back. There is much more light in that room. So that we can sit on the sofa and look into each other's eyes when we talk. The bulb in this room has fused."

When they entered the room at the back, Julia saw her for the first time. Rashid Khan's widow. A strong, handsome woman, the wife of a Pathan, built like one, and looking every regal inch of it. Powerful, hooked nose, large doe-like eyes, full cheeks, and as tall as Julia. Not many women could stand up to Julia, but she did. A full length gharara, with frills on her shoulders falling over her large, matronly breasts, and the flared, frilled skirt that reached to her toes. Mature and stunningly beautiful, without any make-up of any sort whatsoever. The long earrings of pure, filigree gold, and studded with pearls, dangled from her ears. No other jewellery on her, except her gold wedding ring that had a single small diamond set at the very centre of it.

She smiled at Julia to put her at her ease; then without asking disappeared into the kitchen beyond, reappearing minutes later with a tray on which were two cups of hot tea and a plate of the pakoras and kababs Julia had seen being cooked outside.

She waved Julia, silently, to them. They were spicy, but delicious, making Julia truly grateful for the very many lunches and dinners she had had in the Indian restaurant on Finchley Road in Hampstead, that had given her an acquired taste for all foods Indian. Even Heaven couldn't help you, or the marriage either, she thought irrelevantly, if you were married to an East Indian man and didn't like Indian food! But the tea did help to wash down the spiciness.

"They say men eat the kababs and the pakoras, not so much for their taste but because it makes the tea taste so good," the older woman said softly.

She must have been at least fifty years old, though she didn't look it. Julia saw her eyes look her over. Speculatively.

"You wanted to talk to me? What about? Why?" The voice was as soft as ever. Julia searched for signs of suppressed anger in it, and found none.

"Your husband, Colonel Rashid Khan."

"He is dead."

"I know. Who do you think killed him, Begum Khan?"

"Call me Rehana," the older lady said. "If we are to discuss such intimate matters, we might as well know each other better."

"And I am Julia. Do you know who killed him?"

"I know what they tell me."

"And what do they tell you?"

"It was Raja. Do you know who Raja is?"

"Yes. Do you believe Raja killed him?"

"No."

Julia, who had not been expecting that reply, put the cup down with trembling hands on the tray before her. Rehana watched.

"No, Julia. I don't believe your husband killed mine. No matter what they say. I am so very glad you are here, and have come to discuss it with me, so that I can tell you so too. But I have also to tell you that is not what they believe. And they are searching for your husband—like mad men!—to kill him."

"How did you know my husband is Raja?"

"Do you talk to your husband when you are in bed with him?"

"Always."

"And does he tell you things he shouldn't?"

"Sometimes." Julia hesitated before she said: "Have you read THE THAR ARTICLES?"

"Yes. Have you?"

"Yes," Julia said, "I have. But how are you so sure of my husband's innocence?"

Rehana, sitting on the same sofa Julia was sitting on, reached out and held Julia's hand. She stroked it gently; a mother to daughter touch.

"When you get to my age, child, it is easier to rid oneself of such doubts. I am sure Colonel Samuelson didn't murder my husband—not because I know him but because I knew my husband. He was called to Islamabad by the General for this assignment. He was to meet an unknown Indian agent in the Fort on the Indian side of the border to plan and work out the details of the operation, to get the arms through India to the mujahidin. Written, by hand, in THE THAR ARTICLES. Only two copies. The Indian Prime

Minister had insisted on it. It was a very damaging document for India. When he came back from Islamabad he was tense, nervous. About meeting a man he didn't know and could not trust. He slipped a dagger inside his belt. "For safety's sake, never trust a stranger!" he said.'

'Two days later he came back from the meeting and he was a completely changed man. Incredible! He was laughing with mirth at his own fears, it seemed. At first he wouldn't tell me, and I didn't cajole him, but that night, in bed, he couldn't restrain himself. "Guess who is Raja?" he said.'

'Go to bed, Rashid. I have to open the shop early tomorrow. Who is he?"

"The Prime Minister picked the one man he knew I could respect—The Lion of Lahore! He picked Joshua Samuelson."

"Do you know why my husband calls yours 'The Lion of Lahore', or why your husband calls mine 'The Lion of Amritsar'?"

Julia shook her head.

"You do not talk to your husband enough in bed, my child," the older woman said with a laugh, patting the hand she held without releasing it.

"They fought each other in the last war; your husband testing the defenses of Lahore; mine with his eyes set on Amritsar. Both sides threw in virtually everything they had. Both sides claimed victory—naturally. Only there were no victors—only losers. And when a truce was called—to bury the dead—your husband and mine supervised the handing over of bodies to the other side. Can two men ever kill each other after that? Others may believe what they wish, my child, but I know it couldn't be Raja. I could easily have told them who Raja was. Oh, how they asked! Constantly, the same questions, over and over again. Did he say who Raja was? Had he dropped a hint who Raja was? Did I have any thoughts or clues on who Raja might be? But my husband would have wanted me to protect his friend, and I kept his trust. You do not know how much pleasure it gives me to be meeting—and having a cup of tea—with his lovely wife. I have not laughed in almost three months; the sadness will still always be there, but now, maybe, I can live again?" And Rehana raised Julia's hand to her lips and kissed it.

Julia understood. Closure. For Rehana, meeting Julia, the wife of Raja—her husband's 'brother'—had helped to ease the sadness in her heart. All she wanted was to hold Julia's hand, in her fight for Raja's life—and finding her husband's killer! Now there was a meaning and purpose to her own life.

The Begum came through the door. "Ah, there you are, Julia. Do you want to shop? Some lovely jewellery stores here! So you've met Begum Khan."

The two women nodded to each other. Julia guessed they didn't particularly care for each other. Perhaps it was the difference in their stations.

"Rehana," Julia said, "I'd like to buy a burkha. A full length one, with the veil in front and the screen for the eyes. As a keepsake of Pakistan. To take away with me. May I buy it from you? Ask of me whatever price you wish." She rose from the sofa.

The older lady arose too. She held Julia by the arm and led her into the rear of the store where the burkhas were stored and sold. She looked Julia over and then grimaced.

"You will have the same problem I have, child. They're never long enough! Your toes will show—as mine do. But before I show you the best of them, let me confide to you a little secret. Only for dear friends, you understand. Don't let it get out."

Julia assented.

"Whatever I ask for it, you offer me only half. Remember your opening bid must be no more than half! Then we will spend a delightful ten minutes, haggling over the price as I cajole and entreat and, sometimes, even insult you, while you, firm and resolute, inch upwards with your offer, until you wear me out or I wear you out—and the deal is struck. But no more than half again of what you first offered. Yes?"

Julia nodded.

"Now look at this burkha. The finest silk. So light, you will hardly feel its weight on your shoulders. Nor will you feel the heat inside. The material breathes! Important considerations, dear lady, when buying a burkha. Come now, six hundred rupees, shall we say?"

Julia reached into her purse that held the currency she'd changed into Pakistani rupees. She put three hundred rupees on the table and said, in as firm a voice as she could muster: "Three hundred rupees—and that's my final offer! Take it or leave it."

Rehana's eyes flashed in delight at the anticipation of it. The mouth broke into a broad smile that showed white, spotless teeth. A worthy opponent! Not like some of these foreign women who thought it beneath their dignity to haggle with her—a poor shopkeeper.

They had a delightful ten minutes. In that time, Julia heard everything she had to hear about the burkha on the table between them. The magnificence of the cloth, so soft, would she care to touch it? The lightness of it! The fast grey colour that would not run even under a hundred washes. And when Julia refused to budge by more than a few rupees, the long history of the tailor who had made it—poor beyond description, supporting an old, blind and widowed mother, and with six urchin children, all under the age of twelve, constantly begging to be fed—a history designed to bring tears to her eyes and compassion in her heart, that would move her to raise her offer? Did the rich have no heart when they haggled in this unseemly manner over a few rupees for a burkha that was obviously of the finest quality, and made by someone so poor and in desperate need of her compassion and charity?

At which, Julia entering into the spirit of it, said entreatingly that she was only an orphaned granddaughter of a poor Earl, and did the old lady across the counter know what hard times Earls were having in England these days? With the rebellious peasants demanding an ever larger share of the estate revenues and the socialist governments squeezing the rest out with horrendous taxes, they could barely afford a bottle of decent sherry! And did this wealthy burkha shop owner have any idea at all what it cost to keep horses and hounds? Why even the foxes had become uncooperative producing such small litters, there weren't even enough of them to kill! Four hundred and fifty rupees, Julia said, was her very last word! Did the old lady think she'd never shopped for a burkha before? Why, she'd seen better quality garments than the one she was being shown—which was only fit for a camel driver's wife!

At which Rehana, unable to restrain herself any longer, exploded into unseemly laughter quite beaten in the exchange, and reached for the money.

"No more! No more, Julia," she said, "or I shall die laughing. And while that may be a very good way to go—not just yet. A camel driver's wife? Where on earth did you get that one from?"

They spent another pleasant ten minutes trying it out with Julia across the counter as the sales woman and Rehana shopping for it.

Naseem Banu, tired of their exchanges, had disappeared again into the jewellery store next door. Rehana would have wrapped the burkha up in a parcel for Julia to take away, but on the excuse she might want to try it out, Julia led her back into the house.

"What is it, my child?" Rehana asked.

"Please, would you loan me a gun? A pistol or a revolver? Something that will fit in my handbag?"

"Yes, of course. But why? Are you in danger?"

"No. But I need it to bring Colonel Rashid Khan's murderer to justice."

"Ah! Then let me give you—not loan you, but gift you—my husband's service revolver. What purpose for it could be more fitting than that?"

They hugged each other tight, with a love neither could define. Mother and daughter? An older sister and a younger one? The wives of two close brothers?

CHAPTER 11

The party in Julia's honour was held that evening. True to his word, Edward came down from Islamabad for it. He assured Julia the General had promised to be there as well. It was never quite definite, in such matters, because affairs of state could easily intervene—as in England—but the General was already down in Karachi and planned to attend. Edward then left Julia to prepare herself while he closeted himself in a hastily called meeting with some of his associates in Pakistan.

Julia dressed formally. A long, soft-green dress that complimented the white, unblemished skin and the brown in her eyes and hair. It flowed, elegantly, from her shoulders down to her high-heel shoes, the straps spread wide to grip the outside of her shoulders, with scalloping waves of silken fabric across the bodice and past the line of the hip, then plummeting to her toes. She'd been saving that dress for a time when she and Joshua could have been together, but the circumstances now demanded it, and she wore it. The hair was brushed back past the ears, freeing her forehead, framing the beauty in her face, then slipping past the slender neck on to her shoulders; a few of the curls came to rest lightly on her chest.

Edward emerged from his meeting distraught. Julia and Naseem Banu had already left for the hall.

He raced to his car, and, with his Pakistani driver driving at breakneck speed, reached the banquet hall only to find he was too late; the guests had already started to arrive and Julia and Naseem Banu were busy greeting them.

Julia felt perfectly comfortable. This was the life she had grown up to. Important dignitaries often came, from all parts of the world to visit her grandfather at Bromfield House—and she was his one and only hostess. She had greeted friends and strangers, radiating the same charm and warm feeling with which she'd greeted her servants in the lineup when they'd welcomed her back to Bromfield after an absence in London or Oxford. There was one little difference though. In the lineup at Bromfield, everyone curtseyed to her; here most everyone did—including the British High Commissioner to Pakistan and his wife—excepting the General. But he had not yet arrived and so Julia received, graciously, the smiles, handshakes, and curtseys of Pakistani military colonels, ambassadors to Pakistan from friendly foreign countries, their spouses, and the elite of British society in Karachi.

When they were seated, and before dinner was served by the waiters standing in line along one wall of the hall, she went to every single table to inquire if there was anything she could do—as the hostess—to make it a pleasant and happy occasion. The commonest request she got from every one of the unmarried military men was the favour of a dance, and to this she graciously agreed.

Edward fumed in the wings unable to interrupt her in her duties as Lady Julia, but as the food was being served, he rushed in, grabbed her by the arm and thrust her into a little alcove, set apart from the other tables because it was for the General, and security had required the isolation.

"What is the matter, Edward?" she asked, surprised at the rough handling.

"Sit," he said. "We don't have much time because the General will be here any minute—and I don't know how much he knows!"

"Knows, what?"

"I was with my MI-6 Pakistani informants this morning. You know that. Well they have news from Barmer in the Thar Desert. The good news is that Joshua and his man, Mansingh, have located the lost arms shipments and the flatbeds are already on their way to Amritsar."

He stopped, not knowing how to proceed.

"What is the bad news?" she asked quietly.

"The police and the ambulances were called out to a house in Barmer. One body—a man's body—has been recovered. The woman has been wounded and is in hospital; she is in no condition to talk. You might as well have it straight, Julia. She works for the KGB. Apparently she enticed Joshua to the house and after sleeping with him, she killed him."

Julia erupted from her chair.

"That's impossible!" she said. "Joshua would never allow himself to be taken in that way. He has more honour than anyone I have ever known—and that includes you, Edward. He lives by his honour! He would die before he betrayed his country—or me."

"I thought so too. Except that the autopsy report on the dead man—who was naked in bed—showed that sexual activity had occurred. I'm sorry, Julia, but Joshua is dead."

Her husband of three weeks was dead.

That was the news from Barmer. One part of her could not accept it; the other part wept, the tears flowing silently down her cheeks. She blinked rapidly to stem the flow, and failed. She searched in her purse and came up with a lace handkerchief which she pressed to both eyes, but the tears would not be contained. They trickled past her chin, down her neck and then, joining up like a stream, into her blouse. Edward stood by and watched.

"Shall I cancel the evening?" he asked.

She shook her head. "Let me be for a little while, Edward. We'll carry on as if nothing is wrong. Joshua would have wanted it that way too. But make arrangements for me to fly back to Bombay on the earliest flight tomorrow. Joshua's mother is going to need me—and I am going to need her."

Edward left her, signalling to the waiters, she was not to be disturbed.

As she sat and cried, she thought of Joshua. She closed her eyes, using one hand to dab both eyes shut with the handkerchief, but the sobs would not be contained. Her heart wept for the one man she had loved, as no other. The pain she felt was as if half of her had been sliced away, leaving her both in tormented agony and feeling sadly incomplete. The one would heal with time; the other only with death.

She suddenly became aware that her hand on the table was being gently held and stroked. She opened her eyes and found herself looking into the kindly eyes of an elderly East Indian gentleman.

"Sir," she said quietly, "may I know why you are holding my hand and stroking it gently?" She made no attempt to withdraw her hand, and he made no attempt to release it.

He smiled: "Because I thought you were in need of a friendly touch after all the dreadful rumours you've been given about the infidelity of your husband and his death. Both quite untrue, I might add."

She clutched his hand in both of hers. "Untrue?"

"Of course. You were quite right to disbelieve it all. Joshua would never be unfaithful to you—his love for you would not permit it—and he is alive. Though I have to tell you it was touch and go; it could have gone either way. I will live, and relive, the incident as long as I live. The memories will haunt me forever!"

"Please, Sir, please! I do not know who you are, but you have given me new life. For that I will always be in your debt. Sir, will you tell me all you know?"

He nodded, then pointed to the far end of the hall where the General had just entered the room and was being ushered in by Edward towards the alcove.

"I think we should get out of here. Fast. Don't you agree?"

She rose quickly and grabbed him by the arm, afraid to let him go in case he might disappear into thin air—he had appeared out of thin air to breathe new life and hope into her—and she wasn't going to let him go.

"I scouted out the hall before I came in," he said softly. "Through that door there is a patio that encircles the building. At the rear there is a bench we might be comfortable in—at least for a while, until they come out hunting for you."

"What are we waiting for?" she said. "Now I know how the poor fox must feel when hunted by the hounds. For sure, in future, I will ban that sport—if ever it was a sport—in Bromfield."

He laughed as they passed through the door leading to the patio and then around the building to the rear, where the shadowy object of a solitary bench could be seen in the moonlight.

"I'll be quick," he said.

"First tell me, please, where is Joshua? Is he really safe?"

"Yes, Lady Julia. He is safe and alive."

"Oh, please! Call me Julia."

"Very well. Joshua is hiding out in the mud home of his agent in Marwar, Havaldar Mansingh. Mansingh's wife, Rupa Devi, used to be Joshua's cook and servant girl when Joshua was stationed in Ajmer. She was an orphan when Joshua found her, cared for her, raised her, and looked after her as a father might, until his Havaldar fell in love with her. Joshua arranged the marriage and underwrote all the expenses. They have been in his debt ever since. Much more, because during the war, Joshua refused to let the impetuous Mansingh attack an enemy battery—that had brought up heavy artillery during the night—and saved his life too. Rupa Devi thinks of Joshua as a god, and prays for his safety every night—and her prayers were certainly answered that night!"

Julia took the elderly gentleman's hand to her cheek; then kissed it.

"I was waiting outside Devika Rani's house that night. Joshua climbed up the drainpipe and entered from the door leading to the terrace. I was outside the window. He found the dead man—and yes, Devika Rani had slept with him before killing him."

"Who was the man? Do I know him?"

"Yes, you do. Colonel Max Roberts of the CIA. So you see a naked body was taken out of the house."

"Did she surprise Joshua?"

"Yes. She had a gun on him, and she is an excellent shot. Joshua knows that because he trained her. He didn't have a chance. The problem was that I didn't have a chance either, because she was sitting at the dressing table and Joshua was blocking the very small window with his own body—and the three of us were in the same straight line, with Joshua in between. I could hardly shoot her through him!"

They heard the shouts of waiters searching the grounds. Her absence had been discovered, possibly when the General had asked for her and Edward had found her missing.

"She was quite free in her confessions to him; after all he was a dead man as far as she was concerned. And I was outside listening in. She admitted killing Major Patel under instructions from the KGB. She knifed Kantilal. And of course she killed Colonel Roberts."

"And she killed Colonel Rashid Khan too for his copy of THE THAR ARTICLES."

"No! She adamantly denied killing Rashid Khan. Insisted that Joshua—or someone else—had killed him. And I believe her. That was not her doing. So we still have a murderer among us."

The sounds of the waiters could be heard in the kitchens—from where the bench could be seen. Fortunately it was now dark.

"I'll have to go before they find you—or they may accuse me of kidnapping—seeing I've gate-crashed this party. Just to meet with you."

"As you did my wedding reception in Bromfield? Thank God for that!"

"No, actually. I came in with Devika Rani as a gatecrasher, but I did have an invitation for that party. It's a long story—we don't have the time for that. Well, Julia, to make a long story short, Devika Rani offered Joshua two choices in the way he could die. Either groveling on his knees, at her feet, when she would unclasp her blouse from in front, and then, after showing herself to him, execute him with a single bullet to his head—or standing like a soldier, upright, on his two feet. I am so sorry to have to tell you all this. She is a very cruel woman."

"Oh, my poor Joshua! Oh, dear God, how he must have suffered! Didn't he plead with her for his life?"

"Plead with her? He called her a ruthless killer and a bitch! In anger she fired twice at him, past his head, and twice he refused; the third time he went on his knees, leaving the target—Devika Rani—free, and I shot her in the shoulder. Even when hit, she fired at Joshua—the execution bullet—but my shot to her shoulder spun her around, and the bullet went into the wall instead. Joshua was on his feet, gun drawn; Havaldar Mansingh arrived only a few seconds later. The matter was well under control and I melted away. And that, Julia, is the whole truth."

"You didn't kill her? Why? A murderer thrice!"

"Julia, she is the daughter of one of my oldest friends—General Rana Singh—Military Attache to the Indian Embassy in Washington DC. I have known her since childhood—she has dangled on my knee! I could not kill her. I have informed her father who has flown to India to work on her defense. They will work out some sort of deal, where she will be given immunity for her inside knowledge of KGB infiltration of IMI; it will help to weed out those undesirable elements in IMI. I have to go; those voices are uncomfortably close."

"Oh, no, you don't, Sir! This is a party in my honour and you are my honoured guest. You have saved me becoming a widow, given me back my marriage, and my life—and, Sir, I still don't know who you are, but I cannot possibly let you leave without feeding you at my table. Give me the honour, as well, of having the very first dance with you. Please? I think Joshua would also want it that way."

He laughed. "Why not? You were very gracious when you danced with me that day at your wedding reception, because I had no partner—and I was honoured. I will be honoured today as well. But I cannot eat at the General's table."

"Oh, and why not?"

"We were at Sandhurst together, and while he would personally welcome me, there might be uncomfortable questions—for him. Shall we leave it at that?"

"You, Sir, are not leaving without dining with me. I was to eat at the General's table; I am not anymore. Come with me," Julia said, holding him by the hand and leading him in the direction of the back door that led into the kitchen.

When she entered the kitchen, ignoring the staff around, she cleared a table of delicious puddings moving them carefully to one side, pulling two chairs up to it, side by side. She took two clean plates off the counter and handed both to him—one in each hand.

"What would you like?" she whispered.

"That goat biryani looks delicious. May be a trifle spicy for you, though."

"Goat biryani for the both of us. We need some raitha with that," she said, spooning out generously the yoghurt into both plates. "A vegetable curry?"

"You choose," he said. "Then it will be truly a meal for the both of us."

"A cauliflower and potato vegetable. Some dal—to make the food moist?"

He nodded. Julia signalled to one of the waiters for a bottle of non-alcoholic wine, and they sat down to eat, oblivious to the kitchen staff around them.

"Who am I toasting?" Julia asked raising her glass.

He thought about it for a moment. "Your old Uncle Solomon," he said, "but spoken as 'Solomon Uncle', with the name first and the 'Uncle' after—that is if you can think of me as an uncle to you." He would have gone into a detailed explanation of how in India any older person could be called 'Uncle' or 'Aunty' as a sign of respect, but she smilingly cut him short.

"Solomon Uncle it is. I don't have any Uncles or Aunts, and it will be a great pleasure to have you as my very first. Besides I'm going to have to introduce you in a minute, because here comes Edward."

"What the hell are you doing here?" Edward shouted. "The General's waiting for you at his table! There's a whole roomful of people who are asking for you! And who the devil is he?"

"Edward," Julia said sweetly, "may I introduce to you my old Solomon Uncle, who was in town, heard of this party in my honour and dropped by unexpectedly. I was so happy to see him, but when I heard you had no place set for him in the hall, I decided—on the spur of the moment—to feed him here. You don't mind do you?"

"I do mind! And if you were in town why didn't you call on us? I would have invited you. I didn't know you had any Uncles, Julia?"

I didn't either, Julia thought delightedly to herself, but I sure do now!

"Oh, yes. I have a ton of them in India. All from Joshua's side, of course."

"But that still doesn't explain why he didn't call on you for an invitation!"

"I can explain," old Solomon Uncle said, his eyes twinkling with mirth. "I'm one of the, shall we say, poorer members of the family? A not so desirable relative? I would not have dreamed of coming to the big bungalow to see her, but I thought I'd take my chances here. I'm sorry. Please forgive me. I'll leave immediately."

He got up, preparing to leave, but Julia restrained him.

"Solomon Uncle," she said, "as one of the not so desirable members of my family, you will leave when I give you permission to leave. Sir, please sit."

He had half arisen; he sat down with a smile.

Only the two of them knew what an evening this was turning out to be. A rank stranger who had restored her husband and her happiness to her; a tall, elegant and very charming granddaughter of an English Earl who was insisting on eating with him in the kitchens of a banquet hall in Pakistan.

"Edward," Julia said, "you are upsetting my Solomon Uncle's digestion. He suffers from acid reflux when under stress! Now will you please go, and allow us to complete our dinner in peace? I'll be out shortly—when the dancing starts—and after the first dance with Solomon Uncle, I will be your hostess for the rest of the evening. Now go!"

"I don't understand you, Julia. Not twenty minutes ago you were in tears, grieving over the loss of a dead husband. Now you are eating, and drinking, and toasting an Uncle who has come out of nowhere! Did Joshua mean nothing to you?" But he went.

They had, as the both of them confessed to each other, one of the nicest meals they'd ever had. He didn't say much about himself—and she didn't ask—but she did learn that he was seventy-five years old, his wife had died some years ago, he had two elder daughters and one son. True, he had been following Joshua and her in Washington DC. Yes, he had gate-crashed her wedding reception as Devika Rani's companion—but he did have an invitation. And yes, he was on the stairs outside Major Patel's flat when she'd come rushing down the stairs.

He smiled at her questions, took two bowls of flan custard off a passing waiter's tray and they had dessert.

Ten minutes later the band struck up. Julia took him by the hand again, though he hung behind, not quite sure if he had overstayed his welcome with Edward. The music was fast, as would be welcomed by the military colonels who would soon be clamouring for their dances with her. Julia went across to the band leader and whispered in his ear. The music came to an abrupt stop, followed by the lilting strains of soft dance music more appropriate for the elderly.

"I am grateful," she whispered, "for a lot this evening, but may I add one more to that list?"

"I've heard you are a writer, Julia, so I know you won't disappoint me by the mundane!"

She laughed. "I'm grateful I don't wear eye make-up, or I would now be looking an absolute mess!"

And Julia swept her Solomon Uncle into a dance, which if she'd had her way, would have gone on for a lot longer than it did. She hugged him before he left; he patted her back, kissed her on the head, and disappeared into the night. She wondered if she would ever see him again. She kept her word, dancing with anyone who wanted it. Her feet felt airy; so did her heart—all the time thinking of her Joshua, and the kind Uncle who had kept him alive.

The General sent word through Edward he was planning to leave soon, and could she visit with him?

She responded immediately, apologising for the delay, waving her hand at all the youthful colonels who had been dancing with her. The General did not, regretfully, dance, but he had so much he wanted to talk to her about.

They sat in the alcove that had been reserved for the General. He dismissed his entourage.

"They will fuss so," he said. "I have lived with danger all my life; it has left me untouched. But let us talk about you, Lady Julia. I've heard so much about you from Viscount Edward."

"Oh! Nothing damaging I trust," she said, recalling a line Joshua had used with her when they were sitting at a roadside café in Paris, celebrating their togetherness, before they were engaged.

"Except your marriage to an Indian colonel! Could we not have found you a Pakistani colonel who would have been far more suitable?"

The General feigned his deep disappointment at her unpardonable taste in husbands.

Julia laughed openly at his expression.

"Undoubtedly, General, there are many fine brave colonels in the Pakistani army who would have been perfectly suitable, but this Colonel was very special—and still is."

"So I gather. But I feel sorry for you when I tell you what we've found out—about your Colonel."

He stopped. Unsure of whether he ought to proceed. Whether it was right of him to proceed, in matters that were delicate enough to demand more discretion.

"Oh! And what have you found out, General, that I would be sorry about, if I knew?"

"Do you really want to know?"

"Yes."

"Did you know he is Raja?"

"Yes. How did you know?"

"One of his former—shall we say—associates broke with him when he married an English girl. She was not reluctant to make public the information. The power of a jilted woman is like a lightning bolt. It leaves others standing around untouched, but it cremates the one it hits."

Julia looked down at the table cloth. Flowers in a pattern, the stems towards him, curling into a bouquet towards her.

"I'm sorry," he said. "Forgive me. That was crude of me. But if you love him—and you do—you ought to hear the rest."

She nodded.

"He killed Colonel Rashid Khan with an antique revolver that belonged to his grandfather; we have established that. At an emergency meeting called by one of them—we don't know who? We've established that too. And THE THAR ARTICLES—Rashid Khan's copy of it; my copy—was stolen. Tell me, what would you expect me—as Leader of Pakistan and Head of PMI—to do? Rashid Khan was picked by me for this assignment. I loved him like a brother! The Lion of Amritsar, murdered with a bullet in the back of his head—while at prayer."

"What do you plan to do about it?"

"Bring him to justice of course. I cannot bring him to trial in India. That is impossible. And he will not come here willingly to stand trial. So I have to mete out justice to him there. What would you do?"

"Do you believe in justice, General?"

"Yes. But not in clemency. That is what you are begging from me."

"I said 'justice', General; I didn't say 'clemency'. I believe my husband to be innocent of the charges you've made, even though the evidence may certainly appear to be against him. But instead of arranging for his assassination in Bombay—which would equate you to the level of a common murderer—try the real murderer here in Pakistan."

"Strong words, Lady Julia. I have killed many—never murdered."

"Call me Mrs Samuelson," she said.

"And how do you intend to get him—if he is the real murderer—over here? Urge him by your wifely charms to give himself up to us? He may be your husband, Madam, but he is a soldier first, and he would rather take his chances on the streets of Bombay, I think, than in a Pakistani courtroom. I wish you good-day."

"Not so fast, General," Julia said, not rising from her chair. "I have not finished."

The General, who was on the point of rising, settled back with an air of benign tolerance.

"You have said your piece; may I be permitted to speak mine? Give me a military vehicle that can travel the sand dunes of the Thar Desert, and an escort, with safe passage across the border to the Fort. I will have the murderer for you here in seven days. You are a man of justice. You said so, and I believe you. Do I ask for much? A military vehicle and an escort to the Fort?"

The General signalled to a waiter for a pot of tea. He relaxed further back into his padded chair, looking at her with unconcealed admiration.

"I can't say much for your taste in men, my dear," he said, shaking his finger at her, "but I have to compliment Colonel Samuelson on his choice of a wife!"

She blushed, and that set him at his ease. He saw the colour flood into her cheeks.

"Damn these beautiful women!" he thought. "She will now have me eating out of her hand!" But the thought caused him more pleasure than he thought it would.

"And just how do you propose to flush your husband out of hiding—if he is the murderer? The reports I've had indicate that he isn't even in Bombay. He's up in Marwar Junction. Though he's too clever to stay in one place for too long. There is even a rumor being spread that he is dead—I won't go into the details; they would be too painful for you—but I, for one, don't believe it. Colonel Samuelson does not die that easily. How will you get him to the Fort?"

"By arranging for a message to be sent to him—from Rashid Khan. Asking for a meeting. He has never believed Rashid Khan is dead—he thought that was a rumor being spread by PMI. When he gets the message from Rashid Khan, he will come. I guaranty it."

"He will come? Just like that? Without suspecting a trap of some sort? Very naïve, dear Lady Julia. But then, perhaps, you know your husband better than I do the soldier."

"He will come for sure, General, because he will be convinced the message is from Rashid Khan. They had it written down in THE THAR ARTICLES—the method of communicating with each other. The code in which it was to be sent, the way it would be sent, the authentication to make sure that it was only they who could send it and only they who could read it. He will come."

"You, of course, know how to send this message, as if it came from Rashid Khan?"

"Yes."

"How do you know? What the code is? Where to send it? The authentication? How do you know? Unless……."

Julia would not reply. She reached, instead, for her cup of tea, looking round at the dancing couples swirling like water eddies in a river of noise.

"You have to convince me Mrs. Samuelson. Or I am not likely to agree to this scheme of yours. Notice, I haven't derided it—it does seem to have some merit—but I have to be sure. May I assume that you have read THE THAR ARTICLES?"

"Yes."

"And that your husband had possession of them?"

"Yes."

"You have them here with you? Both copies?"

"Yes."

"In your handbag lying on the table between us?"

"Yes."

"I will make a deal with you, Lady Julia. Hand over Rashid Khan's copy—rightfully, my copy—of those documents, and I will call off my agents who are thirsting for your husband's blood to avenge the death of Colonel Rashid Khan."

"No."

"What did you say?"

"I said, no."

"Do you realise that I could reach across the table, look through your handbag, remove the documents, and claim what rightfully belongs to me."

"You could. But you won't."

"And why would I not do that, Madam?"

"Because, Sir, you are a soldier, a General, the Leader of a proud nation, and a gentleman. And you would never look through a lady's handbag without her permission—and I don't give it to you."

The General slammed back into his padded chair in total admiration of her. "Well said, Lady Julia! So near and, yet, so far away. Very well. But you have yet to convince me that you do have those papers, and that you have read them. You will forgive me if I don't just take your word on it?"

"I forgive you, General."

Julia looked up from her tea cup into his crystalline black eyes, below bushy eyebrows that could be very dangerous or very kindly. As now.

"Shall I tell you, General, an exclusive piece of information that is contained in THE THAR ARTICLES, that only you and the Prime Minister of India think you know? Other than my husband who—as you say—is hiding out, somewhere, in Marwar Junction, and Colonel Rashid Khan, who is dead?"

"And Rehana. We must not forget her. She knows and she will not tell! Why?"

"Because she believes, as I do, that Raja did not kill Bahadur. That is why. They were friends! But if I can tell it to you, it ought to convince you I have read them—and possess them."

She pointed teasingly to the handbag between them. He waved his hand to her to proceed.

"General, you are scheduled to meet with the Prime Minister of India on October 25—barely ten days away—at 12:00 noon, in the same Fort, to review the agreement. At which time, each will produce his copy of THE THAR ARTICLES for retention or burning, each having veto powers. If the two of you cannot both agree to their retention, the documents will be burnt."

The General rose from his chair to stand behind Julia. He placed both of his bare hands on the collar bones of her bare shoulders. She did not flinch.

"You are playing a very dangerous game, Lady Julia," he whispered. "But I can see that for you the stakes are at least as high as they are for me—and at a personal level, far higher. All right, I agree. I will appoint another of my trusted soldiers to take Rashid Khan's place as Bahadur. He will be your escort. An army vehicle suitable for desert terrain, and safe passage to the Fort. In return for which I want my copy of THE THAR ARTICLES. The handwritten original! So I can meet with the Prime Minister on the 25th, without loss of face, in the Fort, to review the agreement. Is that agreed?"

"Yes. One small condition."

"Oh!"

"For the journey to the Fort, your soldier will take orders from me."

"Why? I would think you would prefer to leave the military planning to him—he is far more skilled in such matters than you are." The General's voice was almost pleading. "Why?"

"Because he is my escort—and I do not take orders from my escorts—that is why. Agreed?"

He nodded.

"And are you absolutely certain he will not countermand my orders?"

"Lady Julia, he is a soldier. If I order him to take his orders from you, he will die doing so. I trust you will return him back to me alive?"

"That I promise," she said with a smile, rising from the chair and reaching for her handbag.

"Not so fast, Lady Julia. You will, in addition, also hand over to me Rashid Khan's murderer—or your husband—to stand trial in Pakistan."

"Sir, why have you never asked me why I did not trade my husband's life for four handwritten pages, that, quite frankly, are worthless to me? You must think I am a very poor wife. It is because Colonel Joshua Samuelson, the Lion of Lahore, handpicked by the Prime Minister of India, and my husband, would have held me in contempt for the rest of our married life, had I agreed. I value his love and respect—and that is not for trading. Rehana has felt the same way; she has mentored me well. Please have your soldier and the army vehicle outside my bungalow, six days from now, at four o'clock in the morning. I will decide the hour of our leaving Karachi. I wish you, Sir, a very pleasant evening."

He offered her his arm and she took it. He escorted her across the room, plowing through the dancing couples with military abandon, like the parting of the waves in a sea of bodies, as they went towards the main entrance of the hall. Her chauffeured car pulled up. Hafez came out to open the door for her.

As the car swept down the driveway on its way to her bungalow, the General whispered to his aide, who nodded and rushed into a military van, with ten soldiers, to provide her an escort—and a bodyguard—for the rest of her stay in Karachi.

Women, the General knew, carried their precious jewels—diamonds and pearls—in their handbags, when travelling. His wife had done that on many occasions when he'd been moved, in the Pakistani Army, from base to base. He had never arranged for their protection.

But THE THAR ARTICLES were far more precious to him than all the jewels in Pakistan.

CHAPTER 12

Joshua sat in the only chair in Mansingh's house, his head in his hands—and shivered. Even in the warm night, he felt cold. All he could think about was his dishonour. It meant little to those who didn't value it; everything to those who lived by it. Cheating death by dishonour! What would Julia say about it? And even if she didn't voice her feelings, what would she think of him? He had seen the shadow flit across the dressing table mirror. He thought it was Mansingh outside the window. But the window was so small and his body blocked it. Could he have thrown himself to one side and taken his chances that Mansingh would get his shot off before she did?

And as it turned out it wasn't even Mansingh out there. Some stranger had shot Devika Rani in the shoulder and disappeared. Perhaps a past grudge being repaid? Perhaps an old lover? Whoever it was, it did not excuse him from what he'd done. He'd gone on his knees and groveled at her feet. Her diabolical laugh of triumph would haunt him forever! Would Julia ever forgive him, or would she hold him in contempt for the rest of their married life because she'd believe he'd gone on his knees for her to undo her clasp? He hadn't been much of a husband to her. Four weeks of marriage, and here he was imprisoned in Marwar, hunted by PMI, who were convinced he'd murdered a friend. What would she think when she found out he was Raja? Thank God she didn't know! He'd tell her personally. He should have done it a long time ago. Rashid Khan had told his wife Rehana, and had even advised Joshua to confide in Julia—but he had played by the rules. Damn the bloody rules! From now on, for Julia, he was going to break them all.

In the next room, Mansingh and Rupa Devi peered through the open doorway and begged each other for help. To ease their Master's suffering.

"He is suffering from shock," Mansingh whispered to his wife. "I have seen it often enough in battle. Men of great courage on the battlefield, sitting in their barracks after the day was won—just like him—unable to face themselves. The loss of life of some of their men—who didn't come back—was their dishonour. Their nightmares! Do something for him, will you?"

"What can I do?" she said. "I cannot talk directly to him, or look into his eyes—now I am married."

"I know! I know!" Mansingh said impatiently. "But he is our guest, and my Colonel, and at one time you were his trusted cook and servant. You have talked to him before; go talk to him again. We have been married too long for me to be upset by it. And were it not for him we would not have been married at all! Talk to him when you take his tea in to him. I'll do the shopping for the vegetables today. Perhaps a nice bit of fish—to cheer him up?" She nodded.

She brought in his tea at nine o'clock precisely. He had not slept well, in the only bed they had, and which they insisted he have. He was up, bleary eyed, and with the haunted look still in them. All he could think of all night, was how to tell Julia everything—that he was Raja, that he had not one but two copies of THE THAR ARTICLES in his possession in his Mother's flat in Bombay, and how he'd groveled at Devika Rani's feet to save himself. What if she believed he had groveled for another reason?

She set the tray on the table. Normally she would have left the room, her face covered. Instead she returned to the kitchen and returned with a cup of tea for herself, sitting on the floor across from him. She shared a cup of tea with him—Master and servant—as in the old days, when he'd instructed her to get a cup of tea for herself. The cloth was still across her face, shielding it. She slid it backwards to free her eyes, before him, for the first time since she'd been married ten years before.

"Reminds me of the old times in Ajmer, Joshua Saheb," she said, in Hindi, "when I cooked and cleaned house for you and made your morning tea."

"Yes, Rupa Devi, it does. Those were fine times. No cares, no wars, no ties," he replied, also in Hindi.

"Yes, no ties. I often think of them too."

"Do you miss them?"

"Sometimes, Joshua Saheb, when the day has been hard. I have to speak the truth. Yes, I miss them. There was more laughter then; more time for it too."

"Yes, I remember. You were the giggly type! You could never stop laughing, once you started."

"I was young then," she said reproachfully.

"Particularly I remember that day when the donkey strayed into the garden and started to eat the plants. Mansingh chased it all over the place; the donkey braying and Mansingh swearing! Such words from my Havaldar—and in front of you too. That donkey was swift on his four feet."

"Especially when Mansingh got hold of its tail and the donkey stopped. I thought I'd never stop laughing when the donkey kicked and Mansingh threw himself over the donkey's back to avoid his hoofs."

"He might have been hurt!" Joshua remonstrated.

"Not my Mansingh, Joshua Saheb. He knows how to take care of himself."

"He knows how to take care of you too. Tell me, Rupa Devi, do you laugh much these days?"

"There may not be that much laughter in marriage, Joshua Saheb, but it has its compensations. I think of what life would have been all alone—without Mansingh and my children—and I may think longingly of the days when I was single, but I would never go back. Neither, Joshua Saheb, will you."

He nodded in agreement. They talked on for quite a few minutes more. He felt his problems were not only his but hers too—if differently framed. It was a comforting thought to know that he was not alone, that his servant woman sitting on the floor across from him had the same fears and doubts about her marriage, as he had about his. And faith in it too.

Mansingh came in with the vegetables and his bit of fish. Rupa Devi rose from the floor, folded her hands to him, put the cloth back across her head and face, and left the room. Mansingh noticed the difference in his Colonel and was grateful to his wife.

There was a letter in the P. O. Box that Joshua had signed for Mansingh at the local post office. And a phone call from Abdul. He had received a letter too in his P. O. Box in Amritsar.

Joshua sprang to attention. There had to be a third letter in the P. O. Box, in Major Patel's name, in the Central Post Office in Bombay. Each box had two keys. One was with his agent in the field; the other in his Mother's flat in Bombay.

He called his Mother.

"Joshua!" she almost screamed into the telephone. "Where on Earth are you? And where is Julia?"

When he told her, she was even more livid.

"What are you doing in Marwar? You can't be honeymooning in Marwar—and all alone—if Julia is in Karachi! Don't tell me you and Julia have split up already? You'll never find a girl like her, anywhere, no matter who you pick!"

He calmed her down. No, they were still together. And still very much in love. But they had some loose ends in their jobs they had to settle first. And yes, they'd be back in Bombay in a week's time, he promised her. Then he asked to speak to Susan.

There was a complete change in her tone as she turned euphoric about Susan. His sister wanted to consult him on a very important matter and would he please pay close attention to what she had to say? Then Susan came on the line.

"Joshua, I'm in love. I hope to be engaged soon. And then married as quickly as possible."

"Oh! Congratulations, Susan. I'm really happy for you. Who is the lucky man?"

"My professor of meteorology, Dr David Abrams. He's a little older than I am, but he's never been married before because of his studies for a Ph.D. in America. But he loves me too!"

"My dear girl, what has age got to do with it?"

"Then you agree?"

"Susan, dear, you need never feel the need to ask my permission. Mother is the only one who has to agree. But you have my total blessings and support, if that is what you're looking for?"

"Oh, thank you, Joshua! I'm going to call Joe, and get his approval too. The two of you, my two older brothers, have been so wonderful, I just could not be happy if you didn't approve. I knew you would approve—and so will Joe. But I just had to ask."

"Tell me Susan, have you told him all?"

"I was wondering if you'd ask. Yes, I've told him about my defective heart valve, that I may not have many years to live, and that I cannot have children. That is why he wants us to be married as soon as possible. Now what do you want me to do for you in Bombay?"

"Susan, there is a P. O. Box at the Central Post & Telegraph Office in Bombay; the key is in your flat in the office desk in the living room, top drawer, right side—you can't miss it. The number of the Box is on the key. There will be a letter in the box—from Karachi. It will have only six numbers on it. Please go now and retrieve it. I will call you in two hours. Open the letter and read the numbers out to me. Please, do it now."

Two hours later he had three sets of numbers in front of him:

Abdul's read: 593741

Mansingh's read: 634728

Susan's read: 790186

The Code that gave the date, time, and the authentication—that the message was genuine and could only have come from someone who had the documents—was dreadfully simple. Therein lay the genius of the men who had designed it.

First, the time: the first and sixth digit of Abdul's message read '51', reversed '15' or 3:00 PM.

Second, the day: the second and fifth digit of the message in Mansigh's Box read '32', reversed 23rd.

Third, the month: the third and fourth digits of Susan's message read '01', reversed '10' or the month of October.

Finally, the authentication: All the digits in any message, added up, had to be in a sequence of numbers. In his case, they were: 29, 30, 31. The authentication was complete.

He had only one day to reach the Fort. First he had to get to the Army base in Jaisalmer to procure a military vehicle capable of travelling over the sand dunes without being bogged down. It could well be an army battle tank!

He had to go alone—that was their agreement. Each person came alone. Mansingh remonstrated with him.

"Colonel Saheb, the lady you shot in the bungalow in Barmer—the one you called the ambulance for and is now recovering in a hospital in Barmer—has already alerted every enemy agent in the country that you are Raja. They will be waiting for you as you approach the Fort."

"Mansingh, I have already told you, I did not shoot her. I went down on my knees and groveled at her feet—to my eternal shame—but that opened up the line of fire between the window and her—and if you didn't shoot at her, someone who was outside that window did."

"Saheb, if I had shot at her, I would have killed her—for sure!" he said reproachfully. "Perhaps they didn't want you killed in Barmer? Kill you at the Fort and parade your body in Pakistan? Let me come with you, Colonel Saheb," he pleaded.

"You will come with me, Mansingh. You and the vehicle will drop me at the Fort, and then retreat one hundred yards away from the Fort on the Indian side. Bahadur's men will retreat to one hundred yards on the Pakistani side." Joshua paused.

"He and I, we meet alone."

He'd never really believed Rashid Khan was dead. Such a message coming in code, with authentication, could only mean he was alive. He wanted to see Joshua—presumably about the arrangements after Joshua was with Julia in England. Rupa Devi was right. There were compensations for everything—if one looked for them. He was willing to freely admit he was missing Julia. Why did she have to be holed up in Karachi? It had been his bright (stupid?) idea; not hers! Separating them in this way was hard on him; she was probably having a fine time, in an endless series of parties and dances, and hadn't given him a thought all week! Certainly there had been no letter from her; nor a telephone call to his Mother.

Still it would be good to see Rashid Khan again. The first time they had met, he had no idea who Bahadur was going to be. Joshua had come early to the Fort. He had his service revolver inside his military jacket. One always came prepared for such a meeting. Never trust a man you hadn't met before. Strangers were like death—they stalked you without feeling. Until he'd seen Rashid Khan open the door and come into the Fort from the Pakistani side. They stared at each other in disbelief. A coincidence? The Lion of Lahore and the Lion of Amritsar had both been picked for the same assignment! Abandoning all reserve they had embraced with genuine pleasure at seeing each other. Then they sat down to the business of framing THE THAR ARTICLES. Joshua had brought a bottle of sherry for himself and, not knowing who his adversary might be, a bottle of lime juice as well. He congratulated himself on his foresight. Rashid Khan was a religious Muslim and did not touch liquor—though he tolerated, with benign pleasure, Joshua's enjoyment of it.

They embraced once more when they were to part. This time, with the satisfaction of a job well done. Joshua had felt the hardness of the dagger at Rashid Khan's waist.

Rashid Khan reached inside and drew it out. A curved weapon. Barely eight inches long, with a sharpened blade that could slice through a man's military uniform and his guts at the same time. Resting in a pearl and enamel ivory sheath, the handle encrusted with precious stones. A work of art—if a deadly one.

Rashid Khan pleaded forgiveness.

"How was I to know it would be you, Joshua? You took no chances either—I can feel your service revolver at your chest. That is good. We are both careful people—so we stay alive. But I can hardly let you leave without a gift. Here, take the dagger. I won't feel so bad about having brought it—I can truthfully say it was for you!"

"I don't have anything for you, Rashid. But at our next meeting—and I hope there will be a few more—I will bring you a delightful antique, lady's, revolver owned by my grandfather—Major General Sir Isaac Samuelson."

"Ah! I've heard of him. A great soldier! It belonged to him, you say? It will be a pleasure to take it. All right, Joshua. You take the dagger now, and I will accept your antique revolver. Bring a few bullets too, with you, and we'll try it out here. To see how it works after all these years. I love old weapons—they never die."

That is what he had done when he'd received the message, in code, from Bahadur asking for an urgent meeting on July 23.

Julia was in London, and he was travel-weary shuttling between Bombay and London, keeping tabs on the scheme and courting her as well. But he had found an excuse and gone. The most difficult part was being unable to tell her anything. She had worked for MI-6; she had other loyalties too. It was not as if his safety alone was involved—had it been so he would have told her on day one. Any disclosure increased the chances of assassination. Inadvertent disclosure, unintentional! Yet, Rashid Khan had told his wife. And told Joshua, at that next meeting, that he'd told his wife. Joshua made excuses for himself by saying that Rehana was Rashid Khan's wife; Julia was only engaged to him, and engagements often were broken? He'd tell Julia when they were married—and he'd never got around to it.

They met that second time, on July 23, almost to celebrate their success. Joshua saw the burly Pathan's eyes light up with laughter as they recounted the success of the mujahidin with the arms that were getting through to Amritsar and then in to Lahore and on to Peshawar.

"Before you tell me why you've called this meeting, let me tell you, I'm going to be married, Rashid. An English girl, Julia, granddaughter of an Earl. I'll have to give up all of this—this life of Raja and IMI. I'll be a medical doctor again; I've promised her."

He was incredulous. “Just when it’s going so well, you’re going to give it all up? That is not acceptable, Joshua! You made a pact with me, and now you are breaking it—for the sake of a woman?”

Joshua laughed; slapped Rashid Khan’s knee.

“Tell me, Rashid, what pact would you not break for Rehana? My job is done; so is yours. We’ve organised the scheme, and made sure it’s running smoothly. Now all we do is to leave it to others—trustworthy people—to keep it running until the Soviet’s leave Afghanistan. And that may well take years! We—you and I—can’t be tied to the day-to-day running of this sort of thing. We were meant for more intelligence type work. Setting it up was a challenge—and we did it. We can feel proud of it. Managing it for the next few years was never my commitment to it. I have better things to do.”

“Like getting married?”

“Now that you mention it—yes.”

Rashid Khan laughed. “Well, then may I be the first to offer you my congratulations on joining the rest of us married folk, and settling down to domesticity. Because she will domesticate you—you know that, don’t you?”

“I’m looking forward to it.”

“Twenty-five years from now, when you’ve been married as long as I have, write to me and tell me how you feel! For now, I’ll let you bask in your joy.”

“Marriage has its rewards,” Joshua said. “How could I live without her?”

“You’re right, Joshua. Marrying Rehana was the best thing I ever did—even though I might speak disparagingly about marriage. Go! Go your way. Have plenty of children. I have three sons—all in the Army. Two conditions.”

“Oh! All right, let’s hear them.”

“That you are still Raja. Appoint others to do what is necessary, but you will meet me here in this Fort if there is an urgency—so we can relive old times! Be nostalgic? I’m getting old, Joshua, if nostalgia has of late become so important to me. But there is another reason. We have sworn to protect each his copy of THE THAR ARTICLES. I don't trust your copy in the hands of anyone else. You will keep it! Agreed?"

"Yes. I can see how that will continue until we hand over the copies to our respective leaders for retention or burning—as is specified in the documents. What is the second condition?"

"Ah! The reason I called you here today. That you take charge of my copy as well."

"What! You want to hand over your copy to me? In heaven's name, why?"

Rashid Khan placed his copy of THE THAR ARTICLES on the table between them. For the first time since he had known him, Joshua sensed doubt and uncertainty in his friend. Not fear—there could never be fear in this Pathan—but an unsettling confusion. Like taking steps in the dark in an unfamiliar terrain. Unwilling to place the foot firmly on the soft ground, in case the ground disappeared.

"Will you? For a friend."

"Yes. But why? Why?"

"I am a man of honour, Joshua. I prize it above all else. More than my life itself. I may soon be unable to prevent the public disclosure of these documents. Pressure from the Americans, I think, on PMI to leak them. They would like to have their cake and eat it too! Embarrass Indo-Soviet relations at some later date—even as they are getting their arms through to Peshawar. PMI has badgered me twice for these, and I have refused them every time; I will refuse them a hundred times! But if the Soviets know of it—as they must—they will need to secure my copy to prevent disclosure. They will kill if they have to. Will you keep my copy for me? Please?"

Joshua nodded. Folded the papers into his military jacket, bringing out the gun. Not his service revolver—he hadn't brought that with him this time—but the little antique weapon, with the mother-of-pearl handle he'd brought for Rashid Khan.

Rashid Khan was delighted with it. His face lifted; the tensions disappeared as he saw the weapon cradled in Joshua's palm, held out to him for inspection. A lady's gun really, but deadly. Five shots in the weapon. Joshua had brought a box of bullets with him.

Rashid Khan loaded the chambers. Then walking to a slit in the Fort walls, he took aim at an offending scrub fifteen yards away and fired, kicking up the sand in the dead centre of it.

It was time to leave. For Joshua, that is. Usually they came out of the Fort together. They didn't linger long because of the heat reflecting off the sand. Just time for a warm manly embrace, so common to the tribes from up north, feeling the powerful frame and the touch of reassuring hands, and offering his smaller stature, but equal reassurance in return.

This time, it was twelve noon. Rashid Khan's prayer time. After embracing Joshua, he would look West towards Mecca, kneel on the ground with his head bowed, his back facing the door. And pray.

Joshua's gift to him lay on the table.

CHAPTER 13

They met on the western edge of Cholistan, the extension of the Thar Desert into Pakistan. Twelve thousand square miles of it. Arid, dry, barren, except for stunted thorn bushes—and very hot. With the hissing, dry winds, the shallow sand dunes shifted unmercifully—a walking, moving, cholna—inviting suffering to anything else that walked and moved. That gave the desert its name.

They came together. Edward drove Julia to the edge of the desert in his Land Rover, while the military colonel, assigned by the General to be the new Bahadur, drove the military half-track vehicle, that would be capable of travelling over the sand dunes without being bogged down.

At first, they passed a dwelling once in a while; soon there was nothing else but sand, until they passed Dewar Fort at a distance. Julia avoided it. It had once belonged to the Hindu rulers of neighbouring Jaisalmer, now a part of India.

They had to be getting close to the border.

Colonel Sher Ali Khan slowed the half-track and said: "We are getting close to the military checkpoint Lady Julia. We have two choices; approach it and request permission to escort you to the Fort—after all you do have a visa to enter India—and risk being refused that permission. Or avoid it by turning off slightly to the South and entering India illegally. In which case, if we are caught, there will be a diplomatic incident. The instructions of my General are to follow your orders implicitly. What would you have me do?"

"Avoid the border crossing, and risk being caught," Julia said firmly, cradling a brown paper parcel in her lap, her handbag on her shoulder, and clutching a new sun-bonnet round her head, much as she had done in her flight down the stairs and out of Major Patel's flat in Bombay.

He nodded, turning the half-track a little towards the South. She felt the heat more than the Colonel and Edward, the sweat pouring off her into her white blouse, causing her bra to stick to her, delineating her upper body in a sort of sculptured wetness. Her legs protruded under the printed flared skirt, showing the painted toenails. She thought of Joshua when she looked at them, and the sensuous massage he had given her, including her toes. His slender hands had almost made love to them!

Twenty yards from the Fort, Colonel Sher Ali Khan helped her out of the half-track. He glanced at her with considerable admiration. Not many women of his acquaintance would risk doing what she was doing to vindicate a husband.

A youthful colonel. As tall as she was—taller than Joshua—the sun-tanned skin and the handsome jaw making him so alive. A slightly hooked nose; the almost traditional military moustache curling away at the corners, and—unlike Joshua's—without any grey in it. Carrying his service revolver, openly, in the holster at the side of his khaki uniform.

He was striding to the Fort. Julia stopped him.

"Just a minute, Colonel," she said. "You have done an excellent job in following my instructions and bringing us here safely. I congratulate you. Now, for a while, you may be permitted to rest."

He did not understand, stopping in mid-step, turning around to face her. The Fort was barely twenty yards away.

"Aren't we going into the Fort?" he asked.

"I am. You are going to take Viscount Edward and the half-track one hundred yards away from the Fort. As is written in THE THAR ARTICLES."

"But that is impossible!" the Colonel said sharply. "Quite out of the question! I am Bahadur. My orders are to meet with Raja. I cannot allow you to go in there to meet a man who is a killer!"

"I will risk it," Julia said, quietly.

"Impossible!" the Colonel shouted. "I cannot agree!"

"Colonel, are you a good soldier?"

"The best there is."

"Then your General has not let me down—because I asked for the best. How does a good soldier—the best there is—take orders?"

"Are you ordering me to retreat one hundred yards from the Fort? Behind that sand dune?"

"Yes, Colonel. That is an order."

She need not have doubted the outcome. Her father had been in the Army; her husband was in one too.

Colonel Sher Ali Khan saluted smartly; signalled to Edward to enter the half-track. Edward was about to protest, but the tone in her voice told him he had better not risk having Julia order the Colonel to remove him by force.

Julia waited until they were out of sight, before she walked into the Fort. A circular apron, one hundred feet wide of solid concrete, and cleaning by army bulldozers, kept the encroaching sands at bay.

The door, on the Pakistani side, opened directly on to a stone staircase that led to an upper floor. She entered what was the meeting room. The furniture in the room, the adornments on the walls and the carpeting on the floor spoke of hasty arrangements made by both sides for the first meeting between the Prime Minister and the General. Raja and Bahadur would hardly have cared for anything other than a table and two chairs for them to draft THE THAR ARTICLES.

The second door from the apron—on the Indian side—led to a similar staircase entering the meeting room from the opposite side.

There were only two doors into the Fort.

The timing had to be just right. She had called the meeting for 3:00 PM in the afternoon. It was 2:50 PM. Joshua was usually so punctual at such meetings, she could not risk his coming there and reaching the Fort ahead of her.

She unwrapped the burkha from the brown paper parcel, drawing it over her head and body, the bottom frilled edge reaching to her ankles, leaving bare her shoes. Since it would never do to have European-style shoes visible beneath the burkha, she kicked them off, leaving her bare toes peeping out from underneath. She adjusted the veil over her face, seeing, without difficulty, through the silken thread screen, her vision unimpaired by the screen being so close to her eyes; her eyes hidden from other prying eyes by the fineness of the mesh.

She reached into her handbag for Rashid Khan's service revolver, wrapping both shoes and handbag in the brown paper wrapping, to complete her image of a Pakistani matron. Not quite, because this Pakistani matron had a lethal weapon in her left pocket, the safety catch off, and the finger of one hand around the trigger. She sat down to await Raja.

He came at precisely 3:00 PM. She heard the battle tank come noisily to the concrete apron, some words in Hindi; then it went one hundred yards away.

She had not seen Joshua in over a week; had been married to him for a total of just over four weeks. Is this how her married life should begin? Facing him so soon after marriage—with a dismembered honeymoon—in an abandoned Fort in the middle of a foreign desert, dressed in a burkha, and awaiting an explanation of murder. Or was she waiting for a killer?

He came up the staircase from the Indian side. He thought he might be early, and Bahadur was late, so not seeing him as his head came up the stairs did not alarm him—until he turned around and saw the burkha'd figure awaiting him. Her hands were inside the pockets of the burkha, the veil covered her face, her eyes unseen behind the screen.

He has changed, Julia thought. He looked worn, tired, beaten, the gray in his hair looked more aged than before. He seemed, to her, to be in poor health. She longed to rush to him and put her arms around him, but she desisted.

"Begum Rehana?" he said.

Julia did not reply, but the movement of her head could have been construed as a nod by someone who was expecting it.

He folded his hands, to her, in front of his chest, in an Indian 'namaste' of respect. She did not withdraw her hands from the pockets of her burkha.

"I thought it might be you that sent the message," Joshua said. "I couldn't be sure. So my friend Rashid Khan is really dead? I did not kill him, though you have come here to kill me. Will you hear me out? Then you must decide for yourself, whether he would have wanted you to murder me; I will not resist."

Another silence. Another nod.

"I met him here, that day, because Rashid Khan called an emergency meeting. We toasted each other on the success of our mission. I had a glass of sherry; he had a glass of lime juice. I told him I was to give it all up, to marry a very lovely English girl I was desperately, desperately in love with! He didn't like the idea at all—at first. But he agreed, if I took charge of THE THAR ARTICLES. Not just my copy, but his copy too! He was afraid he wouldn't have control over his copy much longer—or, perhaps, he knew he was marked for death. He lived by his honour, and he had sworn to protect his copy of the documents from disclosure. So he entrusted them to me. Your husband, Begum Rehana, died a brave soldier; I am a coward, because I could not.'

'And the gun? I gave it to him! It was my gift to him that day. He had presented me with a beautiful curved dagger on our previous meeting. I had promised him, the next time we met, an antique, lady's, five-chamber revolver that belonged to my grandfather, Major-General Sir Isaac Samuelson. And I did. It was lying right there on the table beside you, as he knelt for prayer."

Joshua pointed with his hand to the low table beside her—looking down at it. Gazing hard at her bare white feet and the painted toenails. Bright red in colour. The sort used by millions of women all over the world.

"Julia!" he exclaimed, throwing up his hands to the heavens, "What are you doing here? And in that outfit!"

She lifted the veil off her face and smiled sweetly. Then she did what she'd been wanting to do for a long time. She ran to him, put both hands around him, clasping him behind the neck and back, putting her mouth to his and kissing him ardently on the lips—the long moist kiss that had always worked wonders for his pulse and his circulation. Far better than any exercise bicycle, he'd told her. The magic hadn't left her still.

"How did you guess?" Julia asked.

"The two white feet, darling. And the toes. When I massaged them and made love to them, I, sort of, got to know them. They are unmistakably yours! Is this a test? Whether I loved you enough to recognise you by your toes? Have I passed the test?"

He stiffened, moved away from her, pointing an accusing finger at her.

"And now, Lady Julia, I would like an explanation for all this! Why have you brought me here?"

"I wanted to meet you, darling. I was missing my husband, who'd cruelly abandoned me after barely three weeks of marriage. Surely you can understand that?"

"Don't be flippant, Julia. Out with it! I know you better than that. What are we doing here?"

"Waiting, darling,"

"Who for?"

"A killer. And if I am not wrong he won't be long."

"Why? He has already murdered Rashid Khan."

"That is not what he came for that day, after you had left Rashid Khan. He came for Rashid Khan's copy of THE THAR ARTICLES. He didn't get them, because they weren't on him; they were with you. He had killed to no purpose. This is his very last chance to get that copy—and he isn't going to let it slip by."

"That's absurd, Julia. Both copies are lying safely in an old cupboard, filled with Mother's nostalgia, in Mother's flat in Shivaji Park in Bombay."

"Are you quite sure, Joshua?" she said, drawing out Rashid Khan's copy and dropping it lightly on the low table beside her. He made no move towards them. Even from where he stood, there could be no doubt he was looking at the real articles.

His face hardened, his eyes held hers. She shifted uncomfortably.

"How did you come by them?"

"Darling," she said, coming up to him again and nuzzling him, her hand caressing the hair at the back of his neck, her eyes pleading for understanding, "there will be plenty of time for such explanations, but they are better given—and easier taken—sitting outside Henri's hotel in Paris, near the Place de La Republique. Will you take me there, Joshua, when this is all over? There is so much we have to confess to each other—and forgive."

He did not have time to reply, though she knew what it would be, by the hungry kissing of a starved husband, as Joshua commenced kissing her and would have continued for some time, had they not been interrupted by a cough.

They found themselves, still in each other's arms, looking into the barrel of a gun held by a masked man—tall, gaunt, and strangely familiar.

"I will take those papers, if I may," he said, waving Joshua and Julia away from the table with the barrel of his gun. "And Colonel Samuelson—or should I say Raja—don't put your hand inside your coat pocket, or I will shoot Lady Julia, who is shielding you. I do not, regrettably, have any problems with killing a woman; I am not a soldier."

"I can see that," Joshua said. "Tell me, how did you get in? The Western door is covered by Lady Julia's escort—she must have come with an escort—and the Eastern door is covered by my man Mansingh."

"That would be telling," he said. "You do not need to know. I have no wish to kill either or both of you—it was never my intention to kill Bahadur—but he was a Pathan and, built the way he was, a formidable adversary who would not have permitted himself to be searched without being incapacitated. Thank you for the little loaded gun on the table, Colonel Samuelson. That was a gift—but to me—and a real stroke of luck! He was at prayer; I was behind him. I fired at his back just off his spine—I had no wish to cripple him either—but he chose at that moment to touch his head to the ground, and the bullet passed through the back of his head instead. I am telling you all this because I want you to know I had no intention of killing him."

"But you did, you bloody bastard!" Joshua said. "You killed my friend and a brave soldier, and God help me, you aren't going to leave this place alive—even if we have to kill each other!"

Julia took her left hand away from Joshua—she still embraced him tight, keeping his hand away from his pocket, because she knew what Joshua would do. She put her hand into her pocket and fired. She aimed for the knee cap, but the pocket of the burkha brought Colonel Rashid Khan's service revolver up short, and the bullet hit him in the foot instead. He screamed in agony, and got off a shot, but the intense pain in his foot, bent him downwards, and the bullet lodged itself in the thick carpet, just ahead of them.

Her second shot hit him in the shoulder. He swung round in a pirouette before dropping to the floor. Joshua kicked the gun out of his hand, drawing his own revolver, but the killer though conscious, was out of action. Julia discarded the burkha, keeping the hand that held the gun as steady as she could, without much success. Joshua took the gun away from her, and sat her down in the chair. The three shots would have been heard, in the silence of the desert, for miles around. Colonel Sher Ali Khan and Viscount Edward raced up one staircase; Mansingh rushed up the other. Guns drawn. Julia placed herself between them.

"Gentlemen," she said, "will you all, please, put your guns away? This is not the Wild West!"

They obeyed. Except Julia herself who retrieved Rehana's gift to her, from Joshua, and slipped it into her handbag. Colonel Sher Ali Khan looked at the man on the floor, and then at Julia. Until his orders were countermanded, or retracted, by his General, she was still in charge.

"Colonel Sher Ali Khan, may I hand over to you, for immediate medical attention, Colonel Rashid Khan's killer." It was almost in the formality of an introduction. "Take him back to Pakistan, Colonel, where you can try him for murder. May I also introduce to you my husband, Colonel Joshua Samuelson, of the Indian Army—who is also Raja. Though he is not going to be Raja much longer because the Prime Minister will appoint someone else to take his place—as you have taken the place of Colonel Rashid Khan."

The two military officers shook hands warmly. A quizzical smile lingered on Colonel Sher Ali Khan.

"I am now Bahadur," he said. "Colonel Samuelson, could I not persuade you to stay on as Raja? I have heard so much about the 'Lion of Lahore'! I was not on that front; regrettably, I was too young. But the stories of that campaign are legendary."

"I am sorry Bahadur—may I call you Sher Ali?—but that is not going to be possible. I have just promised my wife to take her back to Paris, to a hotel owned by a friend, where we got engaged, to complete this shattered honeymoon. Try to put my marriage back together again. Are you married, Sher Ali?"

"Not yet, Sir," the younger man replied. "But I do have someone in mind who feels the same way about me as I do about her."

"Good Luck, my friend. In marriage, you may need as much luck as you need in a war."

"Yes, Colonels," Julia said, "but in a war there are no winners—only losers. In marriage, it need not be that way."

Edward and Mansingh had been attending to the man on the ground; binding up his wounds as best they could with the first-aid kit that Mansingh had retrieved, quickly, from the battle tank outside the Fort.

"What shall we do with him?" Edward said.

"Take him back to Pakistan, and get him to a hospital as quickly as possible. He'll survive. Then charge him!" Joshua said. "I have a battle tank outside, and Julia and I, with Mansingh, will go back to India. Forward Lady Julia's bags to Bombay."

Julia moved to the table, and folded THE THAR ARTICLES into a protective envelope.

"Colonel Sher Ali Khan," she said, "I promised your General that I would hand over to him Colonel Rashid Khan's murderer, whoever he might be. And I have. I promised him also that his copy of THE THAR ARTICLES would be returned to him, so that he can meet with the Prime Minister, two days from now, without loss of face."

She gave the envelope to Joshua.

"Colonel Sher Ali Khan, these are THE THAR ARTICLES—Bahadur's copy. They were given to my husband for safekeeping, when Colonel Rashid Khan realised he was in danger of losing control over them. He was a man of honour—as you are. My husband would like to hand them over to you. They are the property of the Pakistani Government. The General designated you as his agent. Please make sure they reach the General intact, and undisclosed. That is also an order—and until your General countermands or retracts his orders to you, you are still under my command."

But she said it so sweetly, the Colonel laughed even as he saluted her, accepting the envelope from Joshua.

Colonel Sher Ali Khan and Mansingh helped the killer to his feet, and, with him limping between them, they descended the staircase to the Pakistani entrance and the half-track that the Colonel had driven to the door of the Fort.

Edward would have followed them, but Julia motioned him to stay. He lingered behind. She waited until the Colonel was out of earshot.

"I don't have much time," she said urgently. "This has thrown me too! Because I didn't expect it. You'd best get back to Karachi as fast as you bloody well can, and get Naseem Banu and the children on the first plane to London—before he is grilled. He is a faithful servant, Edward, but he will soon break!"

Edward nodded miserably.

"I recognised him as soon as I pulled his mask off. But why, Julia? Why?"

She patted his arm in sympathy. Joshua, too, came round the other side of him for support.

"That only she can tell us. Get her out fast! Then meet us at Henri's hotel in Paris. Off the Place de La Republique. Ten days from now. Agreed?"

He nodded, unable to quite fully comprehend his predicament.

"You will come, Edward?" Joshua said with an edge to his voice.

"Do I have a choice?"

They watched him go down the stairs his head disappearing from view before they turned to each other.

Then they both did what they had been wanting to do for a long, long time. They put their arms tight round each other, their mouths and their lips tight against each other, their thighs between each others, and swayed to the whistle of the wind through the gun slits in the walls.

Mansingh, returning from the half-track, to find out and obey his Colonel Saheb's wishes, discreetly withdrew down the stairs.

He smiled. He would have a lot to recount to his wife, Rupa Devi, that night.

CHAPTER 14

Julia had deliberately asked Edward to meet them at Henri's hotel after ten days. First, two days for a quick trip to Delhi—where Joshua handed over, personally, his copy of THE THAR ARTICLES to the PM—and then the flight back to Bombay. And all this after first riding in a battle tank driven by Joshua to Jaisalmer. Not entirely true, because Joshua had insisted on her being at the controls, while racing at full speed after a fictitious retreating enemy. She was surprised they arrived in one piece, because Joshua insisted on showing her his turret-turning skills, almost flipping the vehicle over and upside down—which he reassured her was almost normal at the speed she'd been going!

Three days with Joshua's Mother and Susan in Bombay. Regrettably, they were unable to meet Susan's fiancé because he was away on a research project. Susan promised them they would certainly meet him the next time they came.

Off to London, where lazing in deck chairs and sleeping in—cuddling in a bed designed for one— eased the tensions of the previous week. There were yet many unanswered questions and doubts to be cleared up between them, but by tacit consent all that had been postponed for Paris—getting to know each other, as they should on a disrupted honeymoon, was their very first priority. Emma and Tomkins—not to mention the eleventh Earl—all respected their need for complete privacy, and kept out of sight, until they were needed. A blissful three days!

But some matters had yet to be settled, and so on to Paris, and old friend Henri's hotel off the Place de La Republique. Henri had sat with them on his pavement café, outside his hotel, presenting them, against their protestations, with free bottles of fine wine for the married couple. Or rather Joshua's protestations, because he said he couldn't afford to pay for them.

For the honeymooning couple—no charge!

Henri didn't sit with them as long as he might otherwise have done. That he would do when they'd been married a few years; not now. He knew they would always patronize his hotel. Where else, Joshua said, were they likely to find a hotel owner who lived as if he was the Emperor of France—without a thought for tomorrow, or how he was going to pay for it—much to the chagrin of his divorced daughter who ran the establishment.

So they'd spent the ninth day, quite recovered from jet lag, unwilling to share it with anyone else, basking in the sunshine, eating the finest French food, and consuming fine wine. Joshua did; Julia declined.

Edward and Naseem Banu were to join them the next day.

"Why don't you tell me, darling?" she said very gently. "And let me tell you too. We will have to find the courage to do it some time. What could be more forgiving than this? Would you like me to start?"

He nodded miserably.

"I'm so very sorry, Joshua to have opened your hidden documents. Please forgive me. The dreadful, dreadful thoughts that would not let me rest—that they might be her letters to you, or worse still, your letters to her! The agony I went through was unbearable. I'm so very sorry, Joshua."

Her eyes filled with tears, but he took her in his arms and kissed her repeatedly until she sank her head on his shoulder and dried her eyes on his shirt.

"There is nothing to forgive, darling. It all worked out well in the end. Besides, if I recall, it was my insistence that we have permission to open each other's personal mail, wasn't it? At the time when I thought that maybe a Duke or an Earl or a Viscount, or even a Prince of some realm, might try to drive a wedge between us? I was insecure then—and I still am. Why, I do not know?"

She cheered up immediately.

"Darling, why are you so insecure? I will tell you as often as you wish, that there will never be, for me, any other man, but you—the Father of my child."

"Yes, you've told me that.......What?"

"I told you. You will soon be 'Pappa'! Isn't that what the father is called in India? I'm so happy!"

"Pappa or Daddy. Are you serious, Julia?"

"Darling, would I joke about being pregnant? Grandfather doesn't know yet. But he'll be the second person to know—as soon as we return to London—so we'll have to keep quiet about it tomorrow with Edward and Naseem Banu. Yes?"

"I will! I will! Though I want to shout it out to the world—I'm going to be a Pappa! Accost every person on the street and share with him, or her, the good news—but I won't; is it Mumma or Mummy?"

"Either is so sweet! Now your turn, Joshua. Tell me what you have to confess. I promise you, no matter what it is, I will forgive. Did you sleep with her?"

"No!"

"Did you ask her for sexual favours, to distract her, so that Solomon Uncle could shoot her through the small window?"

"No! Solomon who?"

"Your Uncle Solomon. Except that in India they put the first name ahead of the Uncle or Aunty—so it becomes Solomon Uncle."

"But I don't have a Solomon Uncle or an Uncle Solomon! Who the hell is he?"

"Well, I wouldn't swear at him, darling, because he's the gentleman who saved your life. He did, didn't he? Or do you have a different version? Did Mansingh shoot her through the window, when you went down on your knees and groveled at her feet?"

"Mansingh didn't shoot her......You know?"

"That you went down on your knees and groveled at her feet? Oh, yes."

"But how could you know? You weren't there!"

"I told you, Solomon Uncle told me. Is that what you've been trying to tell me all this while? Ask my forgiveness for it? Why would you need to do that?"

"I'm so sorry, Julia. I was a coward. She gave me two choices on how to die—I chose the cowardly way. You may forgive me—or you may not—but I will never forgive myself. I heard her diabolical laughter as I slid to my knees, and she pointed the gun at my bent head—it will haunt me forever."

"Darling, there is nothing to forgive. You helped Solomon Uncle have a shot at her—he told me it was touch and go; a few seconds more and she would have drilled you standing. When you slid to your knees, she'd offered to unclasp her braless blouse from in front and let the sides fly apart for your viewing pleasure—before killing you."

"I swear to you, Julia, she was fully clothed, when whoever it was took a shot at her from outside the window. I swear it! How do you know all of this?"

"I told you. Solomon Uncle told me. Wait! I can tell you who he is. He's the elderly Indian gentleman who's been following us all over the world—first in Georgetown, then when he gate-crashed our wedding reception in London—though he insists he had an invitation. I checked with Grandfather and he didn't. He was outside Major Patel's flat when I raced down the stairs, and he gate-crashed Edward's party for me, in Karachi. Edward had just given me the news that you were dead, that your naked body had been taken out of a house in Barmer, and I was weeping, unashamedly—my heart was in shreds—when he sits across me, covers my hand with his own, leads me to a bench outside the kitchens, and tells me all."

"Then you do forgive me?"

"Yes. But on one condition."

"Ask! Anything you ask, I agree."

"That if ever again you are facing a woman with a gun in her hand, you will plead for your life—not call her a ruthless killer and a bitch! That doesn't help."

"What!"

"You heard me, darling. No heroics for you anymore! You have responsibilities to me and our children; they come way ahead of military honour."

"Rashid Khan knew how to die; I didn't," Joshua said sadly.

"Maybe, but poor Rehana is a widow, and I still have you here beside me. Agreed?"

"Agreed. But on one condition."

"Oh! I didn't know conditions had conditions. And what might that be?"

"In a restaurant in Bombay, you once told me that there was a nicer place, and a nicer way, to forgive each other. Shall we?"

She got up with alacrity.

Viscount Edward and Naseem Banu met them outside Henri's hotel, in his sidewalk café, the next morning at eleven. Julia held out her hand to Edward, who shook it morosely; she patted Naseem Banu's hand and held it. She'd seen Indian and Pakistani women regularly comfort each other by holding hands. Unlike in the West where it might be mistaken for unseemly behaviour.

Joshua signalled the waiter for another bottle of wine and a glass of orange juice for Julia.

"What do we do now?" Edward asked.

"First we find out why?" Julia said.

"I know why!" Edward shouted, thumping the table. "Money! That's why. Isn't that the reason you sold me out to the KGB?"

"Yes, dear."

"God! What a bloody fool I've been."

"Yes, dear."

"All those arms shipments through Pakistan before the Thar operation—no wonder the KGB were able to sabotage them on a regular basis. She supplied them with all the information—the types of arms in particular shipments, dates of arrival in Karachi—that the CIA supplied to me. She gave them all they needed to sabotage the bloody shipments. God! I could kill you, Naseem."

"Yes, dear. Why don't you?"

"Because, damn it," Edward shouted, "I love you!"

Naseem smiled for the very first time that morning, disengaging her hand from Julia's and patting Edward's shoulder with it before sliding it up the back of his neck.

"I know that, dear. But there was never enough money for me. I am the daughter of a Raja. I have to support my Mother—a Maharani, no less!—in Rawalpindi. The allowance? It was an insult! This way I was an independent woman. I didn't need to come begging to you anymore. I was a woman of means! Large sums too, Edward. Hundreds of thousands of pounds. But that's all over now. What will happen to Hafez?"

"I don't give a damn what happens to Hafez!" Edwards said. "I hope they put him up against a wall and shoot him! He was your go-in-between with the KGB, wasn't he?"

She nodded. "I'm so very sorry he killed Rashid Khan. Those were never his instructions, believe me. He was to secure Rashid Khan's copy of THE THAR ARTICLES. After killing him, he searched the body—and found nothing."

"Rashid Khan was a very brave man," Joshua said. "He was kneeling, with bent head touching the ground, before God, in prayer. Unlike me."

Julia slid her hand into his. She had him to hold on to; Rehana would have to hold on to her memories.

"Let's all be sensible about this," Julia said. "We are all guilty of some deception in this affair. Hafez must be tried, but not in a public trial."

"That's impossible," Edward said. "They're just about ready to publicly execute him."

"Well, Edward, dear, that's where you will have to use your influence with the General to hold it in 'camera'. For reasons of Pakistan's national security.'

'And it is involved. The entire operation, of sending arms through India to the mujahidin, will come to light. India will, promptly, abandon it, disclaiming any knowledge of it, saying it was a clandestine operation, carried out by the CIA, without their consent. The route through Amritsar, which is now open, will be closed. Surely the General will see that it is hardly worth that risk to put one murderer on public trial? That will keep Naseem out of it."

Edward leaned back. Not quite sure of the soundness of it. He sipped his wine, signalled Joshua, who was doing the honours, for a drop more. Naseem and Julia sipped heir juices.

"Subject, of course, to two conditions," Julia said.

"Oh!" This, from all the other three.

"Oh, yes. There must be conditions. Colonel Rashid Khan's murder can hardly go unavenged, can it? The first condition is that Naseem Banu cannot ever go back to Pakistan. For her own sake, and the sake of her children. They will assassinate her as soon as she steps off the plane—because Hafez will talk."

Naseem set up a wail.

"Oh, do be quiet, darling," Edward said. "Go on Julia."

For the very first time, in more than eight years of marriage, he seemed to be putting his wife in place—and he found himself enjoying it.

"The second condition, the three of us require, to save you, Naseem, is that you disclose all information on the KGB set-up in Pakistan. We might even supply you with some disinformation that you can pass on to them. No risk! All done in London. We'll string them along, until they make fools of themselves. By the time they catch on, poor Edward here will have redeemed himself with MI-6."

Edward looked at Julia with open admiration. He leaned forward and slapped her on the back; then pulled her towards him and attempted to kiss her on the mouth. She moved her head sharply and the kiss ended up on her cheek.

Her lips, she had decided, were reserved only for a select few—her husband, her grandfather, and her children.

Joshua didn't care too much for the back slapping and the kissing, but he didn't say anything. Julia turned to him, and soundly kissed him on the mouth, which helped a great deal.

"What a splendid idea," Edward said. "And, darling, if you can sell them the information, I'll even let you keep the money."

She brightened at the thought of it.

"Make it good," she said, "the disinformation. So I can really bleed them! Oh, you are a sport, Edward. Thanks ever so much."

Edward rose from his chair, pulling Naseem up by her bare arm with him. She rose too.

"Well, you two, we're off. To do some planning. She's such a hot contact, I'll just have to stay very close to her."

"Before you go, two questions to Naseem," Julia said. "How did Hafez get into the Fort? He didn't come in from the front entrances. And how did he know of the first date and time Raja met Bahadur?"

"That Fort," Naseem said, "lies in my Father's old kingdom. Hafez knows it very well. As a child he used to take me there to play. There is a trapdoor in the lower floor, into a tunnel that goes under the concrete apron for about half a mile. After all in early days, under siege, the soldiers had to have a means of retreat. He went by camel and tethered the beast to a post that marks the entrance to the tunnel. The old date and time was sold by Major Patel to the KGB. But how Hafez knew of this day and time, when Julia was going there, I'll never know."

"Oh, that's easy," Julia said. "I told him, while he was driving me back to the bungalow after the party. I made it common knowledge, to one and all, that I was to meet Raja at the Fort—the day and time. He couldn't attack me in the bungalow because the General had a battery of his soldiers protecting me."

"Darling," Naseem said, "couldn't we see some of the sights of Paris first, before dashing off to London for whatever you had in mind? Please! The KGB won't run away; they'll wait for us."

He nodded; took her arm in his, tipped his hat to Julia, winked at Joshua, then massaging her arm, they sauntered off down the street.

"You'd think they were on their honeymoon, and we'd been married eight years," Julia said sadly.

"I know I've behaved badly," Joshua said. "If only I had told you all—as Rashid Khan told Rehana—I could have saved you so much heartache. Forgive me for that too?"

"I'm so happy to have you back alive, Joshua," Julia said, changing seats so that she sat beside him, nudging shoulders and touching knees, "I'll forgive you anything!"

He pretended to heave a sigh of relief; wiping his forehead of mock sweat.

"When you talked, in Bombay, about taking the redeye flight back to London, I was afraid you were talking of divorce, or annulment, or, out of pity for me, something a little less dreadful—like banishing me from the marriage bed for a month!"

She laughed. "That would be cruel and inhuman punishment—for me. No, Joshua, your punishment is to stay married to me for life."

"You're sure?"

"Darling, I've been married to you for just over six weeks. In that short time, I've been confronted by a dead man, been chased in a taxi—driven by a friendly Sikh driver, who treats his taxi as his wife—all over Bombay by a cruel Indian Army Colonel in a Police car with a siren, suffered unimaginable agonies on reading a simple handwritten document, met a widow I will never forget, wept, as never before, on being told that said cruel Indian Army Colonel was dead, found an Indian Uncle who will have a special place in my heart to the day I die, met a fine General, shot a murderer in the foot and shoulder, and brought him to justice, driven an army battle tank—nearly turning it over—in the seventh largest desert in the world, seen some parts of Bombay and Karachi, and I'm now sitting here with said cruel Indian Army Colonel—who has made me pregnant—on this glorious morning, in a roadside café outside Henri's hotel in Paris. Tell me, Joshua, am I ever likely to meet another man who can bring so much living—or loving—into my life?"

"You forgot one thing, Julia?"

"Oh?"

"Worn a burkha! I thought you looked rather nice in it, darling. Gave your figure real mystery; kept it hidden from all those lusting eyes. Maybe you ought to wear it more often?"

She punched him lightly on the shoulder. "I've kept it as a souvenir. The left pocket has two bullet holes in it. But if it turns you on, why, I can always wear it in bed with you?"

They lifted their glasses to each other.

CHAPTER 15

Julia and Joshua soon settled into married life at Bromfield. This was temporary, while looking for a large, three-bedroom flat, with two bathrooms, in Hampstead, where Joshua would resume his practice with the National Health Service. His old partner, Dr Clayborne, was dead, so he was also searching for a partner to share his practice with. Fortunately Amelia, his former receptionist, nurse, and stalwart manager of the surgery, was still available and eager to resume work with him once more.

In the meantime—in the interlude—life had taken a serene turn, for which they were both grateful. Joshua had relented, and they had now a double bed. He had put his foot down, firmly, when Julia had suggested, mildly, that maybe a king-size bed might be more useful in case, when the children were very small, they climbed on it, to sleep in the bed too.

"A double bed is big enough," he growled, "for the both of us and all of them! I may lose you during the day, Julia, but I, for sure, want to be able to find you at night." Then, with a twinkle in his eye, that set her smiling: "All these horrible nightmares I have of Dukes and Viscounts swooping down on you! How can I fend them off, if you aren't even within my reach?"

"Darling," she said, teasingly, "why only royalty? What about young, handsome, Pakistani colonels?"

"You're right," Joshua said. "If I have to fend them off too—in my nightmares—we may have to go back to the single bed. I have to be sure to reach you in time. Pakistani colonels, they swoop quickly!"

"No, no," Julia said hastily. "No colonels of any country! Just the odd royalty or two. I don't even know if there are any eligible ones left. Are there?"

But the double bed was just right. They could reach for each other when the need arose—and she found herself reaching for him just as often as he for her—yet they could pass the night without physically assaulting each other in sleep.

For the first few weeks, they breakfasted in their rooms—it was inevitable because they both slept late and the old Earl had long before left for London—but as the weeks went by, they tried to keep him company at breakfast and dinner as well. It was not always possible, because sometimes the old Earl left at an unearthly hour and returned at an equally unearthly one.

Lunch was always together, and alone, during the weekdays.

One Tuesday, they were breakfasting alone in Julia's suite of rooms. Emma and Tomkins had served breakfast and discreetly withdrawn. They smiled at each other, read the morning paper—they dissected it as soon as it was delivered; Joshua had the sports section to see the cricket scores; Julia went for the Arts and Books—when there was a tap at the door and Tomkins re-entered with a platter and a single sealed envelope on it. He offered it to Joshua, placed the platter on the table and stepped back.

Joshua glanced at it; returned to the cricket scores.

"Tomkins, when will Hertfordshire realise they have to have good bowlers too; stalwart batsmen just aren't enough."

"I couldn't agree with you more, Sir. They say that Vincent has a good leg-break—if only his length was better. He tends to pitch them short of a length, and generally the batsmen make sixers of it."

"Why, Tomkins, I didn't realise you were a cricket lover too?"

"Been one of my loves since childhood, Sir."

He hesitated again as if unsure whether to proceed. Julia who had known him since her childhood sensed his uncertainty, and asked: "What is it Tomkins?"

"If the Young Master would care to take a look at the letter I brought in a moment ago? It has the Royal Crest on it, and it was hand-delivered a few minutes ago. From the Palace."

"Well, Tomkins, then here give it to Lady Julia," Joshua said. "She handles all correspondence from her side of the family."

"I would normally do that, Sir. But this one is addressed to you." And with a bow, and a faint smile that Julia caught but Joshua missed, he left the room.

"It's an invitation from the Queen," Joshua said, "for the both of us to attend a tea party at the Palace. This Sunday, at 4:00 PM. There is an RSVP card. Do we go?"

"If you feel comfortable accepting, I'm all for it. In childhood, I've attended many, many of her tea parties at the Palace, with Grandfather. The cup cakes she serves are delicious!"

"That settles it. Then we accept. I wonder whether she's heard rumors of your pregnancy and wants to confirm it? Don't forget she's promised me a Jane Austen First Edition on the birth of each of our children. She gave me 'Pride and Prejudice' for our wedding; I wonder if she'll let me choose? If she does, which one should I take? 'Emma'?"

Julia burst out laughing.

"We're terrible people, Joshua, you and I—you know that, don't you? All I'm thinking about is food, and all you're thinking about is first editions!"

"You're right, Julia," Joshua said ruefully. "Your Majesty, my wife and I would be delighted to attend your tea party on Sunday at 4:00 PM, because you really are a fine person, and we enjoy meeting you. We are truly humbled that of all your millions of subjects you have chosen us to spend this Sunday afternoon with, and we look forward to it with genuine pleasure."

Julia nodded. "Much better, because she is a fine person and I've always enjoyed being round her. I never had a mother I can remember, so I suppose, as Mother's dear friend, she became mine too."

"There's a little hand written postscript. She's sending a royal car for us, so we don't have to go through all the formalities at the gates of the palace. Now that is really very kind of her."

"And unusual," Julia said, with a puzzled look. "She's never done that for Grandfather and me. Though Grandfather, as one of the Directors of MI-6, knew everyone at the gate. Is he invited?"

Joshua slid the invitation across the table to her. "Not on this card. He may have independently received an invitation. We can check with him. If he has, he can come with us."

The eleventh Earl had not received an invitation. In any case, he had an important meeting on Sunday afternoon—affairs of state—and so he could not have attended anyway.

Julia dressed tastefully, but charmingly, for the occasion. No off the shoulder dress, no short skirt above the knee, no plunging cleavage. She chose a silk dress, with a batik print, a high boat neck, short sleeves, the dress pulled in at the waist and flaring to just below the knee. Around her slender neck, Joshua clasped a two-strand pearl necklace that had belonged to her mother; from her ears dangled gold filigree earrings that were a gift from Joshua's mother. With her brown hair tied up in a pony-tail, she looked so beautiful, Joshua went down on one knee, kissed her hand, and proposed to her all over again, which she graciously accepted.

He then suggested that the burkha would make a fitting, final touch to her ensemble, which, laughingly, she graciously declined.

Yet, she hadn't dressed up the way she had for their wedding banquet, with her hair tied up in a bun in the Grecian style, and wearing a dress of such elegance, as befitting a Queen. She still looked stunningly beautiful, but as a commoner!

Joshua couldn't quite figure out why? The doubt must have shown in his eyes, because she placed a hand on his arm and asked: "Something troubling you, Joshua?"

"No! You look so stunning from head to toe, why should I be troubled? And you're married to me!"

She laughed. "Joshua, you've convinced me over and over again that you love me. While I do appreciate your caring thoughtfulness—

believe me I do—I don't need a new proposal of marriage, every time we go to a royal event, to be convinced of your love. We've been married six weeks; yet I can read your mind—and you can read mine. So why don't we start by me reading yours, and, please, correct me if you think, I've read it wrongly. Yes?"

He nodded, smiling at the game they were about to play—but only with pieces that were the absolute truth! No white lies, no fabrications, no blurring of the edges, no hiding behind shadows that were half-truths.

"What you are uneasy about is why I haven't made myself up today in the sort of regal "queenly" attire that would have been normal for a visit to Her Majesty, the Queen—who, by the way, is related to me from my mother's side, and not too distantly either. Am I right, Joshua?"

"Perfectly correct! Julia, I can have no more secrets from you, ever—not that I want too—if you will read my mind with so much accuracy. Now may I read yours?"

"Not yet. I haven't finished. And what you are thinking is that, perhaps, when we are with the Queen, she might make some remarks on how I would have made a worthy Queen for some Prince of some realm?"

"Right again! And she will—and she should—because you would have made a worthy Queen for any Prince of any realm."

"Thank you, dear. But I'm married to you."

"So is it my turn now?"

"Not yet. So you are thinking that I've dressed prettily, but as a commoner, so that I can come down—condescendingly—to your level, to forestall any such remarks, that might be hurtful to you?"

Joshua was silent. Her reading of his mind had stripped him naked before her. Except at one point where she had erred.

"Did you ever stop to think, Joshua," she said, in almost as much pain as he was, "that I cannot change my royal birth—even if I wanted to—no more than you can change who you are? I love you for who you are; why can't you love me for what I am? Now, if you wish to strip my mind naked, if you feel I've hidden some unspoken truth from you, the floor is yours, Joshua."

He shook his head, smilingly.

"You played both sides of the board admirably," he said. "You spoke your mind at the same time as you were reading mine—with such accuracy, I may, in the future, have to ask you to tell me what I am thinking! Or what I should be thinking?"

"I would never do that. So you don't wish to correct me on anything?"

"Just on one little word, perhaps?"

"I told you, darling, the floor is yours."

"I have been in two wars, Julia. I sent men into battle who didn't came back, and even though I was there with them on the frontlines—I was lucky; like your Father, they weren't—they come back to haunt me. Even in such nightmares—and I have them, Oh! so very often—I would never think you were being 'condescending' to me. You were trying to protect me from being hurt; that is what I thought."

"Yes, of course, Joshua." A troubled look crept into her eyes. "Darling, is that why you need a single bed? So that when you are troubled by such nightmares, you need to reach for me? Why didn't you tell me?"

Joshua was silent. He would not look into her eyes.

"Oh, I've been so blind! Forgive me. It has taken me six weeks to find it out. I feel so ashamed."

"Even a colonel, when asleep, Julia, is just a man. Thank you for being there. These past weeks you have been a great comfort at night—in every way."

"Oh, forgive me, Joshua! We'll go back to a single bed; the double bed can go into the East Wing."

"No! A double bed is fine!" His eyes twinkled. "After all when the little ones come along, I, too, would like them to climb into bed with us. Think of all the pillow fights we can have. Boys against girls?"

He changed the subject abruptly.

"Do you know what I would like for you to do, so that this visit to the Palace is not traumatic for me?"

"Tell me, Joshua. I'll do anything to make you more comfortable with my relatives. You did so much, in Bombay, for me to be comfortable with yours."

"You're sure? No rolling of the eyes, no muttered remarks under your breath, so I can't hear them, about this mad Indian Colonel and his demands?"

She laughed. "I don't recall ever rolling my eyes at you, or muttering under my breath with you."

"No rolling of your eyes, perhaps, darling, but you did mutter under your breath when you placed the ROUTING file in my hands in that restaurant in Bombay? Heavens, Julia, we all mutter under our breath sometimes! Nothing to be ashamed of. Roll our eyes too! But promise me, you won't do it for what I'm going to ask of you today."

"I promise."

"Julia, will you never lose your trust in me? I may ask for something that you will have to live with."

"I will never lose my trust in you, because I love you. Now what is it you wish to ask of me? Do you wish to cancel tea with the Queen?—I'll call the Palace and express our apologies."

"No! That is not what I was thinking—which shows you can't, thank heavens, read my mind all the time either. That in itself makes me feel so much better!"

"Then what, Joshua?" she said, gently. "Tell me, please. I'll do it willingly—I promise."

"What I'd like for you to do," he said, softly, "is to call Emma, put your hair up and change your dress, for a formal elegance as befits a Queen, or a visit to a Queen. Because that is what you are—a worthy Queen for any Prince of any realm—and I am honoured that you have chosen to be my wife, and I would be lacking even in common decency, to ask for you to be something you are not. My military honour does not permit it. So, please, go and change; I will be at the front door. We have the time for it."

She put her arms round him and kissed him on the mouth, swaying as they had done in the Fort; he held her tight. Their most insurmountable marital barrier had been overcome—so thought the both of them, reading each the other's mind with an accuracy, that left them both in delight.

She came back twenty minutes later, transformed in every way. Not just the hair style, where Emma had outdone herself in an elegant bun; not just in the dress—a formal one, light-orange with lace, that covered her down to her toes—but in the sparkle in her eyes as she twirled around before Joshua for his viewing pleasure. She still wore flat-heeled shoes—so as not to tower above Joshua—but the formal gown hid her toes. He offered her his arm and she took it.

"Happy?" she asked, as they entered the royal car.

"Delirious! And you?"

"How can I not be? I have your arm to hold. Since I met Rehana, I've found out how important it is just to be able to touch you—and be touched by you."

Julia had been to the Palace several times before; she knew the exact location of the room where the Queen received her guests for tea. So she was a little surprised, when the royal equerry, escorting them to the receiving room, led them off toward a staircase at the side, leading to the floor above. He opened the door to the room, announced them, and left without entering it.

The Queen and one person, standing at the window with his back to the door, were the only two in the room. Julia and Joshua entered the room; the Queen came forward to meet them. Julia curtseyed; Joshua bowed low over her outstretched, ungloved hand.

"I'm so glad, you could come, Colonel and Mrs Samuelson," she said. "I would like you to meet a dear friend of mine, one who my husband and I have had the pleasure of knowing for many, many years. I've also had the honour of knighting him, some years ago, for his services to the Empire."

The elderly Indian gentleman with silvery white hair, thinning at the top, and with kindly eyes behind his coral-frame spectacles, turned around and smiled at them.

Before the Queen could complete the introductions, Julia, who had been holding on to Joshua's arm, led him straight over to the elderly gentleman; there she gave the now-familiar gentleman a warm hug, while he patted her back and kissed her lightly on the hair.

"Oh, Solomon Uncle," she said delightedly, "I'm so glad you're here, so I can introduce you to my husband, Joshua. I'm very pleased to meet you again. When you left me in Karachi, I never thought I would ever see you again."

She took Joshua's arm once more, turning towards Joshua and the Queen who were looking on with different expressions—the Queen with quiet pleasure; Joshua with astonishment that a 'Solomon Uncle' had in fact materialized, at no less an occasion than tea with the Queen, and in her royal chambers.

"Joshua, darling, meet Solomon Uncle. I don't really know who he is, but he's the Uncle who saved your life—and mine—by shooting that dreadful woman through the window of that house in Barmer." Joshua shook his hand warmly.

"Then let me complete the introductions," the Queen said. "Please meet Retired General Sir Solomon Abrams, Former Director of Indian Army Intelligence, and one of our dearest friends."

"Your Majesty," Sir Solomon said, "I think we owe this beautiful young couple an explanation—long overdue. Would you like to give it—or shall I?"

"Solomon," the Queen said, "I'll give it, but I have to make one request of you first. Tell me what do you call me in private?"

"Elizabeth."

"Then may we, in front of this beautiful couple I hold so dear, dispense with the 'Your Majesty' bit, and revert to our mode of address in private?"

He bowed: "Very well, Elizabeth—if you wish it."

"I do. They are not the only two in your debt—I am too. And I am Aunt Elizabeth to the two of you."

The Queen motioned all of them to sit at a small round table, Sir Solomon to her right and Julia to her left with Joshua facing her.

"When I heard from my officers—who will remain nameless—that they were planning to use Joshua here—may I call you Joshua; Julia is like my child, and as her husband, you are very dear to me too—for such a dangerous assignment, I was appalled! They are just married—and you want to put him in harm's way? I berated everyone—the Viscount, your Grandfather—anyone who even mentioned the project to me.'

'Then they tried a different approach. They said: Your Majesty, the President of the United States, the Prime Minister of India and the Military Dictator of Pakistan have all expressed a desire for the arms to be delivered—safely—into Afghanistan. How can we refuse? And I said to myself: 'if all those leaders are in it, why can't I get into the act too?'

'So I called your Grandfather and Viscount Edward here, to this very room, for a meeting. They thought I'd called them to let them have another piece of my mind. I laid down the terms. If they were going to put my child—and Julia here is like my own daughter; she would have made a worthy Queen to any Prince of any realm—and her new husband at risk, I would assign one of my own to protect them, no matter where they were. Every day, I wanted the best information they had on where you two were; I have a complete log of where Joshua was on any given day—and wherever he went, Sir Solomon was sure to go! Even at your banquet in Bromfield Hall, he was there—on my invitation. Would you care to take over, Solomon? You know the rest better than I do, though you've filled me in on what happened."

"I can tell you, it wasn't easy. Georgetown was a piece of cake; then it became increasingly difficult. Sometimes I was with Joshua, sometimes just behind him and sometimes just ahead of him! And because you two were together, I was providing protection for Julia as well—until you split up, with Joshua going to Marwar Junction and Julia to Karachi. Julia was at no risk; Joshua was, so I stuck to him. A former retired Director of Indian Army Intelligence still has considerable clout with the officers who worked for him. They were handpicked by me and they were only too happy to help, with information."

Sir Solomon thought carefully about how he was going to phrase what came next.

"The most difficult part came when Devika Rani ordered Joshua to his knees, twice—and he refused. His body was blocking the window and my line of fire! She made it more difficult—not easier—for him by offering to release the clasp in front that held the two sides of her braless blouse together. I tried to give him indication in the dressing table mirror that I—he thought it was Mansingh—was outside the window. If he would only go on his knees! It was touch and go. Finally, she was prepared to kill him standing—and there was nothing I could do about it. I prayed. Oh! How I prayed, and God must have answered my prayers because Joshua went down on his knees. She laughed, a diabolical laugh, the gun in her right hand still pointing at him, while her left hand moved to the clasp in front. That is when I shot her. I'm willing to swear to you, on my God above, Julia, that she was fully clothed when she fell."

"Joshua told it to me," Julia said quietly. "I have reassured him it would have been of no consequence. She knew someone was outside! Had she not spent a few seconds reaching for her clasp, she would have killed Joshua as soon as he slid to his knees—before you shot her! Joshua feels he was a coward, for going on his knees, and while I've tried hard to dissuade him from thinking that way, he is still hurting."

"Perhaps I can help," Solomon Uncle said, turning to Joshua. "Tell me, Colonel, is it cowardice to retreat in battle when you know fully well—as you did—that another regiment of your army is going to encircle the enemy and annihilate it? I was another regiment of your army; the fact that you thought it was Mansingh is not relevant. Does the regiment that retreats feel disgraced, when they have, in fact, helped to win the battle—and the war?"

Joshua brightened. Put in military terms made it easier to accept. Julia's arm holding him tight and pressing him into her certainly helped.

"Sir Solomon, I thank you. It is a debt I can never repay. What will happen to Devika Rani?"

"She is still recovering in a military hospital in India. Her father, General Rana Singh, has flown from Washington DC to look after her. I think they will use the same tactic that we are using for Naseem Banu here—she will help IMI to clean up KGB infiltration of IMI; in the meantime she will feed KGB enough disinformation to exonerate herself. In any case, they cannot ever bring her to trial because the whole project would go under, and neither India nor Pakistan wants that, do they now? Oh! And please call me Solomon Uncle, because in just a few weeks, that is precisely what I will be to the two of you. My son David Abrams plans to marry—very soon—your sister Susan. Yes, I will be Susan's father-in-law, and Uncle to the two of you. So you see, when our Queen ordered me to help, I jumped at it; keeping you alive was a top priority. I could hardly have my daughter-in-law grieving on her wedding day, could I, now?"

"Requested you, Solomon," the Queen reproached him, smilingly. "You are an old and valued friend of my family; I would never order you to do anything. A desperate plea for help, perhaps?"

The Queen rang a little silver bell on the table beside her and ordered tea.

"Julia, I've made sure we have some of those cup cakes you used to adore as a child. Your Mother, besides being related to me and my childhood friend, was very, very dear to me. When she died, I promised her I would look after you, and, today, I think I have. This calls for some champagne, doesn't it? Don't you think the British taxpayer should forgive me my excesses on this day?"

Joshua and Sir Solomon accepted readily; Julia declined, opting for tea instead, placing her hand on her stomach. The Queen nodded.

While the champagne and tea were being served, the Queen went to the library cupboards, lining one wall, and invited Joshua to come over.

"Jane Austen First Editions. Choose Joshua," she said, putting an arm round him. "You are a Prince of this realm; which one would you like?"

"Emma," he said. "But we would have such a nice time analysing her complex character, if we got together at Bromfield House, one afternoon for tea? Please, Elizabeth Aunty, would you come?"

She seemed surprised at his mode of address; but there was more warmth and affection the Indian way, so she smiled, tightening her arm round his shoulder, as she said:

"Of course, Joshua. Uncle Philip and I would love to come."